Alexander H. Sands

Practical Forms for the Guidance of Conveyancer, Notaries Public, Justices of the Peace, Commissioners in Chancery,

and Business Men

Alexander H. Sands

Practical Forms for the Guidance of Conveyancer, Notaries Public, Justices of the Peace, Commissioners in Chancery,
and Business Men

ISBN/EAN: 9783337224233

Printed in Europe, USA, Canada, Australia, Japan

Cover: Foto ©Suzi / pixelio.de

More available books at **www.hansebooks.com**

PRACTICAL FORMS

FOR THE GUIDANCE

OF

CONVEYANCERS, NOTARIES PUBLIC, JUSTICES OF THE PEACE, COMMISSIONERS IN CHANCERY, AND BUSINESS MEN;

BY

ALEXANDER H. SANDS,

Of Richmond.

RICHMOND, VA.
PUBLISHED BY WOODHOUSE & PARHAM.
1867.

PREFACE.

The legal profession and business men generally are now without a Form Book in Virginia for their guidance in ordinary business transactions. To supply this want, the present volume has been prepared.

Commissioners in Chancery will find, under the titles "Dower," "Executors, Administrators, &c.," the forms of accounts of these fiduciaries, of Trustees and of Guardians, and the method of calculating Annuities and Dower interests.

If the present series of forms meet with the favor of the public, the writer proposes to follow them by forms in Common Law actions, and in Criminal proceedings in the Courts of Virginia.

ALEXANDER H. SANDS.

Richmond, February 7th, 1867.

PRACTICAL FORMS.

I.

ABANDONMENT.

In Maritime Insurance, when a voyage is entirely defeated or rendered not worth pursuing by the operation of any of the perils insured against, the party insured may abandon all his interest in the subject insured and call upon the insurer for payment as in case of total loss. This places the insurer in the place of the insured, and by operation of law transfers the property to the former, together with all the profit and loss that may be incident to it. *Graydon's Forms*, 19. No especial form of abandonment is prescribed by law or usage, but the word *abandon* should be used. 2 Pars. Mar. Law, 396.

Notice of abandonment.[1]

To : Gentlemen:—Having received a letter from Captain McKnight (the master), informing me that the ship Commerce was lost, I abandon the proportion of the cargo that your office was interested in. Respectfully, &c. A B.

[1]In *Columbian Ins. Co.* v. *Catlett*, 12 Wheat. 386, this notice was held sufficient, 1st, as a notice of the intention to abandon, and 2dly, as an actual abandonment.

Another notice of abandonment.[2]

To :—Take notice, that I, A B, of etc., do hereby abandon, cede and leave to you all my right, title, interest, claim, property and demand of and in the ship called the of ,

[2]Dixon's Mar. Law, 292.

of the burden of tons, or thereabouts, and all and every part of her cargo and the goods laden on board of her by me the said A B, and do demand of you a total loss, of the sum of dollars, lawful money of the United States, by you underwrote on goods and merchandises laden on board the said ship by me the said A B. Value in goods. A B.

II.

AFFIDAVIT.

Affidavit in ordinary cases.

County of H (or City of R), to wit.

This day personally appeared before me, the undersigned, *a justice of the peace*[1] for the county (or city) aforesaid, James Alfred, and made oath that [here state the matter designed to be sworn to] is true, to the best of his knowledge and belief. Given under my hand on this day of , A. D. 18 .

[1]May be made before a notary public, and when made before a notary, insert "a notary public" in lieu of words italicised.

Affidavit of service of notice when party on whom the notice is to be served cannot be found. Code Va., ch. 167, *sec.* 1.

County of H (or City of R), to wit:

This day personally appeared before me, the undersigned, *a justice of the peace*[2] for the county (or city) aforesaid, James Alfred, and made oath that he went on the day of , to the usual place of abode of George S, named in the within notice, and not finding* him at his usual place of abode, but finding his wife there, affiant delivered a copy of the within notice to Sarah, the wife of the said George S, and gave information to her of the purport of said notice. Given under my hand on this day of , A. D. 18 .

[2]See note to next preceding form.

NOTES.

When the service is on a person other than the wife:—Follow the preceding form to the (*), then say: the said George S, nor his wife at the usual place of abode of the said George S; but finding there Jared Ammons, a white person over the age of sixteen years, and a member of the family of the said George S, affiant delivered to the said Jared Ammons a copy of the within notice, and gave information of its purport to the said Jared Ammons. Given under my hand on this day of 18 .

When the service of the notice is made by posting a copy at the front door:—Follow form to the (*), then say: the said George S, nor his wife, nor any white person over sixteen years of age, a member of his family, at the usual place of abode of said George S, affiant posted a copy of the within notice at the front door of the said place of abode. Given under my hand on this day of 18 .

General form of affidavit to a petition, &c.

County of , to wit:—This day personally appeared before me the undersigned [here insert the name and style of the office], A A, named in the above petition (or, *bill*, or according to the fact), and made oath that he believes the statements therein contained are true. Given under my hand on this day of 18 .

R J (*style of office*).

Affidavit to an account against the estate of a deceased person.

County of , to wit:—This day personally appeared before me the undersigned [here insert the name and style of officer], A A, and made oath that the foregoing account is just and true, that the sum of , as above, is justly due and owing to him from the estate of the said , and that he hath never received the same, nor any part thereof. Given under my hand on this day of 18 .

R J (*style of office*).

Affidavit of materiality of witnesses, on which to base an application for a continuance of a pending cause.

County of , to wit:—This day personally appeared before me the undersigned [here insert the name and style of officer],

A A, a party defendant (or plaintiff) to an action pending in the court of , in which R J and M L are plaintiffs (or defendants), and made oath that James R, John C and Alexander R are material witnesses in his behalf, on the trial of said action, and that he cannot safely go to the trial of the said action in the absence of the said witnesses, or of either of them. Given under my hand on this day of 18 .

R J (*style of office*).

Affidavit of appraisers of estate of decedent.

County of , to wit:—This day personally appeared before me the undersigned [here insert the name and style of officer], James R, Benjamin B and Samuel T, three of the appraisers appointed by the court of to appraise the estate of the late D M, and made oath that they would truly and justly, and to the best of their judgment, view and appraise the goods and chattels of the said D M, which shall be produced or shown to them for appraisement [*if personal representative authorized to sell, or receive the rents and profits of the real estate*, add: and also the real estate of the said D M which lies in said county]. Given under my hand this day of 18 .

R J (*style of office*).

Affidavit of general partner in a limited partnership.

See form annexed to certificate of limited partnership, under title PARTNERSHIPS.

Affidavit to require bail.

State of Virginia, County, to wit:

This day personally appeared before me the undersigned [here state name and style of officer], A B, plaintiff in a certain action of (or *suit in equity*), instituted by him against one C D, defendant, which action (or *suit*) is now pending in the court of said county, and made oath that he the said A B has just cause of action against the said C D, for which he has instituted said action (or *suit in equity*) against the said C D, and further made oath that he the said A B has probable cause for believing, and that he does believe, that the said C D, defendant, is about to quit this State, unless he the said C D be forthwith apprehended. Given under my hand and seal this day of 18 .

R E (*style of office*). [Seal.]

☞ The foregoing is the form usually employed; the following is preferred by the author:

State of Virginia, County, to wit:

This day personally appeared before me the undersigned [here state name and style of officer], A B, plaintiff in a certain action of , instituted by him against one C D, defendant, which action or suit is now pending in the court of county; that the said defendant owed and still owes to him the said affiant, the sum of $, *by open account* (or *note* or single bill, as the case may be), for which he hath instituted said action, and that he hath just claim against the said defendant for the said sum of money, with interest thereon at the rate of six per centum per annum from the day of , to recover which, said action has been instituted against the said C D; and affiant further made oath that the said defendant has [if any facts be known to affiant showing an intention to quit the state, here recite them], and that he the said affiant has probable cause for believing, and that he does believe, that the said C D, defendant, is about to quit this State, unless he the said C D be forthwith apprehended. Given under my hand and seal this day of 18 .

——— ——— [Seal.]

If an action of detinue, or of trover, the affidavit should be modified according to the nature of the case.

See *post.*, title Action at Law.

III.

AGREEMENTS.

Agreement for the sale of goods at a price to be ascertained by appraisement.

Articles of agreement made and entered into on this day of , in the year 18 , between T S of the one part, and Arthur B of the other part, witness, that the said T S hath agreed, and doth hereby agree, to sell to the said Arthur B the following articles, viz: [here name them], the price therefor to be ascertained and determined by appraisement, as hereinafter mentioned. These articles farther witness that the said articles shall, at the equal and joint charge of said S and B, be appraised by Robert C and James A, on or before the day of , and the amount of their appraisement is to be the price to be paid for the said articles, and when and as soon as said appraisement is made and the said price paid for the said articles, the said T S covenants to make an absolute bill of sale for the said articles to the said Arthur B, and to deliver full possession thereof to said B. Until such appraisement is made, the said articles are to remain at the risk and costs of the said .[1] In witness whereof, the parties hereto have hereunto set their hands and seals, on the day and year first above written.

T S. [Seal.]
ARTHUR B. [Seal.]

[1] Either of the buyer or of the seller, as the parties may agree. It had better be stated, so that the party who is liable may know definitely his liability, and may, if he choose, *insure* himself against loss.

Contract in writing for the sale of real property; land, &c.

Articles of agreement, made and entered into on this day of , in the year 18 , between John Vendor of the one part, and Robert P of the other part, witness, that the said John Vendor agrees to and with the said Robert P, that he the said John Vendor will sell the said Robert P all that [here describe the property], with the appurtenances, at the price of dollars: the said John Vendor agrees to execute, at his own proper costs and charges, a deed to said P, containing the covenant of general warranty and the usual covenants of title. And the said Robert P covenants that on the execution of the conveyance aforesaid, he will pay to said John Vendor the purchase money aforesaid. The taxes for the year to be paid by the said Vendor; the rents and profits of the premises from the day of to be received by the said P: and if the said conveyance shall not be executed and the purchase money paid on or before the day of , the said Robert P is to pay interest on said purchase money from that day unto the said John Vendor. In witness whereof, the said parties have hereto set their hands and seals on the day and year first above written as the date hereof.

JOHN VENDOR. [Seal.]
R. P. [Seal.]

Agreement for building a house.

Articles of agreement, made and entered into this day of , in the year 18 , between Henry O of the one part, and Benjamin B of the other part, witness, that the said Benjamin B, for the consideration hereinafter mentioned, doth for himself, his executors and administrators, covenant, promise and agree to and with the said Henry O, his executors, administrators and assigns, that he the said Benjamin B shall and will, on or before the day of , in good and workmanlike manner, and according to the best of his art and skill, well and substantially erect, build and complete in the city of , on street, a dwelling-house of the size and materials set forth and specified in the paper marked "A," hereunto annexed, the materials for building the said house to be furnished by the said ;[1] and the said Henry O, in consideration of said covenant by the said Benjamin B, doth for himself, his executors and administrators, covenant and promise to and with the said Henry O, his executors, administrators and assigns, to pay to the said Benjamin B the sum of dollars as follows, to wit: [here state the time or times at which the money is to be paid.] In witness whereof, the said parties to these presents have hereunto set their hands and seals on the day and year first above written as the date hereof.

HENRY O. [Seal.]
BENJAMIN B. [Seal.]

[1]According to the contract, either by the owner or by the builder. Sometimes, the owner furnishes a part, and the builder the balance.

Paper "A," referred to in annexed contract.

The house is to be built of brick, three stories high—on the first floor four rooms; the front room on the first floor to be neatly finished, and to have a marble mantel-piece, &c. &c. (according to the agreement of the parties).

On the second floor, &c.

On the third floor, &c. (Signed) H. O.
B. B.

Agreements for the purchase of growing timber.

Articles of agreement, made and entered into this day of , in the year , between A B of and C D of , witness, that the said A B, in consideration of the sum of , to be paid him by the said C D, on the day of , in the year , and of the agreements and covenants hereinafter mentioned, and which the said C D, his executors, &c., are to observe and perform, doth hereby grant, bargain and sell unto the said C D, his executors, &c., all and singular the timber-trees, and other trees hereinafter mentioned, that is to say: [here describe the trees and their situation], together with full liberty and authority for the said C D, his servants and workmen, or his agents, to fell the said trees at all reasonable and convenient times, and to place and lay the bark of the oak trees in convenient parts of the premises to dry; And the said trees and wood, with the bark of the oak, and boughs, lops and tops of the whole of the said trees, to draw, remove and carry off, and take away in shares, in and by the most usual and convenient ways and parcels, at any time on or before the day of next; And also free liberty and authority to and for the said C D, his executors, &c., and his and their servants, agents and workmen, and other person or persons, to whom he or they shall sell and retail the said timber and wood, or any part thereof, to dig saw-pits, and break up and saw the said timber, in proper and convenient parts of the said premises, in and upon which the said timber and wood stands and grows, at any time before the said day of next, without paying or making any satisfaction to the said A B, his heirs or assigns, or under-tenants.

And the said C D, in consideration of the premises, and the bargain and sale of the said trees and bark, made to him as aforesaid, doth for himself, his heirs, &c., covenant and agree to and with the said A B, his executors, &c., by these presents, that he the said C D, his heirs, &c., shall and will pay to the said A B, his executors, &c., the sum of , as aforesaid; And also that he the said C D, his executors, &c., shall and will fell, hew and cut down the said trees, and remove and take away the same, with the boughs, &c. thereof, within the time before limited and agreed upon for that purpose, and according to the true intent and meaning of these presents. And also shall and will, within months next after the said day of next, at his and their own costs and charges, fill up all such saw-pits as shall for the purposes aforesaid have been made by him or his servants, on any of the said lands; and also fence, amend and repair all the hedges and fences in and about the said lands, in all such places as shall be broken, or otherwise damaged or destroyed, in felling, hewing, or carrying away the said timber, on being allowed wood for that purpose by the said A B.

In witness whereof, the said parties to these presents have hereto set their hands and affixed their seals the day and year first above written.

——— ——— [Seal.]

——— ——— [Seal.]

Agreement to submit a dispute between the parties to arbitration.

Articles of agreement, made and entered into this day of , in the year , between N M of of the one part, and T R of of the other part: Witness, that whereas there are sundry questions and disputes between the said parties hereto, in reference to [here describe the subject matter of difference]. Now, therefore, for the finally ending all such questions and disputes between the said parties, and for preventing all other disputes and differences concerning the same, and the charges of suits which may or might otherwise arise or happen to be occasioned thereby, it is agreed, by and between each of the said parties to these presents, that the rights, titles, claims and demands or pretences of the said parties in relation to the matters in difference between them, shall be and are hereby referred and submitted to the final award and determination of of , so that they may make their award or determination of and concerning the premises, in writing, under their hands and seals, ready to be delivered to the said parties requiring the same, on or before the day of next ensuing the date of these presents. And it is further agreed by and between the said parties to these presents, that they and each of them, if required, within the time before limited for that purpose aforesaid, shall and will produce, or cause to be produced, all such documents and writings relating to or concerning the said premises, or any part thereof, which are in the custody or power of the said parties, or either of them, as they the said shall think or find proper or necessary to be inspected and perused by them for their better information in and knowledge of the premises: and it is further agreed by and between the said parties to these presents, that in case the said , in order to make their award of and concerning the premises, shall find any fact or facts necessary to be ascertained by examination of witnesses, or other due proofs to be made concerning the premises, or any part thereof, that all and every such account, matter and thing shall be performed and taken for that purpose, as by and with the judgment of the said shall most conduce to make out the truth of every such fact or facts, by affidavits or otherwise. And that all and every such fee and fees as the said shall give or find necessary to be given to any counsel or other person or persons for his advice and direction in the premises, or any other matter or thing relating thereto, or in order to the making his award therein, shall be equally borne and discharged by the said parties to these presents, and not otherwise.[1]

In witness whereof, the said parties to these presents have hereto set their hands and affixed their seals on the day and year first herein written. ——— ——— [Seal.]

——— ——— [Seal.]

[1] If the parties desire an umpire to be chosen in case of the disagreement of the two arbitrators, or their failure to make their award in the time limited, then add: "And if the said arbitrators shall fail to agree, or shall disagree of and concerning the proper award to be made on the matters in difference between the said N M and T R, on or before the said day of , then the same shall be and are hereby referred and submitted to the award, determination and umpirage of such third person as said arbitrators shall select, and such third person, umpire as aforesaid, shall make his award, determination and umpirage of such matters in difference, in writing, under his hand and seal, ready to be delivered to the said parties in difference on the day of 18 ."

Agreement for sale and finishing the hull of a ship, from the shipwright.

Articles of agreement, indented and entered into on the day of , in the year , between A B of of the one part, and C D of of the other part: Witness, that the said A B, for the consideration and at the price to be paid him by the said C D, as hereafter is mentioned, doth hereby agree to sell unto the said C D the hull or body of a new ship or vessel lately built by the said A B, at his own charge, and now in at , computed to be of the burden of tons, be the same more or less; and the said A B, for himself, his executors, administrators and assigns, doth covenant and agree to and with the said C D, his heirs, administrators and assigns, that he, the said A B, his executors and administrators, workmen, servants or assigns, shall and will, at his and their own charges, in substantial and workmanlike manner, do and perform the several works in and about the said hull of the said ship, as follows: (that is to say), &c. [here insert the work to be done]; and will find and provide a complete suit of masts and yards fitting for such a ship, and will likewise do and perform all joiners' work, painters' work, glaziers' work, plumbers' work, and all other works for the complete finishing the said hull or body of the said ship, and will launch her into the river , and deliver her safe unto the said C D, his executors, administrators or assigns, on or before the day of . In consideration and for the purchase of which said hull or body of the said ship so agreed to be sold, and of the several works and things to be done and performed as aforesaid, the said C D, for himself, his executors, administrators and assigns, doth covenant and agree to and with the said A B, his executors, administrators and assigns, by these presents, that he, the said C D, his executors, administrators or assigns, shall and will well and truly pay unto the said A B, his executors, administrators or assigns, at and after the rate of dollars, in manner following: that is to say, dollars, part thereof, on the day of , and the residue and remainder thereof on the day of , he the said A B, his executors or administrators, then and at the same time, at the request and at the costs and charges of the said C D, his executors or assigns, executing and delivering a sufficient bill of sale of the said hull of the said ship, with her masts, yards and appurtenances, unto the said C D, his executors, administrators or assigns, or to such other person or persons as he or they shall order and appoint.

In witness whereof, the said parties to these presents have hereunto set their hands and affixed their seals the day and year first above written. ——— ——— [Seal.]

——— ——— [Seal.]

An agreement for making a quantity of shoes.

Articles of agreement, made and entered into this day of , in the year , between A B of of the one part, and C D of of the other part: The said A B, for the consideration hereinafter mentioned, doth covenant, that he will, at his own charge, make for the said C D pair of shoes of the same quality of leather and goodness, as, and in all other respects, according to a pattern agreed between the said parties, and of a size from to , and deliver the same to the said C D at , within from the date hereof. And the said C D, in consideration thereof, doth covenant to pay to the said A B, at the rate of per pair, after months from the delivery of the said shoes as aforesaid. And it is agreed, that if any of the shoes shall not be made agreeably to the said pattern, and for that reason shall be rejected by the said C D, he, the said A B, shall take back such as shall be refused, and deliver the said C D the like quantity of the goodness and make, according to the pattern aforesaid.

In witness whereof, the said parties to these presents have hereunto set their hands and affixed their seals the day and year first above written.

——— ——— [Seal.]

——— ——— [Seal.]

Agreement between a merchant and his clerk.

Articles of agreement, made and entered into this day of , in the year , between A B of of the one part, and C D of of the other part: Witness, that the said C D, for the consideration hereinafter mentioned, doth hereby covenant and agree to and with the said A B, by these presents, that he, the said C D, shall and will, during the space of , to commence from the day of the date hereof, diligently and faithfully serve the said A B, in keeping the books of account of him, the said A B; and therein shall, from time to time, and at all times during the said term, observe, fulfil and keep the lawful and reasonable commands and directions of the said A B, without disclosing the same, or the secrets of his employment, business or dealings to any person or persons whomsoever during the said term; and shall not at any time hereafter, during the said term, correspond with any person or persons corresponding with the said A B, nor use any traffic or dealing in the way of the said A B, either for himself, or for any other person or persons other than the said A B, without the permission and consent of the said A B first had and obtained for that purpose. And the said C D doth hereby further covenant and agree to and with the said A B, that he, the said C D, shall and will, from time to time, during the said term, write and keep a true and perfect account and accounts for him, the said A B; and will not embezzle, purloin, wilfully waste or misspend any of the goods, wares, moneys, merchandise or commodities of the said A B; and will, upon every request to him made for that purpose, make and give unto the said A B a full, true, just and perfect account in writing, of and for all money which he shall receive in or pay out of all goods and commodities which he shall, at any time during the said term, receive in, or deliver, or pay out, for or upon the account and for the use, or by the order of the said A B. And also, that he, the said C D, shall and will well and truly pay unto the said A B all such sum or sums of money as shall appear to be due upon the foot of any such account or accounts. And further, that he, the said C D, shall not nor will, at any time or times during the said term, trust, or deliver forth, or pay upon credit any of the goods, wares, merchandise, moneys or securities of or belonging to, or in the hands, custody or power of the said A B, to any person or persons whomsoever, without the previous consent and direction of the said A B. In consideration of all which said services to be observed, done and performed by the said C D as aforesaid, he, the said A B, doth hereby covenant and promise that he, the said A B, shall and will pay, allow and give unto him, the said C D, the sum of , by the year, for every year during the aforesaid term of years, by even quarterly payments, the first quarterly payment thereof to be made on the day of ; and shall and will, during all the said term, find and provide for the said C D sufficient lodging, &c.

In witness whereof, the said parties to these presents have hereunto set their hands and affixed their seals on the day and year first herein written. ——— ——— [Seal.]

——— ——— [Seal.]

Agreement by executors for letting premises during the minority of a child.

Articles of agreement, made and entered into this day of , in the year , between H C of , and N C of , executors named in and by the last will and testament of R P, late of , deceased, of the one part, and B R of of the other part: Witness, that the said H C and N C, as executors as aforesaid, hereby agree to let unto the said B R, his executors and administrators, all that [here give a description of the property]. To hold the same to the said B R, his executors and administrators, from the day of , now next ensuing, for the term of years, fully to be complete and ended, if J, the son of the said R P, deceased, shall so long live; but if he shall happen to die at any time before the said term of years shall be fully expired, then these presents, so far as relates to that term, shall immediately cease, and become null and void, subject, nevertheless, to the payment by him, the said B R, his executors and administrators, of the yearly rent of dollars, payable half yearly, on the day of and the day of , in every year, and to such proportion of any such half yearly payment as shall accrue up to the day of the decease of the said J P, in case he shall happen to die before the said term of years shall be accomplished, or unto such further day as he, the said B R, his executors and administrators, shall be permitted to remain in possession of the said premises. And the said B R doth hereby, for himself, his executors and administrators, agree with the said H C and N C, executors as aforesaid, and the survivor of them, his executors or administrators, to take the said premises and become tenant thereof, from the day of now next ensuing, and to pay to them the aforesaid rent or yearly sum of dollars as aforesaid, on the days hereinbefore reserved and appointed for the payment thereof; and that he, the said B R, his executors or administrators, shall and will, in case the said J P shall happen to die at any time before the expiration of the said term of years, upon notice thereof in writing from the said H C and N C, and the survivor of them, his executors or administrators, forthwith surrender up to them the said premises. And the said H C and N C do hereby agree that he, the said B R, paying the said rent, and performing these conditions, shall quietly enjoy the said premises for the term of years, if the said J P shall so long live.

In witness whereof, the said parties to these presents have hereunto set their hands and affixed their seals on the day and year first herein written. ——— ——— [Seal.]

——— ——— [Seal.]

Agreement to let a field for building.

Articles of agreement, made and entered into this day of , in the year , between I C of of the one part, and W H of of the other part, as follows: That in consideration that the said W H hath promised and agreed to build a dwelling-house with its appurtenances as hereinafter mentioned, he, the said J C, doth hereby promise and agree to and with the said W H, to grant and execute to him a good and valid lease, as soon as the dwelling-house above mentioned shall be covered in, of certain land now measured and staked out, and being a part of a certain field, situate, lying and being in , adjoining the lands of A B, E F and H T. Bounded as follows: that is to say, beginning [here describe the boundaries of the field], and containing acres, and that the said intended lease shall be made to hold to the said W H, his executors, administrators and assigns, from the day of , in the year , for the term of years then next ensuing, subject to the payment, by the said W H, his executors, administrators or assigns, of an annual rent amounting in the whole to the sum of dollars, besides all charges whatsoever, and that from, and out of the rent which shall accrue due for the three first years of the said term, there shall be allowed and deducted the full and clear amount of one-third part of the said annual rent for the use and benefit of the said W H, and that the said intended lease shall contain all the usual covenants, and also a covenant on the part of the said W H, that no bricks shall be made upon the said premises, and that no inn, tavern, or public house, trade or manufactory whatsoever, shall be carried on there, or any dilapidations or waste be committed or suffered on any part of the said premises. And that the said W H shall and will insure and keep the said premises insured from fire. And the said W H doth hereby promise and agree to accept and take such lease, and to pay the said J C or his attorney, the whole costs and charges of preparing and completing the said lease. And also, that he, the said W H, shall and will, before he shall erect any building upon the said piece of land, submit to the inspection of the said J C a plan and elevation of the dwelling-house, out-offices and appurtenances thereon to be erected as hereinafter mentioned, for his approbation, and when, and so soon as such plan and elevation shall have been approved by him, the said J C, shall and will forthwith proceed to erect, cover in, finish and complete, within the space of months now next ensuing, in a substantial and workmanlike manner, a good and substantial brick built dwelling-house, with suitable carriage-house, stables, offices and appurtenances and fence walls, agreeably to the said plan, so approved, at his, the said W H's own proper costs and charges, and that the dwelling-house shall be placed at not less than feet from a private road, intended to be made on the northeast side of the said land, at the expense of the said J C, and that no building which shall be erected at more than the space of feet beyond the back line of the back front of the said dwelling-house, shall be built of any height above feet from the surface of the ground, and that the said W H shall lay out and expend in the building of the dwelling-house, exclusive of all other erections, a sum not less than dollars, and shall and will, at his own expense, erect forthwith a paling of oak of five feet in height, from the surface of the ground, on the sides of the said piece of land so agreed to be taken by him, the said W H, as aforesaid.

In witness whereof, the said parties have hereunto set their hands and affixed their seals on the day and year first herein written as the date hereof. ——— ——— [Seal.]

——— ——— [Seal.]

Agreement to permit the continuance of an obstruction of ancient lights.

Articles of agreement, made, concluded and agreed upon, this day of , in the year , between A B of of the one part, and C D of of the other part: There being two ancient window lights on the side of the dwelling-house of the said A B, situate in aforesaid, and which lights have been totally obstructed by a dwelling-house which the said C D hath lately erected upon his lot adjoining thereto, it hath been agreed between the said A B and the said C D, for the purpose of preventing disputes between the owners and occupiers of the said two dwelling-houses, in manner following, that is to say: First, the said C D admits and declares, that the said A B was well entitled to the said window lights, and that the said A B voluntarily, and from motives of friendship and good neighborhood, agreed that the said C D might obstruct them, as before mentioned. And the said A B, on his part agrees that the said window lights shall and may forever remain obstructed, as before mentioned; and he hereby releases to the said C D, his heirs and assigns, all actions, suits, claims and demands whatsoever, on account thereof.

In witness whereof, the said parties to these presents have hereunto set their hands and seals the day and year first above written.

——— ——— [Seal.]
——— ——— [Seal.]

IV.

APPRAISEMENT.

In every State in the Union appraisers are appointed to ascertain the value of the property of which a decedent dies possessed. These appraisers, after making affidavit that they will truly and justly, to the best of their judgment, appraise the goods and chattels, &c. of the deceased, and after appraising the same, return a certificate of the appraisement to the court that appointed them.

Form of appraisement.

An appraisement of the estate of John Decedent deceased, in the county of . , made by the undersigned appraisers appointed by the court of the said county; the said appraisers having first been sworn according to law.

One table,..$10 00
Six knives and forks,... 5 00

&c. &c. (Signed) ALBERT A.
PETER V.
ROBERT L.

V.

APPRENTICES.

Indenture of an apprentice bound by his father or mother or guardian.

This indenture, made this day of , in the year 18 , between G H, and J H the child of the said G H, of the one part, and Robert Master of the other part: Witnesseth, that the said J H voluntarily, and with the approbation of the said G H, his parent (or guardian), hath put, placed and bound himself, and by these presents doth put, place and bind himself to be an apprentice with him the said Robert Master, and as an apprentice with him the said Robert Master to dwell, till the said J H shall have attained the age of years,[1] which will be on the day of , in the year 18 . During all which term the said G H and J H do covenant and agree to and with the said Robert Master, that the said J H shall and will well and faithfully serve the said Robert Master in all such lawful business as the said J H shall be put unto by the said Robert Master, according to the best of the power and ability of the said J H, and honestly and obediently behave toward the said Robert Master. And the said Robert Master doth covenant and agree to and with the said J H, that he the said Robert Master will well and truly instruct the said J H in the art and mystery of a *carpenter*, which the said Robert Master now followeth, and will use all due diligence to make the said J H as perfect in the said art or mystery of a carpenter as possible. And that the said Robert Master will allow to the said J H good and sufficient meat, drink, apparel, washing, lodging, and all other things suitable for an apprentice, during the said term.[2]

In witness whereof, the said parties have hereunto set their hands and affixed their seals on the day and year first herein written as the date hereof.

G H. [Seal.]
J H. [Seal.]
ROBERT MASTER. [Seal.]

[1]If a female, until 18 years; if a male, until 21 years.
[2]At this point any other covenants may be inserted.

Indenture of an apprentice bound by the overseers of the poor, under an order of court.

This indenture, made this day of , in the year , between George Oversight and William O, overseers of the poor of the county of , of the one part, and Samuel Master of said county, of the other part: Witnesseth, that the said George Oversight and William O, overseers of the poor as aforesaid, by virtue of an order of the court of , bearing date on the day of , in the year , have put, placed and bound, and by these presents do put, place and bind Oliver Orphan, of the age of years, to be an apprentice with him, the said Samuel Master, and as an apprentice with him, the said Samuel Master, to dwell from the date of these presents until the said Oliver Orphan shall come to the age of *twenty-one years*,[1] according to the act of assembly in that case made and provided. By and during all which time and term, the said Oliver Orphan shall well and faithfully serve the said Master in all such lawful business as the said Oliver shall be put unto by his said master, according to the power, wit and ability of him the said Oliver Orphan, and honestly and obediently, in all things, shall behave himself towards his said master. And the said Samuel Master, for his part, for himself, his executors and administrators, doth hereby promise and covenant to and with the said overseers of the poor, and every of them, their and every of their executors and administrators, and their and every of their successors for the time being, and to and with the said Oliver Orphan, that he, the said Samuel Master, shall, the said Oliver Orphan in the craft, mystery and occupation of a *carpenter*, which he the said Samuel Master now useth, after the best manner that he can or may, teach, instruct and inform, or cause to be taught, instructed and informed as much as thereunto belongeth, or in any wise appertaineth. And that the said Samuel Master shall also find and allow unto the said apprentice sufficient meat, drink, apparel, washing, lodging, and all other things needful or meet for an apprentice, during the term aforesaid. And also that the said Samuel Master shall teach or cause to be taught to the said

[1]A male apprentice until he is twenty-one years of age; a female apprentice until she is eighteen.

Oliver Orphan, reading, writing and common arithmetic, including the rule of three; and will moreover pay to the said Oliver Orphan the sum of dollars at the expiration of the term aforesaid.

In witness whereof, the parties to these presents have hereunto set their hands and seals on the day and year first herein written as the date hereof.

——— ——— [Seal.]
——— ——— [Seal.]
——— ——— [Seal.]

☞ Return to the clerk's office within six months after its execution. Code Va., ch. 126, sec. 8.

VI.

ASSIGNMENTS.

Assignment of a note or other evidence of debt without recourse.

I assign the within *note*[1] to James Buyer, for value received, without recourse to me in any event.

GEORGE ASSIGNOR.

[1]Or single bill, or as the case may be.

General form of assignment.

Know all men by these presents, that I, James Creditor, in consideration of dollars to me in hand paid by James Buyer, have assigned, and do by these presents assign to the said James Buyer, and his assigns, all my interest in the within [here describe the instrument], and in every clause, article or thing therein contained.

Witness my hand and seal this day of in the year .

——— ——— [Seal.]

Assignment of money due upon open account.

Know all men by these presents, that I, James Creditor, of the city of R, in consideration of the sum of dollars to me in hand paid by Benjamin Buyer, of the , do hereby assign and set over unto the said Benjamin Buyer, to his own proper use, without any account to be given for the same, the sum of , and all other sum or sums of money remaining due and payable upon or by virtue of the annexed account, and all my right, title, interest and demand in and to the same; and do give and grant unto the said Benjamin Buyer full power and authority to demand and receive the same to his own use, and upon receipt thereof, to give discharges of the same, or any part thereof; and I, the said James Creditor, do hereby covenant and agree to and with the said Benjamin Buyer, that the said sum of dollars is justly due and owing, and that I have not received or discharged the same, or any part thereof.

In witness whereof, I have hereunto set my hand and seal on this day of 18 .

—— —— [Seal.]

Assignment of a debt.

Know all men by these presents, that I, E M of , in consideration of the sum of , now justly due and owing by me to W P of , and for better securing the payment of the same to the said W P, have assigned, transferred and set over, and by these presents do assign, transfer and set over, unto the said W P, his executors, administrators and assigns, all that debt or sum of which is now due and owing to me from J H of , for goods sold and delivered by me to the said J H, or his order, before the day of the date hereof, and all my right, title, interest, claim and demand in and to the said debt or sum of , and every or any part thereof, to hold to the said W P, his executors, administrators, &c., from henceforth, to his and their own proper use and benefit forever: And I do hereby covenant and agree to and with the said W P, his executors and administrators, that I have not done or suffered, and that I, or my executors or administrators, shall not nor will do or suffer any act, matter or thing, whereby or by reason whereof the said W P, his executors and administrators, shall or may be hindered or prevented from the recovering or receiving the said debt or sum of , hereby assigned, or any part thereof, or such other satisfaction as can or may be had or obtained for the same, by virtue hereof.

In witness whereof, I have hereunto set my hand and seal on this day of 18 . —— —— [Seal.]

Assignment of a bond.

Know all men by these presents, that I, the within named A B of , for and in consideration of the sum of dollars, of lawful money of the United States, to me in hand paid by C D of , at or before the sealing and delivery of these presents, the receipt whereof is hereby acknowledged, have assigned, transferred and set over, and by these presents do assign, transfer and set over, unto the said C D, his executors, administrators and assigns, the within written bond or obligation, and the sum of , mentioned in the condition thereof, and all interest due and to grow due for the same, and all my right, title, interest, claim and demand whatsoever, of, in and to the same.[1] And I do hereby authorize the said C D, in my name, to demand, sue for, receive, have, hold and enjoy the said sum of , with the interest, to his own use absolutely, forever.

In witness whereof, I have hereunto set my hand and seal on this day of 18 . ——— ——— [Seal.]

[1]If without recourse, add: "But it is expressly understood and agreed hereby, that in no event whatever shall the said C D have recourse against me or my heirs, executors or administrators, for the said sum of money and interest aforesaid."

Assignment of annuity for the life of assignee.

This indenture, made this day of , in the year , between E M of of the one part, and I A of of the other part: Witnesseth, that whereas M M, late of , deceased, did, by his last will and testament in writing, devise unto the said E M, one annuity or yearly sum of dollars, of good and lawful money of the United States, to be issuing and payable, yearly and every year, out of all and every the property of him the said M M whatsoever, and to be paid yearly and every year, from and after his decease, unto E M, for and during the natural life of the said E M, as in and by the said last will and testament recorded in the office of , reference being had may more fully appear. Which said annuity hath, ever since the death of the said M M, been satisfied and paid to the said E M, according to the tenor, purport and true intent and meaning of the said will. And whereas the said I A hath contracted and agreed with the said E M for the purchase of the said annuity, at or for the price or sum of dollars. Now, this indenture witnesseth, that for and in consideration of the sum of dollars, and for divers other good causes and considerations him thereunto moving, he the said E M hath granted, bargained, sold, assigned and set over, and by these presents doth grant, bargain, sell and assign unto the said I A, his executors, administrators and assigns, all and every part of the aforesaid annuity, yearly rent or sum of dollars, and all the right, title, interest and benefit which he the said E M now hath, or may or in any wise ought yearly to have, of, in, or unto, or for the said annuity, yearly rent or sum of dollars, before mentioned. To have, hold, receive, enjoy and take the said annuity, or yearly rent or sum of dollars, and all the right, title, interest and benefit, use, possession, claim and demand whatsoever, of him the said E M, of, in and to the same, and of, in and unto every part and parcel thereof, as aforesaid, unto the said I A, immediately from henceforth, for and during the term of the natural life of the said E M, in as large, ample and beneficial a manner, to all intents and purposes, as he the said E M might, could, should or ought to have or enjoy the same, if these presents had not been made. And the said E M doth hereby covenant and agree to and with the said I A, his executors and administrators, that he hath not done or suffered, and that he or his executors or administrators shall not nor will do or suffer any act, matter or thing whereby, or by reason whereof, the said I A, his executors, administrators or assigns, shall or may be hindered or prevented from recovering or receiving the said annuity or yearly sum of dollars, hereby assigned, or any part thereof.

In witness whereof, &c. (as on page 16, before).

——— ——— [Seal.]
——— ——— [Seal.]

Assignment of lease by endorsement by an administrator, with consent of the lessor.

Know all men by these presents, that A B of , administrator of all and singular the goods and chattels, rights and credits of the within named C D, deceased, for and in consideration of the sum of dollars to him in hand well and truly paid by E F of

, at or before the sealing and delivery of these presents, the receipt whereof the said A B doth hereby acknowledge, hath (by and with consent of the within named P R, testified by his executing these presents) bargained, sold, assigned, transferred and set over, and by these presents doth (by and with such consent as aforesaid) bargain, sell, assign, transfer and set over unto the said E F, his executors, administrators and assigns, all and singular the, &c., and premises comprised in the within written indenture, and therein mentioned to be thereby demised, with their and every of their appurtenances, together with the within indenture of lease, and all the estate, right, title and interest which he, the said A B, as administrator of the said C D as aforesaid, or otherwise, now hath, or at any time hereafter shall or may have, claim or demand of, in or to all or any of the said premises, by virtue of the said indenture of lease, or otherwise, as the administrator of said C D. To have and to hold the said, &c., and all and singular other the premises, with their and every of their appurtenances, unto the said E F, his executors, administrators and assigns, for and during all the rest, residue and remainder yet to come and unexpired of the within mentioned term of years, in as full, ample and beneficial a manner, to all intents and purposes whatsoever, as he the said A B, his executors or administrators, might or could in any manner have held and enjoyed the same, if these presents had not been made, subject, and without prejudice, to the yearly rent of dollars, in and by the said indenture of lease reserved and contained, and to become due and payable, and to all and every the covenants, clauses, provisoes and agreements therein contained. And the said A B, for himself, his heirs, executors and administrators, doth hereby covenant and declare, to and with the said E F, his executors, administrators and assigns, that he the said A B hath not, at any time heretofore, made, done, committed or executed, or willingly permitted or suffered any act, deed, matter or thing whatsoever, whereby or wherewith, or by reason or means whereof, the said , &c., and premises hereby assigned, or intended so to be, are, is, may, can or shall be any way impeached, charged, affected or incumbered in title, charge, estate or otherwise howsoever.

In witness whereof, the said A B hath hereunto set his hand and seal on this day of , 18 . ——— ——— [Seal.]

Assignment of mortgage of a lease for years.

This indenture, made this day of , in the year , between J F of the one part, and R G of the other: Whereas F H, by indenture bearing date the day of [here recite the mortgage], which said sum of dollars, or any part thereof, was not paid or tendered to or for the said J F, at the day in the proviso of redemption limited for payment thereof, but yet remaineth unpaid, by reason whereof the said messuage and other premises, and the whole estate, right, title and interest of the said F H in and to the same, became forfeited unto the said J F, and he thereby was and is now lawfully interested in and possessed of the said premises, and every part thereof, during the residue of the term of years therein, which then were and now are to come and unexpired. Now this indenture witnesseth, that the said J F, for and in consideration of the sum of dollars, to him in hand paid by the said R G, the receipt whereof he doth hereby acknowledge, hath granted, bargained, sold, assigned and set over, and by these presents doth grant, bargain, sell, assign and set over, unto the said R G, his executors, administrators and assigns, all the said messuage, &c., and premises, with the appurtenances, granted unto him the said J F, in and by the said indenture as aforesaid, and all the estate, right, title and interest of him the said J F, by virtue of the said indenture of mortgage or assignment above recited, or of any thing therein mentioned or contained, together with the said indenture or demise, and all other writings relating to or concerning the same, now in the custody or possession of him the said J F, to have and to hold the said messuage, &c., unto the said R G, his executors, administrators and assigns, for and during all the rest, residue and remainder yet to come and unexpired of the within mentioned term of years, in as full, ample and beneficial a manner, to all intents and purposes whatsoever, as he the said R G, his executors or administrators, might or could have held and enjoyed the same, if these presents had not been made, subject and without prejudice to the yearly rent of , in and by the same indenture of lease reserved, and to become due and payable, and to all and every the covenants, clauses, provisoes and agreements therein contained.

In witness whereof, the said parties have hereunto set their hands and affixed their seals on the day and year first herein written.

—— —— [Seal.]

—— —— [Seal.]

Assignment of a policy of insurance.

Know all men by these presents, that I, S A, for and in consideration of the sum of dollars, to me in hand paid by J D, at or before the sealing and delivery of these presents, the receipt whereof I do hereby acknowledge, have bargained, sold, assigned, transferred and set over, and by these presents do bargain, sell, assign, transfer and set over, unto the said J D, his executors, administrators and assigns, all that instrument or policy of insurance, dated day of , in the year , numbering , under the hands and seals of , , officers of company, whereby certain houses, situate in , are insured from and against loss by fire, in the sum of dollars, lawful money as aforesaid, for a term of years from the date hereof, which said term hath not yet expired; and all sum or sums of money which may arise or become due or payable thereon, and all benefit and advantage thereof, to have, receive and take the same unto the said J D, his executors, administrators and assigns, to and for his and their own use and benefit.

In witness, &c. (as before, on page 22).

—— —— [Seal.]

Assignment of a bill of sale.

To all persons to whom these presents shall come, A B of , sendeth greeting: Whereas C D of did, by his bill of sale, bearing date the day of , in the year , for the consideration of dollars, bargain and sell unto the said A B the following goods and chattels [here describe them], and all the estate, right, possession and interest of him the said C D, to have and to hold the same, unto the only proper use and behoof of the said A B, his heirs, &c. forever, as by reference being had to the said bill of sale will more fully appear.

Now, know all men by these presents, that I, the said A B, for and in consideration of the sum of dollars, to me in hand paid by H K of , at or before the sealing and delivery of these presents, the receipt whereof I do hereby acknowledge, have granted, bargained, sold, assigned and set over, and by these presents do grant, bargain, sell, assign and set over unto the said H K, his heirs, &c., the above mentioned goods and chattels, together with the bill of sale above referred to, and all my right, title, interest and claim whatsoever, of, in and to the same, to have and to hold the said goods and chattels, together with the said bill of sale unto the said H K, and his heirs, &c. forever, free from all claim or claims, demand or demands, of me the said A B, or of my heirs, &c., or any other person or persons whatsoever; and I the said A B, for myself, my heirs, &c., all and singular the said goods and chattels, and the said bill of sale unto the said H K, his heirs, &c., against me the said A B, my heirs, &c., and against all and every other person or persons whatsoever, shall and will warrant and forever defend by these presents.

In witness, &c. (as before, on page 22).

—— —— [Seal.]

Assignment of a deed.

This indenture, made and entered into this day of , in the year , between H A of of the one part, and R B of of the other part: Whereas M P hath, by a certain deed bearing date the day of , in the year , given, granted and sold unto the said H A a certain lot of ground, situate, lying and being in : Now, this indenture witnesseth, that the said H A, for and in consideration of the sum of dollars to him in hand paid by the said R B, at or before the sealing and delivery of these presents, the receipt whereof he doth hereby acknowledge, hath granted, bargained, sold, assigned, transferred and set over, and by these presents doth grant, bargain, sell, assign, transfer and set over unto the said R B, his heirs, executors and administrators, all that lot of ground, with the appurtenances, granted unto him, the said H A, by M P, as aforesaid, in and by the said deed, together with the said deed, and all other writings relating to or concerning the same, in custody or possession of him, the said H A, to have and to hold the said lot of ground, unto the said R B, his heirs, executors, administrators and assigns, in as full, ample and beneficial a manner, to all intents and purposes whatsoever, as he, the said H A, his heirs, executors or administrators, might or could have held and enjoyed the same if these presents had not been made. And the said H A doth covenant and agree to and with the said R B, his heirs, &c., that he hath not done or suffered, and that he, or his heirs, &c., will not do or suffer any act, matter or thing, whereby, or by reason whereof the said H A, his heirs, &c., shall or may be hindered or prevented from receiving and enjoying the benefits which may or shall arise from the said deed, as above mentioned.

In witness, &c. (as before, on page 16).

—— —— [Seal.]
—— —— [Seal.]

An assignment of an order by endorsement.

I, the within H K, do hereby assign and transfer all my right, title and interest in and to the within written order, and the moneys thereby secured, unto A B, his executors, administrators and assigns, this day of , in the year .

Witness my hand and seal the day and year above written.

—— —— [Seal.]

Assignment of a lease.

Know all men by these presents, that A B of , for and in consideration of the sum of dollars to him in hand paid by E F of , the receipt whereof is hereby acknowledged, hath bargained, sold, assigned, transferred and set over, and by these presents doth bargain, sell, assign, transfer and set over unto the said E F, his executors, administrators and assigns, all and singular, &c., and premises comprised in the within written indenture, and therein mentioned to be thereby demised, with their and every of their appurtenances, together with the within indenture of lease, and all the estate, right, title and interest which he, the said A B, now hath, or at any time hereafter shall or may have, claim, challenge or demand of, in or to all or any of the said premises, by virtue of the said indenture of lease, or otherwise. To have and to hold the said messuage, &c., and all and singular other the premises, with their and every of their appurtenances, unto the said E F, his executors, administrators and assigns, for and during all the rest, residue and remainder yet to come and unexpired of the within mentioned term of years, in as full, ample and beneficial a manner, to all intents and purposes whatsoever, as he, the said A B, his executors or administrators, might or could in any manner have held and enjoyed the same, if these presents had not been made, subject, and without prejudice, to the yearly rent of dollars, in and by the said indenture of lease reserved and contained, and to become due and payable, and to all and every the covenants, clauses, provisoes and agreements therein contained. And the said A B, for himself, his heirs, executors and administrators, doth hereby covenant and declare, to and with the said E F, his executors, administrators and assigns, that he, the said A B, hath not, at any time heretofore, made, done, committed or executed, or wittingly or willingly permitted or suffered any act, deed, matter or thing whatsoever, whereby or wherewith, or by reason or means whereof, the said messuage and premises hereby assigned or intended so to be, are, is, may, can or shall be in any ways impeached, charged, affected or incumbered in title, charge, estate or otherwise howsoever.

In witness, &c. (as before, on page 24).

 [Seal.]

Assignment of a judgment recovered.

Know all men by these presents, that I, A B, of , in consideration of the sum of dollars to me in hand paid by J N, have granted, transferred, assigned and set over, and by these presents do grant, transfer, assign and set over unto J N, his executors, administrators and assigns, a certain judgment by me recovered in the court of , on the day of term, in the year , against C R of , for the sum of dollars, as by the record of the said judgment in the said court doth show, upon which judgment execution hath been lately sued out, as also all benefit, profit, sum and sums of money, and advantage whatsoever, that now can or shall, or may hereafter be obtained by reason or means of the same, or any execution thereupon, now had or to be had, sued, executed or obtained; and all the estate, right, title, interest and demand whatsoever, which I, the said A B, have or ought to have, or claim of, in or to the said judgment, or any sum of money, lands or tenements, which by virtue thereof, or of any process or execution thereupon sued or to be sued, shall or may be recovered, obtained or gotten. And I do hereby authorize the said J N, in my name, to sue and prosecute the said execution upon the said judgment, and to do all and every such act and acts, thing and things whatsoever, as shall be requisite in and about the premises.

In witness, &c. (as before, on page 22).

—— —— [Seal.]

Assignment of debtors' property in trust for creditors.

This indenture, made the day of , in the year , between J S, R W and R G, of , of the first part, J L of , B D of , and S W of , trustees, of the second part, and the several persons, being *bona fide* creditors of the said J S, R W and R G, who shall seal, execute and acknowledge this deed within days from the date hereof, of the third part: Whereas the said J S, R W and R G have for several years past carried on the joint trade of , in partnership together, and by reason of certain losses and misfortunes, they are unable to pay and satisfy to every of their joint and separate creditors the whole of their respective demands, but in order to render to them the utmost satisfaction in their power, they have proposed to convey and assign, as well all their joint property, as also their separate estate and effects, real and personal, to the said trustees, in trust for their said creditors, who shall execute and acknowledge this deed within days from the date hereof, rateably in proportion to the amount of their several debts, in manner hereinafter provided; to which the said respective parties of the second and third parts have consented and agreed: Now, this indenture witnesseth, that for and towards payment and satisfaction of all the debts and demands jointly and severally due to the said respective creditors, parties hereto of the third part, and for and in consideration of dollars, good and lawful money of the United States, to each of them, the said J S, R W and R G, in hand well and truly paid, by the said J L, B D and S W, at or before the sealing and delivering of these presents, the receipt whereof is hereby respectively acknowledged, they, the said J S, R W and R G, in fulfilment of their part of the said recited agreement, have, and each of them hath, bargained, sold, assigned, transferred and set over, and by these presents do, and each of them doth, bargain, sell, assign and set over, unto the said J L, B D and S W, all and singular the leasehold messuages or tenements, warehouses and premises, with their appurtenances, and also all and singular the debt and debts, sum and sums of money, household and other goods, furniture, chattels, wares and merchandise, bonds, bills, notes, securities and vouchers for or affecting the payment of money, and all other the estates and effects of what nature or kind soever and wheresoever, situate and being, and in whosesoever hands, custody or power the same, or any of them, or any part thereof, may now or hereafter at any time may come or be, with their and every of their appurtenances, and all the right, estate and interest, property, claim and demand whatsoever, therein or thereto, of them, the said J S, R W and R G, as well jointly as partners in trade, or as separately and distinctly in their own separate and distinct capacities. To have and to hold, all and singular the said respective premises hereinbefore assigned, and every part thereof, respectively, to them, the said J L, B D and S W, their executors, administrators and assigns, upon trust, nevertheless, that they, the said J L, B D and S W, or the major part of them, and the survivor or survivors of them, his executors, administrators and assigns, do and shall, with all convenient speed, sell and dispose of all and singular the estates and effects hereinbefore assigned, for the most money that can be procured for the same, and use their utmost endeavors, by all lawful ways and means, to obtain, recover and receive the same respectively into their hands and possession, and forthwith convert the same into money, upon and for the most advantageous terms, and from time to time to pay, distribute and divide the whole of such moneys, estate and effects to and amongst all such *bona fide* creditors of the said J S, R W and R G, as shall execute and acknowledge this deed within days from the date of this deed, their respective executors, administrators, agents or assigns, rateably and in proportion to the several amounts of their respective debts, to be verified on oath, if required by the trustees. And the said J S, R W and R G, do hereby jointly and severally covenant, promise and agree, to and with the said J L, B D and S W, their executors, administrators and assigns, in manner following (that is to say): That neither of them the said J S, R W and R G hath, at any time heretofore, made, done, committed or suffered, nor shall or will at any time or times hereafter, during the execution of all or any of the trusts hereby created, or any person or persons by their order or for their use, make, do, commit or suffer to be done, any act whatsoever, whereby to release or discharge any debt or debts, or alienate or conceal any sum or sums of money, estate or effects hereinbefore assigned, or intended so to be, or to obstruct or hinder the due recovery and receiving the said respective estates and effects hereinbefore assigned, or to release or discontinue any process which shall or may be commenced for recovery thereof, or to prevent any defence concerning the same, but, on the contrary, shall and will, at all times permit and suffer, promote and forward the due and regular receipt and recovery thereof, and ratify, allow and confirm all such acts as shall be lawfully done therein, by virtue of these presents, and that they will execute all such further and other acts, deeds, matters and things as shall be requisite and necessary in and towards the carrying on and accomplishing the trusts herein created. And the said J L, B D and S W do hereby, for themselves, their executors and administrators, respectively, covenant, promise and agree to and with the said J S, R W and R G, and to and with all and every their said creditors, parties hereto of the third part, their executors and administrators respectively, in manner following (that is to say): That they the said J L, B D and S W, and the survivor and survivors of them, and the executors and administrators of such survivor, shall and will, from time to time, when and as often as any moneys, estates or effects shall come to their hands by virtue of these presents, after deducting and retaining all such costs and charges as may by them be expended in the premises, well and truly share, divide and pay the same to and among such of the said creditors, parties hereto of the third part, who shall execute and acknowledge this deed within days from the date hereof, in rateable proportions, according to their respective debts. And it is further agreed by and between the said parties, that they the said respective creditors, parties hereto of the third part, in performance of their part of the aforesaid agreement, and in consideration of the assignments and provisions and covenants hereinbefore made and entered into by and on the part of the said J S, R W and R G, and for other good and valuable considerations them hereunto specially moving, do, and each and every of them, for himself and themselves severally and respectively, and for their several and respective executors, administrators and assigns, doth hereby accept and take the said hereinbefore assigned joint and several premises, estates and effects, in full payment, satisfaction and discharge of all their respective debts and demands. And they the said several creditors executing these presents, in further pursuance and full performance of their recited agreement, and for the several considerations aforesaid, have, and each and every of them hath, and by these presents for themselves, severally and respectively, and for their several and respective executors and administrators, do, and each of them doth, freely, clearly and absolutely relinquish, exonerate, discharge and forever quit claim unto the said J S, R W and R G, jointly and severally, and their joint and several heirs, executors and administrators, and their respective lands, tenements, goods and chattels, as well their, and each and every of their respective debts, as also all and all manner of action and actions, suit and suits, cause and causes of action and suit, both at law and in equity, which they the said creditors executing these presents, or any or either of them, their, or any of their executors, administrators or assigns, now have, ever had, or at any times hereafter can, shall or may have, claim, challenge or demand against them the said J S, R W and R G, either jointly or severally, their, or either or any of their heirs, executors or administrators, for or by reason or on account of their said respective debts, so due to them as aforesaid, or for or by reason or on account of any other matter, claim, demand, cause or thing whatsoever, antecedent to the day of the date of these presents.

In witness, &c. (as before, on page 16).

—— —— [Seal.]
—— —— [Seal.]
—— —— [Seal.]
—— —— [Seal.]

A shorter form of assignment of debtor's property, all the creditors sharing equally.

This deed, made this day of , between J H of the city of , party of the first part, M M of the said city, party of the second part, and the creditors of the said J R, of the third part: Whereas the said J R is embarrassed in his pecuniary affairs, and desires to secure his creditors the payment of their respective claims against him, as far as his property will admit of, and with that object in view, he has determined to convey his said property in trust, as hereinafter contained: Now, therefore, this deed witnesseth, that the said J R, in consideration of the premises, and of the sum of five dollars to him in hand paid by the said M M, the receipt whereof is hereby acknowledged, hath granted and conveyed, and doth hereby grant and convey, unto the said M M, all his the said J R's property and rights of property, real, personal and mixed, of every kind and description, the same being enumerated and described, as far as remembered, in the schedule hereunto annexed, marked "Schedule A." To have and to hold the said property and rights of property aforesaid, unto the said M M, his heirs and assigns forever. In trust to collect, sue for, demand, receive and recover all such sum or sums of money as may be due and owing to the said J R, and to sell and dispose of all the real and personal property embraced in said "Schedule A;" and from the proceeds of such sales and collections as aforesaid, after paying all reasonable and proper costs, charges and expenses, including a reasonable commission to himself, the said trustee M M, shall pay to each and all of the creditors of the said J R, the full sum that may be due and owing to the said creditors, a full and complete list of which creditors is, as far as now remembered, contained in "Schedule B," hereunto annexed. Should any creditor or creditors of the said J R not be embraced in said Schedule B, his or their rights hereunder are not to be prejudiced thereby, and if such sales and collections shall not be sufficient fully and entirely to pay off and satisfy each and all of the said creditors of the said J R, then the said trustee shall pay them *pro rata*, in proportion to the amount due and owing, or to become due and owing to each.

In witness whereof, the said parties of the first and second parts have hereunto set their hands and affixed their seals the day and year first herein written as the date hereof.

—— —— [Seal.]
—— —— [Seal.]

SCHEDULE A—referred to in annexed deed.

One wardrobe.
One table, &c.
Bond of M L to J R, dated day of , for $.
Open accounts of J R against the following persons, and for the following sums, to wit:

A C..............................$45 00
D M..............................30 00
J Q..............................560 00

Negotiable note of D T for $

(Signed) J R.

SCHEDULE B—referred to in annexed deed.

L C D, open account against J R, for..............$300 00
M N O, bond of J R for..............1000 00
L Q P, negotiable note, dated day of , for........ 630 00

(Signed) J R.

Assignment of debtors' property, making preferred classes of creditors.

This deed, made this day of , 18 , between J L and James D, partners under the firm and style of L & Co., parties of the first part, M M, party of the second part, and the several creditors of the said L & Co., enumerated and specified in the schedule hereunto annexed, parties of the third part: Whereas the said L & Co. are justly indebted in sundry and considerable sums of money, and have become unable punctually to pay and discharge the same, and are desirous of conveying their property and rights of property, as hereinafter mentioned: Now, therefore, this deed witnesseth, that the said J L and James D, partners under the firm and style of L & Co., in consideration of the premises, and of the sum of five dollars to them in hand paid, the receipt whereof is hereby acknowledged, have granted, sold and conveyed, and do by these presents grant, sell and convey unto the said M M, all and singular the goods, chattels, rights and credits of the said L & Co., and all other property of every kind and description belonging to them, or to either of them, a list of which property, and of such rights and credits, is hereto annexed, marked Schedule A, and is hereby specially referred to. To have and to hold such goods, chattels, and rights and credits and other property of every kind and description as aforesaid, unto him the said M M, his heirs and assigns forever. In trust, nevertheless, and for the following uses and purposes, to wit: *First*, to pay and satisfy from the same the several and respective debts, notes, bonds and obligations and sums of money due from the said parties of the first part, to the several persons mentioned in the class of creditors denominated and described as "First class creditors," of the said parties of the first part, in the Schedule B, hereunto annexed (if not sufficient, then *pro rata* among them), and after fully paying and satisfying such first class creditors as aforesaid, their whole debts and claims as aforesaid, against the said parties of the first part, then, *Secondly*, to pay and satisfy from the said rights, chattels and property hereby conveyed, the several and respective debts, notes, bonds and obligations and sums of money due or to become due from the said parties of the first part, to the several persons mentioned in the class of creditors denominated and described as "Second class creditors" of the said parties of the first part in the said "Schedule B (if not sufficient, then *pro rata* among them); and after fully paying and satisfying such second class creditors as aforesaid, their whole debts and claims as aforesaid, against the said parties of the first part, then, *Thirdly*, to pay and satisfy, from the said rights, chattels and property hereby conveyed, the several and respective debts, notes, bonds and obligations, and sums of money due or to become due from the said parties of the first part to the several persons mentioned in the class of creditors denominated and described as "Third class creditors" of the said parties of the first part, in said "Schedule B," and if not sufficient, then *pro rata* among them.

In executing this trust, and to carry out the purposes thereof, the said trustee is to proceed to collect, himself, or by agents and attorneys appointed by himself, all and singular the notes, bonds, bills and evidences of debt, and to make sale of the said property of every kind mentioned in "Schedule A;" and is to pay all the just and reasonable expenses, costs, commissions and charges attending the collection and management, or sale and disposition of the said notes, bills, evidences of debt, property and rights of property; these costs and charges and commissions to be borne and paid before any distribution of such collection or of the proceeds of said trust property is to be made to any class of creditors hereby secured.

In witness whereof, the parties hereto have hereunto set their hands and seals on this day of 18 .

J L. [Seal.]
JAMES D. [Seal.]

SCHEDULE A—referred to in annexed deed.

[Here describe the claims, property, &c. conveyed.]

J L.
JAMES D.

SCHEDULE B—referred to in annexed deed.

"First class creditors" of J. L. & Co.

M N, negotiable note dated day of , for......	$6,200 00
P Q, bond dated , for..............................	3,000 00

"Second class creditors" of J. L. & Co.

R B C, a note dated day of , due on the day of , for..................................	$1,120 00
L J M, single bill dated day of ,..............	350 00

"Third class creditors" of J L & Co.

A B, open account..	$25 00
C D, note..	100 00
E F, bond for...	420 00
	&c. &c.

And all other creditors of the said J L & Co., if any; whose names would be inserted here, in this third class, if remembered.

J L.
JAMES D.

VII.

POWERS OF ATTORNEY.

A general power of attorney.

Know all men by these presents, that I, James G, of the city of , have made, constituted and appointed, and do by these presents make, constitute and appoint C D of the said city, my true and lawful attorney, for me and in my name to ask, demand, sue for, recover and receive, of and from all and every person or persons whatsoever, all and every sum or sums of money due and owing, or that may become due and owing to me on any and every account, whether due or to become due or payable on bill, bond, note, open account, will, deed or otherwise, to give receipts and acquittances for the same, or at his discretion to compound, compromise and agree for the same, and give discharges; and also for me and in my name to sign any bond, obligation, contract or agreement, or other paper whatsoever, to draw and endorse promissory notes, and the same to renew from time to time, to draw upon any bank or banks, or any banker or bankers, or other individual or individuals, for any sum or sums of money that may be to my credit, or which I may be entitled to receive, and the same to deposit in any other bank, and again at his pleasure to draw for from time to time, as I myself might or could do; and also for me and in my name to sell any part or parts of my real or personal estate which I am entitled to in my own right, or in common with others, or howsoever I may be entitled to the same; and to make all necessary deeds, conveyances and assurances thereof, sealing, acknowledging, executing and delivering the same; and also for me and in my name to do all such other acts, matters and things in relation to my property, estate, affairs and business of every kind, in the said city, or elsewhere in the State of , as I myself might or could do if personally present, and acting therein, it being my intention, by this power of attorney, to commit to the said C D the entire management, care and disposition of my property and affairs, as fully and absolutely as I have now the management, care and disposition of the same, in the State aforesaid; and that this power should be understood and taken in the most comprehensive sense. And I authorize my said attorney one or more attorneys under him to substitute, and again at his pleasure revoke; hereby ratifying and confirming whatever my said attorney may lawfully do hereunder.

In witness whereof, I have hereto set my hand and affixed my seal on this day of 18 . ——— ——— [Seal.]

Power of attorney to mercantile agent.

Know all men by these presents, that I, E M, have made, constituted and appointed, and do hereby make, constitute and appoint J P my true, sufficient and lawful agent and attorney, to sell all or any part of my goods and merchandise entrusted to the said J P—said goods and merchandise to be mentioned and expressed in invoices or particulars thereof, and which my said agent and attorney, by his receipt, shall acknowledge to have received from me—said sales to be made at such times and places, and on such terms as my said agent and attorney may deem most to my advantage, the proceeds of such sale or sales to be remitted to me in good bill or bills of exchange, payable to me, or to my order, or returns thereof to be made in specie, as may be most conducive to the furtherance of my interests: Giving and granting unto my said agent and attorney full power and authority in the premises, to make sales by himself or through the agency of others, to deliver possession, receive the purchase money or good bills as aforesaid, and grant receipts therefor, and generally to do all lawful acts and things whatsoever concerning the premises, as fully, in every respect, as I myself might or could do if I were personally present, hereby ratifying and confirming whatever my said agent or attorney shall, in my name, legally do or cause to be done in and about the premises, by virtue of these presents.

In testimony whereof, I, the said E M, have hereto set my hand and seal this day of . ——— ——— [Seal.]

Power of attorney to sell and convey lands.

Know all men by these presents, that I, B C, of , have made, constituted and appointed, and do hereby make, constitute and appoint A F of , my true, sufficient and lawful attorney, for me and in my name, to bargain, sell, grant, release and convey, to such person or persons, and for such sum or sums of money, or other consideration or considerations as my said attorney shall deem most for my advantage and profit, all that parcel of land situate, lying and being in [here describe the property], and upon such sale or sales, convenient and proper deeds, with such covenant or covenants, general or special, of warranty, as to my said attorney shall seem expedient, in due form of law, as my deed or deeds, to make, seal, deliver and acknowledge, and for me, and in my name, to accept and receive all and every the sum or sums of money, or other consideration or considerations whatsoever, which shall be coming to me on account of the said sale or sales, and upon the receipt thereof, suitable acquittance or acquittances, in my name and stead, to make, seal and deliver, and generally, giving to my said attorney full power and authority touching the premises, to do, execute, proceed and finish in all things, in as ample a manner as I might do if personally present: Hereby ratifying and confirming all lawful acts done by my said attorney by virtue hereof.

In testimony whereof, I, the said B C, have hereto set my hand and seal this day of , in the year .

—— —— [Seal.]

Power of attorney to acknowledge a deed.

To all persons to whom these presents shall come, C E of , sendeth greeting: Whereas I, the said C E, have signed, sealed, and as my deed delivered, a certain deed bearing date the day of , and made between and , as by the said deed may appear: Now know ye, that I, the said C E, have made, ordained and constituted, and do hereby make, ordain and constitute H A of , my true, sufficient and lawful attorney, for me, and in my name, place and stead, to appear before any justice of the peace of county, or any other officer authorized to receive such acknowledgment, and for me, and in my name, place and stead, to acknowledge the said deed to be my own proper act and deed.

In testimony whereof, I, the said C E, have set my hand and seal this day of , in the year .

—— —— [Seal.]

Power of attorney to sell stock, and receive dividends.

Know all men by these presents, that I, B D of , have made, ordained and constituted, and do hereby make, ordain and constitute H A of to be my true, sufficient and lawful attorney, for me and in my name, place and stead, to sell and transfer unto any person or persons whatever, and for such price as my said attorney shall think fit, shares of stock of the company (or bank), and also for me and in my name, place and stead, to make and pass all necessary acts of assignment, and to receive and give receipts for the consideration money arising from the sale thereof; and also for me and in my name, place and stead, to receive and give receipts for all interest and dividends now due, or that shall become due on the stock as aforesaid, until the sale and transfer thereof: Hereby ratifying and confirming all lawful acts done by my said attorney by virtue hereof.

In testimony whereof, I the said B D have hereto set my hand and seal this day of , in the year .

——— ——— [Seal.]

Power of attorney to prosecute an execution upon a judgment recovered by verdict, and receive the proceeds, &c.

Know all men by these presents, that whereas I, B C, lately recovered judgment in the court of , against B D of , for the sum of dollars cents, as by record of the said judgment, recorded in the said court, doth appear, upon which judgment execution hath been lately sued forth: Now, know ye, that I, B C, have made, constituted and appointed, and by these presents do make, constitute and appoint J F of to be my true and lawful attorney, for me and in my name to sue and prosecute the said execution upon the said judgment; and upon composition or agreement made concerning the said premises, to acknowledge satisfaction, or to make and give any other release or discharge for the same; and all and every other such act and acts, thing and things whatsoever, do, as shall be requisite about the premises, as fully and effectually as if I the said B C was myself present and did the same; I the said B C hereby ratifying, allowing and confirming, and agreeing to hold, ratify and confirm all and whatsoever my said attorney shall lawfully do, or cause to be done by virtue of these presents.

In witness, &c. (as before, on page 22).

——— ——— [Seal.]

Power of attorney to draw, negotiate and endorse bills of exchange, &c.

Know all men by these presents, that I, F C of , have made, constituted, authorized and appointed, and by these presents do make, constitute, authorize and appoint R B of my true and lawful attorney, for me and in my name, place and stead, to make and draw bills of exchange upon any person or persons, on account of moneys due me for the sale of any goods, wares and merchandise, and as my attorney, in my name, place and stead, to subscribe the same; selling and negotiating them for my best advantage, and receiving and holding the proceeds to my use. And I do hereby give and grant unto my said attorney full power and authority, for me, in my name, place and stead, to endorse any bill or bills of exchange or other notes, which shall be drawn payable to me, and the same to sell or negotiate for my best advantage, receiving and holding the proceeds resulting from such sale or negotiation, to my use. And generally, for me the said F C, in my name and to my use, to do or cause to be done all other lawful acts, deeds, matters and things, which shall or may be requisite and necessary to be done in and about the premises, as fully and effectually, to all intents and purposes, as I, the said F C, might or could do if personally present and did the same: Hereby giving and granting to my said attorney my whole power and authority in the premises, and hereby ratifying, allowing and confirming all and whatsoever my attorney shall lawfully do or cause to be done in and about the premises, by virtue of these presents.

In witness, &c. (as before, on page 22).

——— ——— [Seal.]

Power of attorney from one executor to the other to act in his absence, execute writings, &c.

To all to whom these presents shall come, W W of , executor named and appointed in and by the last will and testament of

A W, late of , deceased, sendeth greeting: Whereas the said A W, in and by his last will and testament, in writing, bearing date the day of , in the year (and which is recorded in the office of the clerk of , Will Book, vol. , page , where, for further information, reference can be had), did nominate, constitute and appoint the said W W and F W executors of his said last will and testament: And whereas the said A W departed this life on or about the day of , in the year , without having revoked or altered his said last will and testament in all or in any of the matters aforesaid, and since his death the said W W and F W have duly proved his said will in the court of , and taken upon themselves the execution thereof: And whereas the said W W is shortly to depart from for , and is desirous of enabling, so far as he lawfully can, the said F W, the other executor of the said will, to act in the management and conduct of the estate and affairs of the said testator, during his absence, as fully and effectually as if he, the said W W, were present, and actually joining in all and every such act and acts as may be necessary for that purpose: Now, know ye, that in order to carry such, the desire of the said W W, into execution, and for the purposes aforesaid, he, the said W W, hath made, deputed, constituted and appointed, and by these presents doth make, depute, constitute and appoint the said F W to be his true and lawful attorney of him, the said W W, in his name, on his behalf, as one of the executors of the said last will and testament of the said A W, to transact, manage and negotiate all and singular, matters and things whatsoever, which in any wise relate to or concern the management, disposal or conduct of the estate and affairs of the said testator, and to that end for him, the said W W, and in his name, and on his behalf as executor as aforesaid, to settle, sign and seal if necessary, and as his act and deed in due form of law, to deliver all and every or any account and accounts, receipts, deeds, writings and instruments whatsoever, which shall or may be, or to him, the said F W, shall seem necessary or expedient for that purpose; and generally to do, execute and perform, or cause and procure to be done, all and every or any acts, deeds, matters and things whatsoever, any wise necessary or expedient to be done by or on behalf of him, the said W W, in or about the management, disposal or conduct of the said testator's estate and affairs, or any part thereof, and all and whatsoever his said attorney shall do or cause to be done, in pursuance of the powers hereby granted, he, the said W W, doth hereby, and at all times hereafter shall and will ratify, confirm and allow. In witness, &c. (as before, on page 24).

—— —— [Seal.]

Power of attorney to acknowledge satisfaction on a mortgage.

To all persons to whom these presents shall come, H B of , sendeth greeting: Whereas W P of , by indenture of mortgage under his hand and seal, bearing date the day of , in the year , for the purpose of securing the payment of the sum of dollars, which he was justly indebted unto the said H B, did give, grant, bargain and sell unto the said H B, his heirs, &c., the premises in the said indenture described. To have and to hold the same until the said sum of dollars, with the interest thereon, should be paid him, the said H B, his heirs, &c. (as by reference being had to the said indenture, recorded in the clerk's office of the court, Deed Book, vol. , page , will more fully and at large appear): And whereas the said W P hath paid and satisfied the said debt of dollars, with the interest thereon accruing, unto the said H B: Now, know ye, that the said H B hath made, ordained, constituted and appointed, and by these presents doth make, ordain, constitute and appoint A R of , his true and lawful attorney, for him and in his name, to appear in the office aforesaid, and there acknowledge satisfaction of the mortgage, and note the same on the margin of the said Deed Book, for the debt and interest, in full discharge of the said mortgage. And for so doing, this shall be his lawful authority. In witness, &c. (as before, on page 24).

—— —— [Seal.]

Power of attorney to receive the distributive share of an intestate's estate.

Whereas J C, my sister, lately died intestate, by means whereof, and by virtue of the statutes made for better distributing intestate estates, I am become legally entitled to a distributive share of my sister's personal estate: Now, know all men by these presents, that I, B C, having and reposing great confidence in A W of , have made, constituted and appointed, and by these presents do make, constitute and appoint the said A W my true and lawful attorney, for me, and in my name, to sue for, ask and demand, recover and receive of and from N T, administrator of the said J C, all my distributive share of the personal estate of my said sister, which I am by law entitled unto, and all other sum and sums of money, goods, chattels and personal estate whatsoever, which by my said sister's dying intestate, or on any other account, belong, or of right ought to belong to me; and upon receipt thereof, acquittances and other legal discharges for me and in my name, to give to the administrator of my said sister, for what my said attorney shall receive, and to make any agreement or composition for my said distributive share of my said sister's personal estate, or for any other matter or thing due to me from her estate, and [here insert clause for executing refunding bond]: whatsoever my said attorney shall do or cause to be done in and about the premises, I do hereby ratify and confirm the same as fully, to all intents and purposes, as if I were personally present and did the same.

In witness, &c. (as before, on page 22).

——— ——— [Seal.]

Power of attorney to receive and recover rents, and to give discharges.

Know all men by these presents, that I, H S, of , for divers good causes and considerations, me hereunto especially moving, have made, ordained, constituted and appointed, and by these presents do make, ordain, constitute and appoint, and in my place and stead, put and depute N O of , my true and lawful attorney, for me and in my name, and to my use, to ask, demand, levy, recover and receive of and from B M of , the lessee of all that messuage or tenement and premises situate in , and also of and from all other tenants or occupiers thereof, respectively, all sum and sums of money now in arrear for rent, or hereafter to grow due for rent for the same respective premises in ; and on receipt thereof, or of any part thereof, good and sufficient receipts and acquittances in the law, for me, the said H S, and in my name, or in his own name, as my attorney, to make and give for the same, as the case shall require, and on refusal or non-payment thereof, or of any part thereof, to commence and prosecute one or more action or actions, or to make one or more distress or distresses for rent, and to proceed therein as he shall be advised, and to take all other lawful ways and means to compel the payment thereof, that he shall judge expedient. And generally, for me, and in my name, and to and for the uses and purposes aforesaid, to do and perform all and whatsoever other acts, matters and things which shall be requisite and necessary in the premises, as fully and amply, to all intents and purposes, as if I, the said H S, were present and did the same. And I do hereby ratify and confirm whatsoever the said N O, my attorney, shall lawfully do or cause to be done therein by virtue hereof.

In testimony whereof, I, the said H S, have set my hand and seal this day of , in the year .

——— ——— [Seal.]

Power of attorney to recover debts.

Know all men by these presents, that I, M P of , for divers good causes and considerations, me hereunto especially moving, have made, ordained, authorized, constituted and appointed, and by these presents do make, ordain, authorize, constitute and appoint R N of , my true and lawful attorney, for me, in my name, and to and for my sole use and benefit, to bring to account and reckoning, and to ask, demand, sue for, levy, recover, and to receive of and from all and any person or persons whomsoever and wheresoever, all sum and sums of money whatsoever, which they or any of them shall or may be any ways indebted unto me, on any account whatsoever, and on receipt thereof, or any part or parts thereof, for me, in my name, and to my use, such good and sufficient receipts and discharges to make and give for the same as the nature of the case shall require, and to liquidate and discharge the same, and on neglect or refusal from or by any such person or persons to pay all or any such sum or sums of money, so due and owing unto me as aforesaid, to take and use all such usual and customary legal ways and means for compelling or securing the due payment thereof, by action, suit, attachment or otherwise, howsoever, in my name, as my said attorney shall be advised, and for me, in my name and for my use to prosecute and defend all or any actions or suits, either at law or in equity, attachment or other legal process, now brought, or to be brought and commenced by, for or against me, in any court or courts of judicature in , and therein to proceed to judgment and execution thereon, or to discontinue or compromise the same, as my said attorney shall be advised, or to do any other act, matter or thing which shall be required and necessary to be done on my part and behalf, in the proceedings, or carrying on or defending any such action or suit, so brought or to be brought, as aforesaid, and also for me, and to or for my use, to defray, pay and discharge all sum and sums of money, debts, dues, claims and demands which shall or may be justly due and owing from, or accrue against me to any person or persons whomsoever, on any account whatsoever, and to take and receive for the same, such receipts and discharges as the case may require, and also for me, in my name, and to and for my use and benefit, to do, transact, execute and perform all and whatsoever other act, matters and things which shall or may arise, and be requisite and necessary to be done in and about, touching or concerning the management of my affairs and concerns, or any of them, or in any manner relative thereto, and generally, for me, in my name, and to my use, to do and perform and execute all and whatsoever other acts, matters and things which my said attorney shall judge requisite and necessary, or to be advised to be done in and about the premises, as fully and effectually, to all intents and purposes, as if I myself were present and did the same: I, the said M P, hereby ratifying, allowing and agreeing, for myself, my heirs, executors and administrators, from time to time, and at all times hereafter, to ratify, allow and confirm as good and valid, all and whatsoever my said attorney shall lawfully do or cause to be done in and about the premises by virtue hereof.

In testimony whereof, I, the said M P, have set my hand and seal this day of , in the year .

——— ——— [Seal.]

A shorter form of power of attorney to recover debts.

Know all men by these presents, that I, B M of , for divers good causes and considerations me hereunto moving, have constituted and appointed, and by these presents do constitute and appoint W P of to be my true and lawful attorney, giving and granting unto him full power and authority, in my name, to ask, demand, sue for, levy, recover, receive, compound, acquit and discharge any debt or debts, sum or sums of money, now owing, or that may hereafter become owing me, the said B M, and upon receipt of the same, or any part thereof, acquittances or other proper discharges to make, and generally, for me and in my name, to make, do, perform and execute all and every such further and other acts, matters and things touching the premises, as to the said W P shall seem requisite, and that as fully and effectually, to all intents and purposes, as I myself could or might have done if I had been present: Hereby ratifying and confirming all and whatever he shall lawfully do or cause to be done in or about the premises.

In testimony whereof, I, the said B M, have hereunto set my hand and seal this day of , in the year .

——— ——— [Seal.]

Power of attorney to receive a legacy.

Know all men by these presents, that whereas M S, late of , by her last will and testament, did give and bequeath unto me, A T of , dollars, to be paid unto me: And whereas the said will of the said A T having been duly admitted to probate, and E F is the executor thereof: Now, know ye, that I the said A T have made, ordained, constituted, deputed and appointed, and by these presents do make, ordain, constitute, depute and appoint B H of my true and lawful attorney, for me and in my name, and to my use, to ask, demand and receive of and from the said E F, the said legacy of , so given and bequeathed to me the said M S, by her said will as aforesaid, and upon receipt thereof by my said attorney, to deliver a receipt and release for the same, or to give such other discharge as shall be sufficient: And I do further nominate, constitute and appoint the said B H my true and lawful attorney, for me and in my name, place and stead, to execute and deliver all and every proper refunding bond or bonds, with security, which may be required on the payment of said legacy: Hereby ratifying, allowing and confirming all and whatsoever my said attorney shall lawfully do in the premises.

In witness whereof, I, the said A T, have hereunto set my hand and seal this day of , in the year .

——— ——— [Seal.]

Substitution under a power of attorney.

Know all men by these presents, that I, A B of , in pursuance and by virtue of the powers invested in me by P H of , by a power of attorney under his hand and seal, bearing date the day of , in the year , have substituted, deputed and appointed, and by these presents do substitute, depute and appoint E F of , to be my true and lawful attorney to [here insert the power contained in the original letter], giving, and by these presents granting unto the said E F my full and whole derived power and authority in the premises, in as full and ample manner, to all intents and purposes, as I have received the same from the said P H, by the said hereinbefore mentioned power of attorney. I, the said A B, as well for the said P H as for myself, hereby agreeing to ratify, allow, indemnify and confirm all and whatsoever the said E F shall lawfully do therein, by virtue of this, my substitution.

In testimony whereof, I, the said A B, have hereunto set my hand and seal this day of , in the year .

——— ——— [Seal.]

A seaman's power of attorney.

Know all men by these presents, that I, A B, for divers good causes and considerations, me hereunto moving, have and do hereby name, and in my stead and place put and constitute C B of , my true and lawful attorney, revocable, for me, in my name and to my use, to ask, claim, demand and recover, and receive of and from and , or whom else it may concern, all and singular such salary, wages, tickets, bounty money, prize money, short allowance money, smart money, pensions, and all other sum and sums of money whatsoever, as now is, or at any time or times hereafter, shall be due, payable or belonging unto me for my own or any other service or otherwise in any of the United States ships, frigates or vessels, or any merchant ship or ships. And also, of all other person or persons whatsoever, all and singular such other sum or sums of money, salary, wages, goods, wares, merchandises, freights, profits, rents and arrears of rents, debts, dues, duties, claims and demands whatsoever, which now is or at any time hereafter shall be due, owing and payable, and belonging unto me by any ways or means, right or title whatsoever, or howsoever, giving and hereby granting unto my said attorney, his substitutes and assigns, all my authority and lawful power in the premises for receiving, recovering, obtaining, compounding and discharging the same, as fully and effectually as I myself might or could do, being personally present, and acquittances, releases or any other discharges in my name, to make, seal and deliver, and one attorney or more to make, substitute and at pleasure revoke: Hereby ratifying and confirming all and whatsoever my said attorney, his substitutes and assigns, or any of them, shall lawfully do or cause to be done in and about the premises by virtue of these presents.

In witness whereof, I have hereunto set my hand and affixed my seal this day of , in the year .

—— —— [Seal.]

Revocation of a power of attorney.

Know all men by these presents, that I, H B of , for divers good causes and considerations me hereunto especially moving, have revoked, countermanded, annulled and made void and of no effect, and by these presents do revoke, countermand and make void and of no effect, a certain power of attorney under my hand and seal, bearing date the day of , in the year , to A C of , given, delivered and executed, and all powers and authorities whatsoever therein expressed and declared.

In testimony whereof, I, the said H B, have hereunto set my hand and seal this day of , in the year .

—— —— [Seal.]

VIII.

AWARDS.

NOTE.

An award cannot be binding, unless due notice of the time and place of meeting of the arbitrators is served on the parties, and all reasonable opportunity of being heard is granted to them. The arbitrators may proceed *ex parte*, if the party fails to attend after receiving such notice.

The laws of Virginia provide, that persons desiring to end any controversy, whether there be a suit pending therefor or not, may submit the same to arbitration, and agree that such submission may be entered of record in any court. Upon proof of such agreement out of court, or by consent of the parties given in court, in person, or by counsel, it shall be entered in the proceedings of such court, and thereupon a rule shall be made that the parties submit to the award made in pursuance of such agreement.

Form of agreement for award.

Whereas certain questions and disputes, between A B of , of the one part, and E G of , of the other part, have arisen and are now depending: Now, therefore, for the finally ending all such questions and disputes, and deciding the same, it is consented, concluded and agreed, by and between the said A B and E G, that the matters in controversy shall be, and are hereby referred and submitted to the final award and determination of H K of , M P of , and J S of , or any two of them, arbitrators indifferently chosen by the said parties, so as the said arbitrators, or any two of them, do make their award or determination of and concerning the premises, in writing under their hands and seals, ready to be delivered to the said parties requiring the same, on or before the day of next ensuing the date of these presents. And it is hereby mutually agreed by and between the said parties, that this submission shall be entered of record in the court of the county of .

In testimony whereof, the parties to these presents have hereunto set their hands and seals this day of , in the year .

——— ——— [Seal.]
——— ——— [Seal.]

Form of an award.

Whereas J J of , of the one part, and A S of , of the other part, have mutually entered into, and reciprocally executed bonds or obligations to each other, bearing date the day of , in the penal sum of , conditioned that the said parties should, in all things, well and truly stand to, abide, observe, perform, fulfil and keep the award, order, final end and determination of R B of , and N O of , arbitrators indifferently chosen by the said parties, of and concerning all and all manner of disputes and differences existing between the said parties, so as the said award of the said arbitrators should be made on or before the day of , in the year , in writing, and ready to be delivered to the said parties: Now, know ye, that we, the said arbitrators, whose names are hereunto subscribed, having duly examined into the cause or causes of difference existing between the said parties by hearing the statements, proofs and allegations of both, do make and publish this, our award between the said parties, in manner following: [The remainder of the award must be filled up as the circumstances of the particular case require.]

In testimony whereof, the parties to these presents have hereunto set their hands and seals this day of , in the year .

——— ——— [Seal.]
——— ——— [Seal.]

An award by an umpire.

To all to whom these presents come, I, S T of , send greeting:—Whereas P O of , of the one part, and A B and D C of , of the other part, have mutually entered into and reciprocally executed bonds or obligations to each other, bearing date the day of , in the year , in the penal sum of , conditioned that the said parties should, in all things, well and truly stand to, abide, observe, perform, fulfil and keep the award, order, final end and determination of R S of , and B W of , arbitrators indifferently chosen by the said parties, of and concerning all and all manner of action and actions, cause and causes of action and actions, suits, bills, bonds, specialties, covenants, contracts, promises, accounts, reckonings, sums of money, judgments, executions, extents, quarrels, controversies, trespasses, damages and demands whatsoever, both in law and equity, committed or depending by or between the said parties, so as the said award of the said arbitrators should be made on or before the day of , in the year . But if the said arbitrators should not make such their award of and concerning the said differences and disputes, by the time aforesaid, then if the said parties should in all things well and truly stand to, abide, observe, perform, fulfil and keep the award, order, arbitrament, umpirage, final end, and determination of such person, as should thereafter be chosen by the said arbitrators between the said parties, of and concerning the said differences, so as the said umpire should make his award or umpirage of or concerning the same, on or before the day of : And whereas the said R S and B W met upon the said arbitration, and did not make their award between the said parties by the time limited in and by the conditions of the said bonds, and in pursuance of the said bonds have chosen and appointed me as umpire to settle and determine the matters in difference between the said parties: Now, know ye, that I, the said S T, the umpire named and chosen as aforesaid, having taken upon me the burden of the said arbitrators, and having heard and examined, as well the said parties as their respective attorneys, and their respective witnesses, proofs and allegations on both sides, of and concerning the said disputes and differences between them, and fully considered the same, and the matters to me referred, do make this my award and umpirage, in manner following, that is to say [here the award must be inserted, according to the various cases, the conclusion may be as follows]: And upon the payment of the said sum of (or the performance of the required condition), I do award and direct that the said parties shall duly execute and deliver to each other mutual relinquishments in writing, of all and every action and actions, cause or causes of action, damages, claims and demands whatsoever, subsisting or depending on or before the said day of last.

In testimony whereof, I, the said S T, have set my hand and seal this day of , in the year .

——— ——— [Seal.]

A nomination of an umpire by two arbitrators.

Know all men by these presents, that we the undersigned, A and B, arbitrators chosen to award and determine the matters in difference between L P and J M, as appears by articles of agreement made between the said L P and J M, and dated the day of , 18 , not having concluded and agreed upon the premises to us referred as aforesaid, do hereby, according to and in pursuance of the power to us granted by the said articles of agreement, nominate and appoint F R of the city of , the sole umpire in the premises, to conclude and determine and make his final award and umpirage of all the matters, demands and differences in controversy between the said parties, referred to in said articles of agreement aforesaid.

In witness whereof, we have hereunto set our hands and seals on this day of , 18 .

—— —— [Seal.]
—— —— [Seal.]

IX.

BARGAIN AND SALE.

Of goods and chattels.

Know all men by these presents, that I, A B of , in consideration of the sum of , to me in hand paid by C D of , at or before the sealing and delivery of these presents, the receipt whereof I do hereby acknowledge, have granted, bargained, sold and confirmed, and by these presents do grant, bargain, sell, convey and confirm unto the said C D, all the goods, household stuff and implements of household mentioned in the following schedule, to wit [here describe the articles]: to have and to hold all and singular the said goods, household stuff and implements of household, and every of them, by these presents bargained and sold, unto the only proper use and behoof of the said C D, his executors, administrators and assigns, forever, freely, quietly, peaceably and without any contradiction, claim, disturbance or hindrance of any person whatsoever, and without any account to me, or to any other whatsoever, to be made, answered, or hereafter to be rendered, so that neither I, the said A B, nor any other for me, or in my name, any right, title, interest or demand, of, in, to or for the said goods, household stuff, and implements of household, or any part or parcel thereof, ought to exact, challenge, claim or demand, at any time or times hereafter, but from all action, right, estate, title, claim, demand, possession and interest thereof, shall be wholly barred and excluded by force and virtue of these presents. And I, the said

A B, for myself, my executors and administrators, all and singular the said goods and household stuff, unto the said C D, his executors and assigns, against me the said A B, my executors, administrators and assigns, and against all and every other person or persons whatsoever, shall and will warrant, and forever defend by these presents.

In witness whereof, I, the said A B, have hereunto set my hand and seal this day of , in the year .

A B. [Seal.]

X.

BILLS OF EXCHANGE.

A bill of exchange is a written order for the payment of money, issued from one place, and directed to another. If payable in the same State or country in which it is drawn, it is "an inland bill." If addressed to a party residing in a different State or country, requiring him to pay a certain sum to his order, or to a third or fourth party at a specified time, it is a "foreign bill of exchange."

By the law of Virginia, as it stood in the Revised Code of 1819, p. 483, ch. 125, § 1, "All bills of exchange, or drafts for money in the nature of bills of exchange, drawn by any person or persons residing in this State, or any person or persons in the United States, or in the Territories thereof, or in the District of Columbia, shall be considered, in all cases whatsoever, as inland bills of exchange." But this provision has been omitted from the present Code (1860), with the view to make such bills *foreign* bills. See Code, ch. 144, § 9, and note of revisors on that section. The present statutes of Virginia concerning bills of exchange and negotiable notes, are contained in chapter 144 of the Code, sections 1–9. These sections are as follows:

"1. If a person accept a bill of exchange, payable at the house of a banker or other place, without further expression in his acceptance, such acceptance shall be deemed a general acceptance, and the presentment of the bill for payment may be either at such place, or as it might have been if no such place had been specified in the acceptance. If an acceptor shall, in his acceptance, express that he accepts the bill, payable at a banker's house or other place only, and not otherwise or elsewhere, such acceptance shall be deemed a qualified acceptance, and in such case the presentment of the bill for payment shall be at the place specified in such qualified acceptance. But as against the maker of a note or the acceptor of a bill, whether the acceptance be general or qualified, it shall not be necessary to aver or prove presentment for payment at the time or place specified in the note, bill or acceptance. Such maker or acceptor may, however, set up, as a matter of defence, any loss sustained by him, by reason of the failure to make such presentment.

"2. If a bill of exchange, wherein the drawer shall have expressed that it is to be payable in any place other than that by him mentioned therein to be the residence of the drawee, shall not, on the presentment thereof for acceptance, be accepted, such bill may, without further presentment to the drawee, be protested for non-payment in the place in which it shall have been, by the drawer, expressed to be payable, unless the amount thereof be paid to the holder on the day on which the bill would have become payable, had it been duly accepted.

"3. A bill or note which becomes due on a Sunday, shall be payable and may be protested on the preceding day, and a bill or note which becomes due on a Christmas day, or the first day of January or fourth day of July, shall be payable and may be protested on the preceding day, or if that be Sunday, then on the preceding Saturday.

"4. When a bill or note is protested, either under the preceding section or otherwise, on the day preceding any Sunday, Christmas day, first day of January or fourth day of July, notice of the dishonor thereof need not be given until the first day afterwards, which is not Sunday, Christmas day, or the first day of January or fourth day of July.

"5. When a bill of exchange is accepted supra protest for honor, or has a reference thereon in case of need, it shall not be necessary to present such bill to such acceptor for honor, or to such referee, until the day following that on which such bill shall become due, and if the place of address on such bill of such acceptor for honor, or of such referee, shall be in any town or place other than in the town or place where such bill is therein made payable, then it shall not be necessary to forward such bill for presentment for payment to such acceptor for honor or referee, until the day following that on which such bill shall become due.

"6. If the day following that on which such bill shall become due shall happen to be a Sunday or Christmas day, or the first day of January, or the fourth day of July, then it shall not be necessary to present it or forward it for presentment for payment to such acceptor for honor or referee until the first day afterwards, which is not Sunday or Christmas day, or the first day of January, or fourth day of July.

"7. Every promissory note, or check for money, payable in this State at a particular bank, or at a particular office thereof for discount and deposit, or at the place of business of a savings institution or savings bank, and every inland bill of exchange, payable in this State, shall be deemed negotiable, and may, upon being dishonored for non-acceptance or non-payment, be protested, and the protest be in such case evidence of dishonor, in like manner as in the case of a foreign bill of exchange.

"8. The protest, both in the case of a foreign bill, and in the other cases mentioned in the preceding section, shall be *prima facie* evidence of what is stated therein, or at the foot, or on the back thereof, in relation to presentment, dishonor and notice thereof.

"9. When a bill of exchange drawn or endorsed within this State is protested for non-acceptance or non-payment, there shall be paid by the party liable for the principal of such bill, in addition to what else he is liable for, damages upon the principal, at the rate of three *per centum* if the bill be payable out of Virginia and within the United States, and at the rate of ten *per centum* if the bill be payable without the United States."

FORMS OF BILLS OF EXCHANGE, CHECK, DRAFTS AND PROMISSORY NOTES.

Form of foreign bill of exchange.

New York, May 8th, 18 .

£500 Sterling.

Sixty days after sight (or at days after date), pay to this, my first bill of exchange (second and third of the same tenor and date not paid), to Messrs. , or order (or bearer), five hundred pounds sterling, value received of them, and place the same to account, as per advice from R H.

To Mr. , in London.

Form of check.

Baltimore, Nov. 5th, 18 .

$200 00.

Pay to H K, or order (or bearer), two hundred dollars. L M.

Cashier of Bank.

Forms of drafts.

Boston, Jan. 1st, 18 .

$500 00.

Six months after date, pay to my order, five hundred dollars, for value received. B F.

To Mr. T J, Albany.

New York, Aug. 5th, 18 .

$100 00.

Sixty days after sight, pay to C B, or order, one hundred dollars, for value received. J H.

To W F & Co., Philadelphia.

Promissory notes.

New York, Feb. 7th, 18 .

$375 00.

Three months after date, I promise to pay A B, or order, three hundred and seventy-five dollars, for value received.

H B.

Baltimore, March 8th, 18 .

Thirty days after date, I promise to pay B R, the sum of six hundred dollars, with interest thereon, at the rate of six *per centum per annum*, from this date till paid, for value received.

T S.

Form of negotiable note.

Ninety days after date, I promise to pay W E, or order, the sum of three hundred and fifty-nine dollars, negotiable at the bank, without offset, for value received. C P.

XI.

BILLS OF SALE.

Bill of sale of a ship.

Know all men by these presents, that I, B A, of , for and in consideration of the sum of dollars, good and lawful money of the United States, to me in hand well and truly paid, at and before the sealing and delivery hereof, by D C of , the receipt whereof I do hereby acknowledge, have granted, bargained, sold, assigned, transferred and set over, and by these presents do fully and absolutely grant, bargain, sell, assign, transfer and set over unto the said D C, all that ship or vessel called the , and now lying within the port of , together with all and singular the masts, sails standing and running, rigging, ropes, cable, anchors, boats, oars, tackle, apparel, furniture and appurtenances whatsoever to the said ship or vessel belonging. To have and to hold the said ship or vessel called the , and all and singular the premises hereinbefore mentioned, and hereby bargained and sold or intended so to be, and every part and parcel thereof, with the appurtenances, unto the said D C, his executors, administrators and assigns, to and for his and their own proper use and benefit, and as his own property, goods and chattels from henceforth forever. And I, the said B A, do for myself, my heirs, executors and administrators, and for every of them, covenant, promise and agree to and with the said D C, his executors, administrators and assigns, in manner following (that is to say): that I, the said B A, at the time of the sealing and delivery hereof, have in myself good right, full power, and lawful and absolute authority, by these presents, to grant, sell, assign, transfer and set over the said ship or vessel called the

, and premises, with the appurtenances, unto the said D C, his executors, administrators and assigns, in manner and form and according to the true intent and meaning of these presents. And also, that the said ship or vessel, and premises hereby bargained and sold, and every part and parcel thereof, with the appurtenances, shall from henceforth forever after remain, continue and be unto the said D C, his executors, administrators and assigns, free and clear, and freely and clearly acquitted, exonerated and discharged of and from all other bargains, sales, gifts, grants, titles, judgments, debts, charges and incumbrances whatsoever.

In witness whereof, I hereto set my hand and affix my seal this day of , in the year . B A. [Seal.]

Bill of sale of a ship, from two persons, each of a moiety.

Know all men by these presents, that we, A B, of , owner of one full moiety or half part, of and in that good ship or vessel called the , and C D, of , owner of the other full and equal moiety or one-half part of the said good ship or vessel, for and in consideration of our several full and equal half parts or moieties of the sum of dollars, lawful money of the United States, to us in hand paid, at or before the sealing and delivery of these presents, by E F of , the receipt whereof we do hereby severally acknowledge, have severally granted, bargained, sold, assigned, transferred and set over, and by these presents each of us doth respectively, fully and absolutely grant, bargain, sell, assign, transfer and set over unto the said E F, his heirs, executors or administraters, forever, the one full or equal moiety or half part of and in all the aforesaid ship or vessel called the , of the burden of tons, or thereabouts, now lying in , whereof each of them is declared to be owner, as aforesaid, and also of and in all and singular the masts, rigging, sails standing and running, ropes, cables, anchors, boats, oars, tackle, furniture and appurtenances whatsoever, to the said ship or vessel belonging or in any wise appertaining: to have and to hold the said moieties or half parts of and in the said ship or vessel called the , and all and singular the other premises hereinbefore mentioned, and hereby bargained and sold or intended so to be, and every part and parcel thereof, with the appurtenances, unto the said E F, his heirs, executors and administrators, to and for his and their own proper use and benefit, and as his own proper goods and chattels, from henceforth, forever. And we, the said A B and C D, do hereby severally and respectively and not jointly nor one for the other, nor for the other's act, but each for himself only, his heirs, &c., covenant, promise and agree that each of us, the said A B and C D, at the time of the sealing and delivery of these presents, have in ourselves good right, full power, and lawful and absolute authority to grant, bargain, sell, assign, transfer and set over the said moiety or half part of us, the said A B and C D, in the said ship or vessel, with the appurtenances, by us respectively sold unto the said E F, his heirs, &c., and that our said several moieties or half parts of and in the said ship or vessel, with its appurtenances, by us respectively sold, as aforesaid, now are, and so from henceforth, forever, shall be and remain and continue unto the said E F, his heirs, &c., free and clear from all claim or claims of us, the said A B and C D, or any other person or persons whatsoever.

In witness whereof, we have hereto set our hands and seals this day of , in the year .

A B. [Seal.]
C D. [Seal.]

XII.

BONDS.

Bond for the payment of money by installments.

Know all men by these presents, that I, Daniel D, am held and firmly bound unto Cornelius C, in the just and full sum of one thousand dollars, to the payment whereof well and truly to be made to the said Cornelius C, his executors, administrators and assigns, I promise and bind myself, my heirs, executors and administrators, firmly by these presents. Sealed with my seal and dated on this day of , in the year 18 .

The condition of the above obligation is such, that if the above bound Daniel D shall well and truly pay to the said Cornelius C, (*) the sum of one hundred and twenty-five dollars on the first day of , in the year 18 ; the farther sum of one hundred and twenty-five dollars on the first day of , in the year 18 ; the farther sum of one hundred and twenty-five dollars on the first day of , in the year 18 ; and the farther sum of one hundred and twenty-five dollars on the first day of , in the year 18 , then the above obligation is to be void, otherwise to remain in full force and virtue. DANIEL D. [Seal.]

Short form of single bill or bond to the same effect as the preceding.

On the first day of , in the year 18 , I promise to pay to Cornelius C the sum of one hundred and twenty-five dollars; on the first day of , in the year 18 , I promise to pay to the said Cornelius C the farther sum of one hundred and twenty-five dollars; on the first day of , in the year 18 , I promise to pay to the said Cornelius C the farther sum of one hundred and twenty-five dollars, and on the first day of , in the year 18 , I promise to pay to the said Cornelius C the farther sum of one hundred and twenty-five dollars; to the payment of which several sums well and truly to be made to the said Cornelius C, at the respective periods aforesaid, *I bind myself and my heirs, executors and administrators, firmly by these presents.*

Witness my hand and seal[1] on this day of , in the year 18 . ——— ——— [Seal.]

[1] *If given by two persons:*—Substitute "we" in lieu of "I," wherever it occurs; and in place of words in italics, say: "we bind ourselves and our heirs, executors and administrators, jointly and severally, firmly by these presents. Witness our hands and seals," &c.

Bond for the payment of money by installments, given by two persons.

Know all men by these presents, that we Daniel D and Samuel S are held and firmly bound unto Cornelius C in the just and full sum of one thousand dollars, to the payment whereof well and truly to be made to the said Cornelius C, his executors, administrators or assigns, we promise and bind ourselves and our heirs, executors and administrators, jointly and severally, firmly by these presents. Sealed with our seals and dated this day of , in the year 18 .

The condition of the above obligation is such, that if the above bound Daniel D and Samuel S shall well and truly pay to the said Cornelius C, &c., &c., (as in form on page 61, from the (*) to the end).

DANIEL D. [Seal.]
SAMUEL S. [Seal.]

☞ This bond may be used, whether the obligors are both of them debtors to the obligee, or one of the obligors is surety for the other; or, in lieu thereof, the following:

Know all men by these presents, that we A B and R M are held and firmly bound unto C D, in the just and full sum of dollars; to the payment whereof, well and truly to be made to the said E F, his executors or administrators, we bind ourselves, our heirs, executors and administrators, jointly and severally, firmly by these presents. Sealed with our seals and dated this day of , in the year 18 .

The condition of the above obligation is such, that if the above bound A B and R M, or either of them, or their or either of their heirs, executors or administrators, shall well and truly pay to the above named C D, his heirs, executors or administrators, the full sum of dollars, with interest thereon after the rate of dollars for every one hundred dollars for a year, on the days and times, and in manner following (that is to say): the sum of dollars, part thereof, with interest thereon after the rate aforesaid, on the day of , next ensuing the date of the above written obligation, and which will be in the year of our Lord ; the sum of dollars, other part thereof, with interest for the same after the rate aforesaid, on the day of , then next following; the sum of dollars, residue thereof, with interest for the same after the rate aforesaid, on the day of , then next ensuing, and which will be in the year of our Lord , then this obligation to be void: but if default shall be made in payment of any or either of the said several and respective sums of money, with the interest thereof respectively, in manner aforesaid, or any part of them, on any of the said days and times above mentioned for payment thereof, according to the true intent and meaning of these presents, then this obligation is to remain in full force and virtue.

A B. [Seal.]
R M. [Seal.]

Arbitration bond.

Know all men by these presents, that I, H K of , am held and firmly bound unto F G of , in the sum of dollars, lawful money of the United States, to be paid to the said F G, or to his certain attorney, executors, administrators or assigns, for which payment, to be well and truly made, I bind myself, my heirs, executors and administrators, firmly by these presents. Sealed with my seal and dated the day of , in the year .

The condition of the above obligation is such, that if the above bound H K, his executors and administrators, and every of them, do and shall, for his and their part and behalf, in and by all things well and truly stand to, obey, abide, observe, perform, fulfil and keep the award, order, arbitrament, final end and determination of (or any two of them), arbitrators indifferently chosen, elected and named, as well by and on the part and hehalf of the said H K, as by and on the part and behalf of the above named F G, to arbitrate, award, order, judge, determine and agree, for, upon, touching and concerning all manner of action and actions, cause and causes of actions, suits, bills, bonds, specialties, covenants, contracts, promises, accounts, reckonings, sums of money, judgments, executions, quarrels, controversies, trespasses, damages and demands whatever, both at law and in equity, at any time heretofore had, moved, brought, commenced, sued, prosecuted, done, suffered or committed by or between the said parties, so as the award of the said arbitrators (or any two of them) be made and set down in writing, indented under their (or any two of their) hands and seals, ready to be delivered to the said parties in difference, on or before the day of (*), THEN this obligation shall be void, otherwise the same shall remain in full force and authority.

H K. [Seal.]

When to be made before an umpire:—Follow preceding form to the (*), then say: "And if the said arbitrators shall not make such their award of and concerning the premises, within the time limited as aforesaid, then if the said H K, his heirs, executors and administrators, and every of them, for his and their part and behalf, do and shall well and truly stand to, observe, perform, fulfil and keep the award, determination and umpirage of G (being a person indifferently named and chosen by the said parties for umpire), in and concerning the premises, so as the said umpire do make and set down his award and umpirage in writing, indented under his hand and seal, ready to be delivered to the said parties in difference, on or before the day of , in the year , then this obligation shall be void, otherwise the same shall remain in full force and authority."

When to be made a rule of court:—Follow preceding form to the (*), then say: "And it is hereby agreed by and between the said parties, that these presents, and the submission hereby made of the said matters in controversy, shall be made a rule of the court of , to the end the said parties in difference shall be finally concluded by the said arbitration by these presents intended, pursuant to the statute in that case made and provided."

Indemnifying bond given to sheriff on making a levy of fieri facias. (*Code Va.*, *ch.* 152, § 4.)

Know all men by these presents, that we, Robert C and Samuel S, are held and firmly bound unto Lemuel L, sheriff of the county of H, in the sum of dollars;[1] to the payment whereof, well and truly to be made unto the said Lemuel L, sheriff as aforesaid, we bind ourselves, and our heirs, executors and administrators, jointly and severally, firmly by these presents. Sealed with our seals and dated this day of , in the year 18 .

The condition of the above obligation is such, that whereas the above named Robert C, upon a judgment obtained by him in the court of the county of , against Daniel D, has sued out a writ of *fieri facias* for taking the goods and chattels of the said Daniel D, to satisfy him, the said Robert C, the sum of dollars, with interest thereon, at the rate of six per centum per annum, from the day of , 18 , till paid, and dollars costs; which writ is directed to the sheriff of the said county; and J K, deputy for Lemuel L, sheriff of the said county, has levied the said execution on the following property, to wit [here specify it]: and a doubt arising whether the said property is liable to such levy, the said sheriff has applied to the said Robert C for an indemni-

[1] A penalty equal to double the value of the property levied on.

fying bond, according to the statute in such case: Now, if the said Robert C and Samuel S, their heirs, executors and administrators, shall indemnify the said Lemuel L, the sheriff aforesaid, against all damages which he may sustain in consequence of the seizure or sale of the property on which the said execution has been levied, and moreover shall pay to any claimant of such property all damages which he may sustain in consequence of such seizure or sale, and shall warrant and defend to the purchaser or purchasers of the property such estate or interest therein as shall be sold under the said execution, then the above obligation is to be void, otherwise it is to remain in full force and virtue. ROBERT C. [Seal.]
SAMUEL S. [Seal.]

Usual forthcoming bond.

Know all men by these presents, that we Daniel D and Samuel S are held and firmly bound unto Cornelius C, in the sum of dollars, to the payment whereof, well and truly to be made to the said Cornelius C, his executors, administrators or assigns, we bind ourselves and our heirs, executors and administrators, jointly and severally, firmly by these presents. Sealed with our seals and dated this day of , 18 .

The condition of the above obligation is such, that whereas the above named Cornelius C, upon a judgment obtained by him in the court of county, against Daniel D, has sued out a writ of *fieri facias* for taking his goods and chattels, which writ is directed to the sheriff of the said county, and by virtue thereof the following goods and chattels, to wit [here specify them], have been taken by J K, deputy for Lemuel L, sheriff of the said county, to satisfy the said execution, the amount whereof at this time, including the sheriff's fee and commissions, is dollars, and the said Daniel D, the owner of the goods and chattels so taken, desires that the said goods and chattels should be suffered to remain in his possession and at his risk until the day of sale, and has offered to give sufficient security to the sheriff to have the same forthcoming at that time: Now, if the said Daniel D shall have the said goods and chattels forthcoming on the day of next, at , being the day and place of sale appointed by the sheriff, then the above obligation is to be void, otherwise it is to remain in full force and virtue. DANIEL D. [Seal.]
SAMUEL S. [Seal.]

Suspending bond. (*Under Code Va., ch.* 152, § 6.)

Know all men by these presents, that we, C C and Robert S, are held and firmly bound unto Lemuel L, sheriff of the county of , in the just and full sum of dollars, to the payment whereof, well and truly to be made to the said Lemuel L, sheriff as aforesaid, his heirs, executors and administrators, we bind ourselves and our heirs, executors and administrators, jointly and severally, firmly by these presents. Sealed with our seals and dated this day of , 18 .

The condition of the above obligation is such, that whereas Cornelius R, upon a judgment obtained by him in the court of county, against Daniel D, has sued out a writ of *fieri facias* for taking his goods and chattels, which writ is directed to the sheriff of said county, and by virtue thereof the following goods and chattels, to wit [here specify them], have been taken by J K, deputy for Lemuel L, sheriff of the said county, to satisfy the said execution: and whereas the above named Cilly C, at the time of the levy aforesaid, claimed the said goods and chattels, and the sheriff having required of the said Cornelius R an indemnifying bond, the said Cornelius R has executed such indemnifying bond, with Benjamin P as his surety; and the said Cilly C now desiring to suspend the sale of said property, agrees to execute his bond, with the said Robert S as his security: Now, therefore, if the above bound Cilly C and Robert S shall well and truly pay to all persons who may be injured by suspending the sale of the said goods and chattels so levied on, until the claim thereto can be adjusted, such damages as they may sustain by such suspension, then the above obligation shall be void, otherwise to remain in full force and virtue.

CILLY C. [Seal.]
ROBERT S. [Seal.]

Forthcoming bond given (after a suspending bond has been given), so as to permit property to remain in such possession as it was before the levy. (*Code Va., ch.* 152, § 7.)

Know all men by these presents, that we, C C and Robert S, are held and firmly bound unto Cornelius R in the sum of dollars, to the payment whereof, well and truly to be made to the said

Cornelius R, his executors, administrators or assigns, we bind ourselves and our heirs, executors and administrators, jointly and severally, firmly by these presents. Sealed with our seals and dated this day of , 18 .

The condition of the above obligation is such, that whereas the above named Cornelius R, upon a judgment obtained by him in the court of county, against Daniel D, has sued out a writ of *fieri facias* for taking his goods and chattels, which writ is directed to the sheriff of the said county; and by virtue thereof, the following goods and chattels, to wit [here specify them], have been taken by J K, deputy for Lemuel L, sheriff of the said county, to satisfy the said execution, the amount whereof at this time, including the sheriff's fee and commissions, is dollars; and the said C C having claimed as his property the said goods and chattels, the said Cornelius R indemnified the said sheriff, by executing an indemnifying bond, and the said C C has executed a suspending bond to suspend the sale of the said goods and chattels until the claim thereto can be adjusted; and the said claimant C C desiring the said goods and chattels to remain in such possession as they were immediately before the levy, executes this bond, with said Robert S as his security, according to law: Now, therefore, if the said goods and chattels so levied on, shall be forthcoming at such day and place of sale, as may hereafter be lawfully appointed, then the above obligation shall be void, otherwise it is to remain in full force and virtue. C C. [Seal.]

ROBERT S. [Seal.]

Refunding bond to executor on his paying a legacy.

Know all men by these presents, that we, B C and R M, are held and firmly bound unto C D, executor of the last will and testament of H K deceased, in the just and full sum of dollars, to the payment whereof, well and truly to be made to the said C D, executor as aforesaid, his executors, administrators or assigns, we bind ourselves, our heirs, executors and administrators, jointly and severally, firmly by these presents. Sealed with our seals and dated this day of , in the year 18 .

Whereas H K, late of , deceased, did, by his last will and testament, bearing date the day of , in the year , give and bequeath unto B C, the sum of dollars, as by reference being had to the said will, recorded in the clerk's office of court, Will Book, vol. , page , will more fully appear; and the said B C now desires the said legacy to be paid to him, and C D, the executor of said will, having agreed to pay the same to him, and has paid the same to said C D, cotemporaneously with his the said B C's executing this refunding bond, as required by law, and the said B C executes this his refunding bond, with the said R M his surety: Now, therefore, if the said B C shall refund a due proportion of any debts or demands which may hereafter appear against the decedent H K, and of the costs attending their recovery, then the above obligation shall be void, otherwise to remain in full force and virtue.

B C. [Seal.]
R M. [Seal.]

Bond from lessee and his surety to pay rent according to lease.

Know all men by these presents, that we, G T, principal, and R M, surety, are held and firmly bound unto M P, in the just and full sum of dollars, to the payment whereof, well and truly to be made to the said M P, his executors, administrators or assigns, we bind ourselves, our heirs, executors and administrators, jointly and severally, firmly by these presents. Sealed with our seals and dated this day of , in the year 18 .

Whereas the above named M P, by his indenture of lease, bearing even date with, and executed before the above written obligation, for the consideration in the said lease mentioned, hath leased to the above bound G T, a messuage or tenement, with the appurtenances, situated in , to hold unto him the said G T, his executors, &c., for the term of years, from thence next ensuing, determinable, nevertheless, at the end of the first years of the said term, if the said G T, his executors, &c., shall give months notice thereof, in manner therein mentioned, at and under the yearly rent of dollars, payable quarterly, in manner as is therein expressed, as by the said lease may more fully appear: Now, the condition of this obligation is such, that if the above bound G T and R M, or either of them, or either of their heirs, executors, &c., shall and do, during the continuance of the said recited lease, well and truly pay, or cause to be paid, the said yearly rent or sum of dollars, unto the said M P, her heirs, &c., on the four quarterly days following, viz: on the day of next ensuing the date of this obligation, on the day of , on the day of , and on the day of , in the year , by four even and equal portions, or within days next after every of the said quarter days, according to the true intent and meaning of the lease above referred to (subject, nevertheless, to the determination thereof, in manner as aforesaid), then the above written obligation to be void and of no effect; but if default shall happen to be made of or in any of the said quarterly payments, then the same shall remain in full force and virtue.

——— ——— [Seal.]
——— ——— [Seal.]

Bond to one bound for the obligor in a bond for the payment of money.

Know all men by these presents, that we, C D, principal, and R M, surety, are held and firmly bound unto A B, in the just and full sum of dollars, to the payment whereof, well and truly to be made to the said A B, his executors, administrators or assigns, we bind ourselves, our heirs, executors and administrators, jointly and severally, firmly by these presents. Sealed with our seals and dated this day of , in the year 18 .

Whereas the above named A B, at the special instance and request of the above bound C D, together with him the said C D, is, in and by one obligation, bearing even date with the above written obligation, held and firmly bound unto E F of , in the penal sum of dollars, lawful money of the United States, conditioned for the payment of the sum of dollars, with interest thereon after the rate of *per centum*, on the day of , next ensuing the date of the said recited obligation, as in and by the said recited obligation and condition thereof may more fully appear: Now, the condition of this obligation is such, that if the said C D, his heirs, executors or administrators, do and shall well and truly pay or cause to be paid unto the said E F, his heirs, executors, administrators or assigns, the said sum of dollars, with interest for the same, after the rate of *per centum per annum*, on the day of , next ensuing the date of the said recited obligation, according to the true intent and meaning thereof, and in full discharge and satisfaction of the said recited obligation, and if the said C D, his heirs, executors or administrators,

shall also, from time to time, and at all times hereafter, save harmless and indemnify him the said E F, his heirs, executors and administrators, and his and their lands and tenements, goods and chattels, of and from all damages, sums of money, and costs and charges which he, they or any of them, shall or may at any time hereafter be put unto, by reason of the said A B's being bound with the said C D, for the payment of the sum of money and interest aforesaid, then this obligation to be void, else to remain in full force and virtue. ——— ——— [Seal.]
——— ——— [Seal.]

Bond to make and deliver conveyances, and to permit the obligee to receive the rents in the mean time.

Know all men by these presents, that we, B A, principal, and R M, surety, are held and firmly bound unto C D, in the just and full sum of dollars; to the payment whereof, well and truly to be made to the said C D, his executors, administrators or assigns, we bind ourselves, our heirs, executors and administrators, jointly and severally, firmly by these presents. Sealed with our seals and dated this day of , in the year 18 .

The condition of this obligation is such, that if the above bound B A do and shall, upon, and at the request of the said C D, his heirs or assigns, on or before the day of next ensuing the day above written, convey and assure, or cause to be well and sufficiently conveyed and assured, unto the said C D, his heirs and assigns, or to such other person and persons, and his and their heirs, as the said C D shall nominate and appoint, and to such uses as he shall direct, one messuage or tenement, &c., situate, lying and being in , now in the possession of , by such conveyances and assurances in law, as by the said C D, his heirs and assigns, or his and their counsel, shall be devised, advised and required, freed and discharged of and from all incumbrances whatsoever. And also if the said B A, his heirs, executors or administrators, do and shall, until such conveyance and assurance be made and executed as aforesaid, permit and suffer the said C D, his heirs and assigns, peaceably and quietly to have, receive and take to his and their own proper use and uses, the rents, issues and profits of all and singular the said premises, and of every part and parcel thereof, without any manner of let, suit, trouble, disturbance, hin-

drance or denial of the said B A, his heirs, executors or administrators, or any of them, or of any other person or persons whatsoever, by his or their, or any of their means, right, title or procurement, then the above obligation to be void, or else to remain in full force and virtue. ——— ——— [Seal.]
——— ——— [Seal.]

Bond of indemnity, on paying a lost bond.

Know all men by these presents, that we, A A, principal, and R M, surety, are held and firmly bound unto H K in the just and full sum of dollars; to the payment whereof, well and truly to be made to the said H K, his executors, administrators or assigns, we bind ourselves, our heirs, executors and administrators, jointly and severally, firmly by these presents. Sealed with our seals and dated this day of , in the year 18 .

Whereas the above named H K did, by his bond or obligation, under his seal, and bearing date on the day of , in the year , become bound to the above bound A A, in the penal sum of dollars, conditioned for the payment of dollars unto the said A A, his heirs, executors, &c., on or before the day of , in the year ; as in and by the said bond, when produced, will more fully appear: And whereas the said bond is alleged to be lost, or so mislaid that the same cannot be found: And whereas the said H K, the day of the date hereof, at the request of him, the said A A, and on his promise of indemnity, hath made him full satisfaction of and for the said bond: Now, the condition of this obligation is such, that if the above bound A A, his heirs, executors or administrators, or any or either of them, do and shall, in case the said bond or obligation shall happen to be found, or come to his, their or any of their hands, custody or power, or of the hands, custody or power of any other person for them, deliver or cause the same to be delivered unto the said H K, his heirs, executors or administrators, in order to be made void, cancelled and destroyed, and also shall and do, from time to time, and at all times hereafter, save, keep harmless and indemnified, the said H K, his heirs, executors and administrators, of and from all actions, suits, costs, charges, damages and expenses whatsoever, which shall or may at any time hereafter happen or come to them, for or by reason of the said bond or obligation, or any of the money thereby paid, or for, touching and concerning the same: then this obligation to be void, else to remain in full force and virtue.

——— ——— [Seal.]
——— ——— [Seal.]

Bond that a person, when of age, shall convey.

Know all men by these presents, that we, R S, principal, and D M, surety, are held and firmly bound unto J B in the just and full sum of dollars; to the payment whereof, well and truly to be made to the said J B, his executors, administrators or assigns, we bind ourselves, our heirs, executors and administrators, jointly and severally, firmly by these presents. Sealed with our seals and dated this day of , in the year 18 .

Whereas T S, late of , deceased, by his last will and testament in writing, bearing date on or about the day of , in the year , did, among other things, give, devise and bequeath all that messuage or tenement situate in , unto his sons R S and H S; which will more fully appear by reference being had to the said will, recorded in the clerk's office of the county of , Will Book, vol. , page : And whereas the above named J B hath agreed with the said R S and H S, for the absolute purchase of the said messuage or tenement and premises so devised to them as aforesaid, at and for the sum of dollars; but the said H S, not being yet of age, cannot join in conveying the same to the said J B: And whereas the said J B hath, at the request of the above bound R S, and on his promise and undertaking that the said H S should, when and so soon as he should have attained the age of twenty-one years, at the costs and charges of the said J B, convey and assure to the said J B, his heirs and assigns, all his right, title and interest in and to the said messuage or tenement and premises, that being an undivided moiety, paid into the hands of R S the whole of the purchase money, and the said R S hath, by his deed, conveyed his undivided moiety thereof to the said J B, his heirs and assigns: Now, the condition of this obligation is such, that if he, the said H S, do and shall, when and so soon as he shall have attained the age of twenty-one years, at the costs and charge of the said J B, convey and assure unto the said J B, his heirs and assigns, by such deeds and conveyances as the counsel of the said J B shall approve of, his undivided moiety of and in the said messuage or tenement and premises, devised to him and the said R S as aforesaid, and that without any consideration to be paid him by the said J B for so doing: and also, if, and in case the said R S, his heirs, executors or administrators, do and shall, in the mean time, and until the said H S shall have executed such conveyance as aforesaid, save, defend, keep harmless and indemnified, the said J B, his heirs, executors and administrators, and his and their goods and chattels, lands and tenements, and the said messuage or tenement and premises, to be conveyed by the said H S to the said J B as aforesaid, and the rents, issues and profits thereof, of and from all claims and demands to be made thereto, by or on the part and behalf of the said H S, then this obligation to be void and of none effect, else to remain in full force and virtue.

—— —— [Seal.]
—— —— [Seal.]

Bond to indemnify an endorser of a note.

Know all men by these presents, that we, A B, principal, and R M, surety, are held and firmly bound unto C E in the just and full sum of dollars; to the payment whereof, well and truly to be made to the said C E, his executors, administrators or assigns, we bind ourselves, our heirs, executors and administrators, jointly and severally, firmly by these presents. Sealed with our seals and dated this day of , in the year 18 .

Whereas the above bound A B did, by a certain note, under his hand, dated the day of , promise to pay unto H K, or order, months after the date thereof, the sum of dollars, with interest thereon till paid: And whereas the above named C E hath endorsed the said note above mentioned, at the request and for the only debt of the said A B, and thereby become chargeable with and for the payment of the said sum of dollars, with interest as aforesaid, as by the said note and endorsement will at large appear: Now, the condition of this obligation is such, that if the said A B, his executors and administrators, or any of them, do and shall well and truly pay, or cause to be paid unto the said H K, or to any person or persons whom he shall direct, the above mentioned sum of dollars, for which the said note is given, and the interest that may or shall have accrued thereon on the day of payment therein mentioned, and in full discharge thereof and therefrom, and from all actions, suits, charges, payments and damages by reason thereof, shall and will, at all time and times hereafter, save, defend, keep harmless and indemnified, the said C E, his heirs, executors and administrators, and all and every of them, then this obligation to be void, else remain in full force and virtue.

——— ——— [Seal.]
——— ——— [Seal.]

Bond to save harmless from paying rent when the title is in question.

Know all men by these presents, that we, C R, principal, and R M, surety, are held and firmly bound unto F H in the just and full sum of dollars; to the payment whereof, well and truly to be made to the said F H, his executors, administrators or assigns, we bind ourselves, our heirs, executors and administrators, jointly and severally, firmly by these presents. Sealed with our seals and dated this day of , in the year 18 .

Whereas there is a suit depending between the above bounden C R and others, touching the right and interest in the dwelling-house of the above named F H situated [here describe its location]: And whereas the said F H hath nevertheless agreed to pay the rent of the said house to the said C R, yearly, as the same shall grow due, upon his agreeing to indemnify him therefrom: The condition, therefore, of the above written obligation is, that if the said C R, his heirs, executors and administrators, do and shall well and truly pay, or cause to be paid to the said F H, his executors, administrators or assigns, all rent, sum and sums of money, charges and damages whatsoever, as shall by due proceedings in law be adjudged or decreed against him the said F H, his executors, administrators or assigns, and all other costs and damages whatever, which he the said F H, his executors, administrators or assigns, shall sustain or be at, by reason of any action, suit or forfeiture whatsoever, which shall or may happen, or be, to the said F H, his executors, administrators or assigns, as by reason of paying the said rent, or any part thereof, to the said C R, his executors, administrators or assigns, in manner aforesaid, then this obligation shall be void, or else remain in full force and virtue.

——— ——— [Seal.]
——— ——— [Seal.]

Bond given for the performance of covenants.

Know all men by these presents, that we H S, principal, and R M, surety, are held and firmly bound unto C D, in the just and full sum of dollars, to the payment whereof, well and truly to be made to the said C D, his executors, administrators or assigns, we bind ourselves, our heirs, executors and administrators, jointly and severally, firmly by these presents. Sealed with our seals and dated this day of , in the year 18 ..

Now, the condition of the above obligation is such, that if the above bounden H S, his heirs, executors and administrators, do and shall well and truly observe, perform, fulfil and keep, all and every the covenants, clauses, articles and agreements specified and contained in a certain indenture, bearing even date with the above written obligation, and made, or mentioned to be made, between, &c., which, on the part and behalf of the said H S, his heirs, executors and administrators, is, are and ought to be observed, performed, fulfilled and kept, according to the true intent and meaning of the same indenture; then the above written obligation shall be void and of no effect, otherwise the same shall remain in full force. ——— ——— [Seal.]

——— ——— [Seal.]

Bond of indemnity from a vendor to a purchaser, where title-deeds were lost.

Know all men by these presents, that we, A B, principal, and R M, surety, are held and firmly bound unto C D, in the just and full sum of dollars, to the payment whereof, well and truly to be made to the said C D, his executors, administrators or assigns, we bind ourselves, our heirs, executors and administrators, jointly and severally, firmly by these presents. Sealed with our seals and dated this day of , 18 .

Whereas the above named C D hath lately purchased of and from the above bounden A B, certain messuages, &c., situate, lying and being in , for the price or sum of , and the same premises, by a certain deed bearing even date with the above obligation, and made between the said A B of the one part, and the said C D of the other part, have been conveyed and assured unto the said

C D, his heirs and assigns, but the title-deeds and evidences of title to the said premises, are either lost or mislaid, and cannot at present be found, and the said A B hath therefore agreed to save harmless and keep indemnified the said C D, his heirs and assigns, against all persons whomsoever, claiming any right or title to the said premises, or any part thereof, and all costs and charges attending the same: And also, that in case the said title-deeds and evidences to the said premises, shall at any time hereafter be found, the same shall be delivered to the said C D, his heirs or assigns, whole and uncancelled: Now, the condition of this obligation is such, that if the said A B, his heirs, executors or administrators, do and shall, from time to time, and at all times hereafter, save harmless and keep indemnified, the said C D, his heirs, executors, administrators and assigns, of, from and against all mortgages and other charges and incumbrances, anywise affecting the said messuages, &c., and premises, and against all and every person and persons whomsoever claiming any estate, right or title of, in or to the same, or any part thereof. And if the said title-deeds and evidences, forming a perfect and complete title to the said premises, shall at any time hereafter be found, and the same be delivered up to the said C D, his heirs or assigns, whole and uncancelled, without fraud or delay, then this obligation shall be void, or else shall remain in full force and virtue. ——— ——— [Seal.]

——— ——— [Seal.]

Bottomry bond.

Know all men by these presents, that I, A B, commander and two-thirds owner of the ship E, for myself, and C D, remaining third owner of said ship, am held and firmly bound unto E F, in the penal sum of dollars; for the payment of which, well and truly to be made unto the said E F, his heirs, executors, administrators or assigns, I hereby bind myself, my heirs, executors and administrators, firmly by these presents. In witness whereof, I have hereunto set my hand and seal this day of , in the year 18 .

Whereas the above bound A B hath taken up and received of the said E F, the full and just sum of dollars, which sum is to run at respondentia on the block and freight of the ship E, whereof the said A B is now master, from the port or road of B, on a voyage to the port of L, having permission to touch, stay at, and proceed to all ports and places within the limits of the voyage, at the rate or premium of twenty-five *per cent.* (25 *per cent.*) for the voyage. In consideration whereof, usual risks of the seas, rivers, enemies, fires, pirates, &c., are to be on account of said E F. And for the further security of the said E F, the said A B doth by these presents mortgage and assign over to the said E F, his heirs, executors, administrators and assigns, the said ship E and her freight, together with all her tackle, apparel, &c. And it is hereby declared, that the said ship E and her freight is thus assigned over for the security of the respondentia taken up by the said A B, and shall be delivered to no other use or purpose whatever, until payment of this bond is first made, with the premium that may become due thereon: Now, the condition of this obligation is such, that if the above bound A B, his heirs, executors or administrators, shall and do well and truly pay or cause to be paid unto the said E F, or to his attorney in L, legally authorized to receive the same, their executors, administrators or assigns, the just and full sum of dollars, being the principal of this bond, together with the premium which shall become due thereon, at or before the expiration of days after the safe arrival of the said ship E at her moorings in the river T, or in case of the loss of the said ship E, such an average as by custom shall have become due, on the salvage, then this obligation to be void and of no effect, otherwise to remain in full force and virtue. Having signed to three bonds of the same tenor and date, the one of which being accomplished, the other two to be void and of no effect.

Signed, sealed and delivered in the presence of . } A B, for self and C D. [Seal.]

Respondentia bond.

Know all men by these presents, that we, A B, commander of the ship M, in the service of C D, and H L of , are held and firmly bound to P R of , merchant, in the sum of dollars, good and lawful money of the United States of North America, to be paid to the said P R, or to his certain attorney, executors, administrators or assigns; to which payment, well and truly to be made, we bind ourselves, jointly and separately, our heirs, executors and administrators, firmly by these presents. Sealed with our seals and dated this day of , in the year 18 .

Whereas the above named P R has, on the day of the date above written, advanced and lent unto the said A B and H L the sum of dollars, upon the goods and merchandises and effects laden and to be laden on board the good ship or vessel called the M, of the burden of tons, or thereabouts, now riding at anchor in the river T, outward bound to C, and whereof A B is commander, by his acceptance of a bill of exchange to that amount at months date, for the account of them, the said A B and H L: Now, the condition of this obligation is such, that if the said ship or vessel do, and with all convenient speed proceed and sail from and out of the said river T, on a voyage to any port or place, ports or places in , and from thence do and shall sail, return and come back into the said river T, at or before the expiration of months, to be accounted from the day of the date above written, and there to end her said intended voyage (the dangers and casualties of the seas excepted): and if the said A B and P R, or either of them, their or either of their heirs, executors or administrators, do and shall, within days next after the said ship or vessel shall be arrived at her moorings in the said river T, from her said intended voyage, or at or upon the end and expiration of the said months, to be accounted as aforesaid (which of the said times shall first and next happen), well and truly pay or cause to be paid unto the said P R, his executors, administrators or assigns, the full sum of dollars, lawful money of the United States of North America, together with dollars of like money per calendar month, for each and every calendar month, and so proportionably for a greater or lesser time than a calendar month, for all such time and so many calendar months as shall be elapsed and run out of the said calendar months, over and above months, to be accounted from the day of the date above written, or if during the said voyage, and within the said calendar months, to be accounted as aforesaid, an utter loss of the said ship or vessel by fire, enemies, men-of-war, or any other casualties, shall unavoidably happen, and the said A B and P R, their heirs, executors or administrators, do and shall, within calendar months next after such loss, well and truly account for (upon oath, if required) and pay unto the said H L, his executors, administrators or assigns, a just and proportionable average on all the goods and effects of the said A B, carried from the United States on board the said ship or vessel, and the net proceeds thereof, and on all other goods and effects which the said A B shall acquire during the said voyage, for or by reason of such goods, merchandises and effects, and which shall not be unavoidably lost, then the above written obligation to be void and of no effect, else to stand in full force and virtue.

—— —— [Seal.]
—— —— [Seal.]

XIII.

DEEDS.

Deed of bargain and sale of land, &c., from husband and wife to purchaser.

This indenture, made this day of , in the year , between J C of , and E (formerly E N), his wife, of the one part, and H M of , of the other part: Witnesseth, that the said J C, and E, his wife, for and in consideration of the sum of dollars, good and lawful money of the United States, to them in hand paid by the said H M, at or before the sealing and delivery of these presents, the receipt whereof they do hereby acknowledge, and thereof acquit and forever discharge the said H M, his heirs, executors and administrators, by these presents have granted, bargained, sold, aliened, enfeoffed, released and confirmed, and by these presents do grant, bargain, sell, alien, enfeoff, release and confirm unto the said H M, and unto his heirs and assigns forever, a certain lot, piece or parcel of land, situate, lying and being in , and containing acres—bounded as follows, to wit: Beginning at the [here describe the land], together with all the estate, right, title, interest and property, claim and demand whatever, of them, the said J C, and E, his wife, in law or equity, or otherwise however, of, in, to or out of the same: To have and to hold the said lot, piece or parcel of land, and every part and parcel thereof, with their appurtenances, unto the said H M, his heirs and assigns, forever, and unto the only proper use and behoof of him, the said H M, his heirs and assigns, forever. And the said J C, for himself, his heirs, executors and administrators, and for and in behalf of the said E, his wife, and her heirs, doth covenant, promise, grant and agree to and with the said H M, his heirs and assigns, by these presents, in manner and form following, to wit: That he, the said J C, and his heirs, the said lot, piece or parcel of land and premises hereby granted, or intended so to be, with the appurtenances, unto the said H M, his heirs and assigns, against him, the said J C, and his heirs, and against the heirs of the said E, his wife, and against all and every person or persons whatever, will warrant and forever defend by these presents.

In witness whereof, &c. (as before, on page 16).

Signed, sealed and delivered in our presence. } —— —— [Seal.]
—— —— [Seal.]

Deed of bargain and sale of land by executrix.

An indenture, made this day of , in the year of our Lord , between P C, widow, and executrix of the last will and testament of R C, late of , deceased, of the one part, and H A of , of the other part:—Whereas the said R C became in his lifetime lawfully seized in fee simple, of and in a certain parcel and tract of land, situate and being in [here describe the land], and containing acres, which said land was conveyed to said R C, in his lifetime, by M W of , by deed of the day of , in the year , as fully appears by said deed, which is of record in the court of : And being so thereof seized as aforesaid, the said R C, on the day of , in the year , made his last will and testament in writing, whereby he did will and direct, that all his just debts should be paid, and for that purpose his real property should be sold, and then the remainder of his estate, both real and personal, should be in fee and in absolute property to the said P C, of the first part in this indenture mentioned, and said R C did, by said last will and testament, constitute and appoint the said P C to be the sole executrix of said will and testament, and departed this life without altering or revoking the same, as in and by the said will duly proved, and recorded in the office of the court of (Will Book, No. , fol.), reference being had thereto, will more fully appear:

Now, this indenture witnesseth, that the said P C, as widow, and executrix and residuary legatee, for and in consideration that it behooveth her in the due discharge of her trust as aforesaid, the just claims on the estate of said R demanding this exercise thereof, and she, the said P, in her character of widow and residuary legatee, acquiescing therein, and for the further consideration of the sum of dollars, good and lawful money of the United States, to her in hand paid by the said H A, at and before the execution of this indenture, the receipt whereof she doth hereby acknowledge, and thereof acquit and forever discharge the said H A, his heirs, executors and administrators; doth by these presents grant, bargain and sell, by virtue of the powers and authority aforesaid, unto the said H A, his heirs and assigns, all the above mentioned and described tract or tracts of land, together with the privileges and appurtenances to the said land in anywise appertaining and belonging; together with all and singular the estate, right, title, interest, property, claim and demand whatever, of the said R C, in his lifetime, at and immediately before the time of his decease, of, in or to, out of the same; and of all right of dower, in or out of said property, which she, the said P C, has or may at any time be entitled to, as widow of said R C: to have and to hold the said tract or tracts of land, privileges and appurtenances, hereby granted, bargained and sold unto the said H A, his heirs and assigns forever. And the said P C doth hereby promise, covenant and agree, to and with the said H A, his heirs and assigns, that she, the said P, hath not committed or suffered to be done, any act, matter or thing whatever, whereby the premises aforesaid, or any part thereof, is or shall be impeached, charged or incumbered in title, charge or estate, or otherwise, howsoever. And for the consideration aforesaid, and for the further consideration of one dollar in hand paid to the said P, as widow of the said R C, by the said H A, the receipt whereof is hereby by the said P acknowledged, she doth grant, remise, and forever quit claim unto the said H A, his heirs and assigns forever, all the right which she, the said P C, hath to dower or thirds of and in the aforesaid conveyed premises, whereof her husband, the said R C, died seized: to have and to hold the same to the said H A, and his heirs and assigns, forever; and the said P, as widow aforesaid, for herself, her heirs, executors and administrators, doth hereby covenant with the said H A, and his heirs and assigns, that he and they shall henceforth have, and quietly enjoy the released premises, without any claim or demand had or made, or to be had or made by her, the said P C, or any persons claiming the same, or any part thereof, from or under her, the said P, as widow aforesaid.

In witness whereof, the said parties to these presents have hereto signed their names and affixed their seals the day and year first above written.

Signed, sealed and delivered in our presence. ——— ——— [Seal.]
——— ——— [Seal.]

Deed of gift to feme covert, free from claim, &c. of husband.

Know all men by these presents, that I, T P of , in consideration of the natural love and affection which I have and bear unto my daughter M R, wife of S R, of , and also for other good causes and considerations, me, the said T P, hereunto moving, have given, granted and confirmed, and by these presents do give, grant and confirm unto the said M R [here describe the property given], to have, hold and enjoy the said , unto the said M R, for *her own use, livelihood and support,* free and clear of and from all debts and contracts of every and any description whatever, of her present or any future husband; it being the express intent and meaning of me, the said T P, to transfer said property to my said daughter, exclusively and absolutely, as though she were a *feme sole,* entirely free and clear of and from any marital rights whatever of her said husband, or of any future husband. And I, the said T P, the said property unto the said M, and her assigns, against me, the said T P, my executors, administrators and assigns, and all and every other person or persons whatever, shall and will warrant and forever defend by these presents; of which said property, I, the said T P, have put the said M in full possession.

In witness whereof, I have hereunto set my hand and seal this day of , in the year . T P. [Seal.

☞ See Code of Virginia, ch. 116, § 1.

Deed of gift of personal estate.

Know all men by these presents, that I, B A of , in consideration of the natural love and affection which I have and bear unto my beloved brother C B, and also for divers other good causes and considerations me, the said B A, hereunto moving, have given, granted and confirmed, and by these presents do give, grant and confirm unto the said C B all and singular the following goods and chattels [here enumerate them]: to have, hold and enjoy all and singular the said goods, chattels and personal estate unto the said C B, his executors, administrators and assigns, to the only proper use and behoof of the said C B, his executors, administrators and assigns, forever. And I, the said B A, all and singular the said goods, chattels and personal estate to the said C B, his executors, administrators and assigns, against me, the said B A, my executors and administrators, and all and every other person or persons whomsoever, shall and will warrant and forever defend by these presents, of all and singular which said goods, chattels and personal estate, I, the said B A, have put the said C B in full possession.

In witness whereof, I have hereunto set my hand and seal this day of , in the year .

B A. [Seal.]

☞ See Code of Virginia, ch. 116, § 1.

Note.—It is much better to convey property, when designed for the separate use of married women, to trustees for their benefit. See the next Form.

Deed of gift of land to trustees for the benefit of feme covert and her children, and free from all interest or claim of husband.

This indenture, made the day of , in the year , between C H of , of the first part, G D and M N, trustees, of the second part, and N R, wife of A R of , of the third part: Witnesseth, that in consideration of the love and affection which the said C H hath and beareth for his daughter, the said N R, and for and in consideration of the sum of dollars, good and lawful money of the United States, to the said C H in hand paid by the said trustees, at or before the sealing and delivery of these presents, the receipt whereof is hereby acknowledged, he, the said

C H, hath granted, bargained, sold, aliened, released and confirmed, and by these presents doth grant, bargain, sell, alien, release and confirm unto the said trustees, and to the survivors and survivor of them, and the heirs of such survivor, the tract or parcel of land situate, lying and being in the county of , containing acres, more or less, being the same land bargained, sold and conveyed to the said C H by F D of , by deed bearing date the day of , in the year , and of record in the clerk's office of court. To have and to hold the said tract or parcel of land unto the said trustees, and to the survivors and survivor of them, and the heirs of such survivor, upon trust, that they, the said trustees, and the survivors and survivor of them, and the heirs of such survivor, shall permit the said N R to occupy, possess and enjoy the said tract or parcel of land, and the rents, issues and profits thereof, to take, free and clear of and from all manner of charge and incumbrance of her said husband, or any husband she may hereafter take: and on this farther trust, that whenever directed so to do by the said N R, by a writing under her hand and seal, attested by two witnesses, the said trustee shall sell, convey in trust, mortgage, or otherwise dispose of said property: in the event of a sale, the proceeds of sale may, if directed so to be by the said N R, be invested in other property, to be held upon the trusts of this deed: and if the said N R should leave a will, or paper testamentary in the nature of a last will and testament, the said property hereby conveyed, or such as may be substituted therefor, shall go and pass to such persons, and in such proportions and manner as said N R shall thereby direct: and on this farther trust, that if the said N R shall depart this life without having sold the said property, either in whole or in part, and without leaving a will, or a paper testamentary in the nature of a last will and testament, they the said trustees, and the survivors and survivor of them, and the heirs of such survivor, shall hold the said tract or parcel of land hereinbefore conveyed, for all and every the children and child of the said N R, who being a son or sons, shall attain the age of twenty-one years, or being a daughter or daughters, shall attain the age of twenty-one years, or marry, to be divided between or among them, if more than one, in equal shares and proportions, and if there shall be but one such child, the whole to be in trust for that one child, and his or her heirs.

And if any such child or children shall depart this life before he or they shall attain the age of twenty-one years, if son or sons, or be unmarried, if daughter or daughters, then the share or shares of him, her or them so dying, shall go and accrue to the survivor or survivors of such child or children, and be equally divided amongst them, if more than one, share and share alike. And in case of the death of any other of the said children before they arrive to the age of twenty-one years, if son or sons, or be unmarried, if daughter or daughters, every such accruing or surviving part or share shall again be subject and liable to such condition or contingency, or accrue to and amongst the survivor or survivors, as hereinbefore is provided, touching the said original shares and proportions: aud on this farther trust, that in the event the said N R die intestate, leaving no child or children by her said husband A R, who shall attain the age of twenty-one years, if son or sons, or the age of twenty-one years, or be married, if daughter or daughters, the said tract or parcel of land hereinbefore conveyed, shall, on the death of the said N R, and the death of said children, or the survivor, before the age of twenty-one years, or marriage, if a daughter, be transferred and conveyed to the said C H, or his heirs, by the said trustees, or the survivors or survivor of them, or the heirs of such survivor. And the said C H of the first part, his heirs, executors and administrators, doth covenant, promise and agree, to and with the said trustees, of the second part, their heirs and assigns, by these presents, in manner and form following, to wit: That he, the said C H, the said tract or parcel of land hereby given, or intended so to be, unto the said trustees, for the benefit of the said N R, of the third part, and her children as aforesaid, against him, the said C H, and his heirs, and against all and every person or persons whatever, will warrant and forever defend by these presents.

Witness the following signatures and seals.

C H. [Seal.]
G D. [Seal.]
M W. [Seal.]

Deed of lease of house.

An indenture, made this day of , in the year , between B J of the one part, and T H of the other part: Witnesseth, that in consideration of the rents, provisoes and agreements hereinafter contained, and which, on the part of the said T H, are to be done and performed, he, the said B J, hath demised and leased, and doth hereby demise and lease to the said T H, his executors, administrators and assigns, the tenement situate in , with all the cellars and appurtenances whatsoever to the said tenement belonging, or in any wise appertaining. To have and to hold the said tenement and appurtenances, unto the said T H, his executors, administrators and assigns, from the day of the date hereof, for and during the full term of years next ensuing, and fully to be complete and ended, yielding and paying therefor, yearly, the sum of dollars, good and lawful money of the United States, to the said B J, his heirs and assigns, by four equal and quarterly payments; the first thereof to be made on the day of next ensuing the date hereof. And the said T H, for himself, his heirs, executors and administrators, doth covenant to and with the said B J, his heirs and assigns, that he shall and will pay unto the said B J, his heirs and assigns, the said yearly rent of dollars, in manner hereinbefore limited and appointed; except the premises, or some part thereof, shall happen to be burnt down, blown up, or damnified, by reason of fire or tempest, or unavoidable accident, in either of which cases said rent is to cease. And the said B J, for himself, his heirs, executors and administrators, doth hereby covenant to and with the said T H, his executors, administrators and assigns, that he, paying the rent hereby reserved, shall peaceably and quietly hold and possess the said tenement hereby demised, with its appurtenances, for and during all the said term of years, hereby granted, without any hindrance or eviction, molestation or interruption whatever. And the said T H, his heirs, executors and administrators, doth covenant to and with the said B J, his heirs and assigns, that he or they will yield up said tenement in good repair, the casualty of fire which may destroy the said tenement, or any part thereof, and reasonable wear and tear, excepted.

In witness whereof, the parties to these presents have hereto set their hands and affixed their seals the day and year first above written.

B J. [Seal.]
T H. [Seal.]

Another form of lease.

This indenture, made the day of , in the year , between W F of the one part, and C B of the other part: Witnesseth, that for and in consideration of the rents, covenants; agreements and provisoes hereinafter reserved and contained, and which on the part of the said C B, his executors, administrators and assigns, are to be paid, done and performed, he, the said W F, hath demised, granted, and to farm let, and by these presents doth demise, grant, and to farm let, unto the said C B, his executors, administrators and assigns, all that lot, messuage and tenement, situate in the [here describe the property particularly], together with all houses and buildings, easements, alleys, ways, profits and appurtenances whatsoever, to the said lot, messuage and tenement belonging, or in anywise appertaining: To have and to hold said lot, messuage and tenement, and all and singular the premises hereby demised, with the appurtenances thereto belonging, unto the said C B, his executors, administrators and assigns, from the day of the date hereof, for and during the term of years, next ensuing, and fully to be complete and ended, yielding and paying therefor, dollars, yearly, in equal quarterly payments—the first quarter of which will be due and payable on the day of , next ensuing the date hereof; the second on the day of ; the third on the day of ; and the fourth on the day of , during said term, unto the said W F, his heirs or assigns. And the said C B doth hereby, for himself, his heirs, executors, administrators and assigns, covenant, promise and agree, to and with the said W F, his heirs and assigns, in manner following, that is to say:—That he, the said C B, his heirs, executors, administrators or assigns, shall and will well and truly pay, or cause to be paid unto the said W F, his heirs and assigns, the said yearly rent of dollars, in the manner hereinbefore limited and appointed, according to the reservation thereof, and the true intent and meaning of these presents, except the said messuage, tenement and premises, or some part thereof, shall happen to be burnt down, or damnified, by fire, tempest, or unavoidable accident. And also, that he, the said C B, his heirs, executors, administrators or assigns, or some of them, shall and will, at his, their, or some of their proper costs and charges, from time to time, and at all times hereafter, during the said term, well and sufficiently repair, and cleanse said messuage and tenement, and all and singular other the premises, with the appurtenances hereinbefore demised, and every part and parcel thereof, in, by and with, all and all manner of needful and necessary reparation (customary between tenant and landlord), the casualty by fire, which may consume said messuage, tenement and premises, or any part thereof, excepted, it being hereby clearly understood by and between the parties hereto, that such loss is to be sustained by the said W F, and that on the happening of such destruction, said C B is to be entirely discharged from the obligations of this indenture, as hereinbefore expressed. And the said W F, for himself, his heirs, executors and administrators, doth covenant, promise and agree to and with the said C B, his executors, administrators and assigns, that he, the said C B, his executors, administrators and assigns, paying the said yearly rent hereinbefore hereby reserved, and observing, performing and keeping all and singular the covenant and agreement herein contained, on his and their part to be observed, according to the true intent and meaning of these presents, shall and may lawfully, peaceably and quietly, have, hold, use, occupy, possess and enjoy the said lot, messuage, tenement and premises, hereby demised, with the appurtenances, and every part and parcel thereof, for and during the said term of years, hereby granted, without any let, suit, hindrance, eviction, ejection, molestation or interruption whatsoever, of, or by the said W F, or his heirs, or of or by any person or persons whatsoever, lawfully claiming, from or under him, them, or any or either of them. And it is also agreed by and between the parties, that if at the expiration of said term of years, he, the said C B, shall desire to retain said lot, messuage and tenement and appurtenances, for years, next after the expiration of said term of years, he, the said C B, shall have, and power is hereby given him, so to retain, on the terms and stipulations hereinbefore expressed, respecting the term of years, next ensuing the date hereof.

In testimony whereof, the parties to these presents have hereto set their hands and affixed their seals the day and year first above written.

W H. [Seal.]
C B. [Seal.]

Lease from tenants in common.

This indenture, made and entered into the day of , in the year , between A B of the first part, C D of the second part, and E F of the third part: Witnesseth, that for and in consideration of the rents, covenants and agreements hereinafter reserved and contained, and which, by and on the part and behalf of the said E F, his heirs, executors, administrators and assigns, are to be paid, done and performed, he, the said A B, as to one undivided moiety or half part, the whole into two equal parts to be divided, of all that messuage or tenement, with the appurtenances hereinafter particularly described, and the said C D, as to one undivided moiety or half part, the whole into two equal parts to be divided, of all that messuage or tenement, with the appurtenances, hereinafter particularly described, have, and each of them hath (according to their several and respective shares and proportions aforesaid) demised, leased, set, and to farm letten, and by these presents do, and each of them doth demise, let, set, and to farm let, unto the said E F, his heirs, executors, administrators and assigns, all that messuage and tenement, with the appurtenances thereto appertaining or belonging, situate, lying and being in [here describe]. To have and to hold the said messuage or tenement, and all and singular the premises hereby leased, or intended so to be, with their and every of their appurtenances, unto the said E F, his heirs, executors, administrators and assigns, from henceforth, for and during the term of years, fully to be complete and ended, yielding and paying therefor yearly, and every year during the estate and term hereby granted, on the day of , and the day of , unto the said A B and C D, their heirs, executors, administrators or assigns, the sum of dollars, lawful money of the United States, in manner and form following (that is to say): The sum of dollars, lawful money as aforesaid, being one moiety or half part of the above sum of dollars, to be paid by the said E F, his heirs, &c., unto the said A B, his heirs, &c., and the sum of dollars, lawful money as aforesaid, being the other moiety or half part of the above sum of dollars, to be paid by the said E F, his heirs, &c., unto the said C D, his heirs, &c. And the said E F, for himself, his heirs, executors, administrators and assigns, doth covenant, promise and agree to and with the said A B and C D, and their heirs, executors, administrators and assigns, in manner following (that is to say): That he, the said E F, his heirs, executors, administrators and assigns, shall and will well and truly pay, or cause to be paid unto the said A B and C D, their heirs, executors, administrators or assigns, yearly and every year during the said term of years, the yearly rent or sum of dollars, lawful money of the United States, on the day of , and the day of , as aforesaid, and in the manner and form as the same is hereinbefore reserved and made payable. And the said A B, for himself, his heirs, executors and administrators, doth covenant, promise and agree, to and with the said E F, his heirs, executors, administrators and assigns, in manner following (that is to say): That he, the said E F, his heirs, executors, administrators and assigns, paying the rent hereby reserved, and performing the covenants and agreements hereinbefore mentioned and contained, and which, on his and their parts, ought to be paid and performed, shall and may peaceably and quietly have, hold, occupy, possess and enjoy the said messuage, &c., with the appurtenances, hereby leased, as to one undivided moiety or half part thereof, only for and during the said term hereby granted, without the let, suit, trouble, molestation or interruption of him, the said A B, his heirs, executors or administrators, or any other person or persons lawfully claiming or to claim by, from or under him, them, or any of them. And the said C D, for himself, his heirs, executors and administrators, doth covenant, promise and agree to and with the said E F, his heirs, executors, administrators and assigns, in manner following (that is to say): That he, the said E F, his heirs, exeeutors, administrators or assigns, paying the rent hereby reserved, and performing the covenants and agreements hereinbefore mentioned and contained, and which, on his and their parts, are or ought to be paid and performed, shall and may peaceably and quietly have, hold, occupy, possess and enjoy the said messuage, &c., with the appurtenances, hereby leased, as to one undivided moiety or half part thereof, only for and during the said term hereby granted, without the let, suit, trouble, molestation or interruption of him, the said C D, his heirs, executors or administrators, or any other person or persons lawfully claiming, or to claim, by, from or under him, them, or any of them.

In witness, &c. (as before, on page 16). A B. [Seal.]

C D. [Seal.]

E F. [Seal.]

Lease of water power.

An indenture, made this day of , in the year , between M P of the one part, and R A of the other part, all of : Witnesseth, that the said M P, in consideration of the rents and covenants hereinafter reserved and stipulated, on the part of the said R A, to be paid and performed, hath granted, demised and leased, and by these presents doth grant, demise and lease unto the said R A, his executors, administrators and assigns, the right and privilege of using the water passing from the mill of the said M P, situate on , after it has worked the said mill, or fed the same, in the construction or propelling of any kind of machinery at the factory of the said R A, or for any other purpose to which the said R A may choose to apply the same, except for that of working a mill for the grinding of grain, and with this reservation and restriction, as fully and amply, to all intents and purposes, as the same may now be applied and used by the said M P. To have and to hold the said right and privilege of the water aforesaid, and use and enjoy the same, subject to the exception and restriction aforesaid, unto the said R A, his executors, administrators and assigns, for and during, and until the full end and term of years from the day of , in the year : Yielding and paying therefor, unto the said M P, his heirs and assigns, during every of the said years, the annual sum of dollars, by quarterly payments of dollars; the first whereof is to be paid on the day of , in the year . And the said R A, for himself and heirs, executors and administrators, doth covenant, promise and agree, to and with the said M P, and his heirs and assigns, that he will well and truly pay the said rent, at the periods aforesaid, unto him. And the said M P doth, for himself, his heirs and assigns, hereby covenant and agree, to and with the said R A, his executors, administrators and assigns, that he, the said R A, his executors, administrators and assigns, shall have and enjoy the water as aforesaid, except such casual hindrance and interruption as may be caused by the needful repair and necessary reparations of the said mill, or any appurtenance thereto belonging, which shall be effected without delay, after due notice of the intended interruptions of the regular flow of the water, given to the said R A, his executors, administrators or assigns. And it is by these presents further agreed and provided, that the right and privilege of using the said water for any purpose whatsoever, shall *ipso facto* cease, if the said R A, his executors, administrators or assigns, shall, in violation of the provisions in this indenture contained, proceed to apply the same to the purpose hereinbefore inhibited, to wit: For the working a mill for the grinding of grain.

In witness, &c. (as before, on page 16).

M P. [Seal.]
R A. [Seal.]

Deed for land sold under decree of court.

This indenture, made this day of , in the year , between D H of , commissioner as hereinafter mentioned, of the first part, and R H of , of the second part: Whereas, on the day of , in the year , it was decreed and ordered by the court of , in a certain cause in equity then depending in the said court, between A L and C L, complainants, and G S and L S, defendants, that the said D H, commissioner appointed by said court, should, at public auction, upon the following terms, to wit—One-half of the purchase money to be paid in cash; the remainder to be paid in twelve months; the payment whereof to be secured by bond or bonds with approved security, make sale of a certain lot or piece of land, lying and being in [here describe the land], having advertised the time, terms and place of sale, for the period of , in some newspaper published in : And whereas the said D H, commissioner, in pursuance of the decretal order aforesaid, did, on the day of , in the year , on the premises, offer for sale at public auction, the hereinafter described lot or piece of land, being the lot or piece of land mentioned in the said decretal order, having advertised the time, terms, and place of sale, in the , a newspaper published in , for the period of ; at which sale, the said lot or piece of land was struck off to the said R H, for the sum of dollars, that being the highest bid for the same: And whereas the said sale having been reported to the said court, the court, by its decree of the day of , confirmed the said sale, and directed that on the payment of the whole purchase money to the said commissioner D H, the said commissioner should convey the said land to the said purchaser; and the whole of the purchase money having been paid the said commissioner, according to the said decretal order: Now, this indenture witnesseth, that the said D H, commissioner as aforesaid, and party to the first part of this indenture, to carry into effect the said sale, as aforesaid made, in pursuance of said decretal order, in consideration of the premises, and of the said sum of   dollars, to him in hand paid by the said R H, at or before the sealing and delivery of this indenture, which he, the said D H, commissioner, party of the first part, doth hereby acknowledge, hath given, granted, bargained and sold, and by these presents doth give, grant, bargain and sell, unto the said R H, his heirs and assigns, the lot or piece of land, situate, lying and being in   , it being the same land that was conveyed to   , by   , by deed bearing date   day of   , in the year   , and of record in the clerk's office of   , to which deed reference is hereby made for a more particular description of the premises; which said land was sold by the said D H, commissioner, at public auction, as aforesaid, under the power given him as aforesaid: to have and to hold the said lot or piece of land, with the appurtenances thereto belonging or appertaining, to the said R H, his heirs and assigns, to the only proper use and behoof of the said R H, his heirs and assigns forever. And the said D H, commissioner aforesaid, the said lot or piece of land, against himself and his heirs, and all other person or persons claiming or to claim, by, through, or under him, unto the said R H, his heirs and assigns, shall and will, by these presents, warrant and forever defend.

Witness the following signature and seal.

D H. Com'r. [Seal.]

Deed of mortgage of land, for securing payment of money due on a bond.

This indenture, made the   day of   , in the year   , between T S of   , of the one part, and H B of   , of the other part: Whereas the said T S stands bound unto the said H B, in and by a certain obligation, or writing obligatory, under his hand and seal, bearing even date herewith, in the sum of   dollars, conditioned for the payment of dollars, on the day of , next ensuing the date hereof, with lawful interest for the same, as in and by the said recited obligation, and condition thereof, as by reference being thereunto had, will more fully and at large appear: Now, this indenture witnesseth, that the said T S, as well for and in consideration of the aforesaid debt, or sum of dollars, and for the better securing the payment thereof, with its interest, unto the said H B, his executors, administrators and assigns, in discharge of the said recited obligation, as of the further sum of one dollar, to him in hand paid by the said H B, at and before the sealing and delivery hereof, the receipt whereof is hereby acknowledged, hath granted, bargained, sold, released and confirmed, and by these presents doth grant, bargain, sell, release and confirm unto the said H B, his heirs and assigns, all that lot, piece or parcel of land, situate, lying and being in [here describe the land], together with all and singular the buildings, improvements and appurtenances thereto belonging, or in any wise appertaining; and the reversions and remainders, rents, issues and profits thereof: to have and to hold the said lot, piece or parcel of land, the buildings, improvements and appurtenances hereby granted or mentioned, or intended so to be, with the appurtenances, unto the said H B, his heirs and assigns, to the only proper use and behoof of the said H B, his heirs and assigns, forever: Provided always, nevertheless, that if the said T S, his heirs, executors or administrators, shall and do well and truly pay, or cause to be paid unto the said H B, his executors, administrators or assigns, the aforesaid debt, or sum of dollars, on the day and time hereinbefore mentioned and appointed for payment thereof, with lawful interest for the same, according to the condition of the said recited obligation, without any fraud or further delay, and without any deduction therefrom—then and from thenceforth, as well this present indenture, and the estate hereby granted, as the said recited obligation, shall cease, determine, and become absolutely null and void, to all intents and purposes, anything hereinbefore contained to the contrary, in anywise, notwithstanding.

In witness, &c. (as before, on page 16).

T S. [Seal.]
H B. [Seal.]

Deed of mortgage to secure endorsers.

This indenture, made this day of , in the year , between A B of , of the one part, and C D and E F of , of the other part: Whereas the said C D and E F have endorsed for the said A B a promissory note for the sum of dollars, bearing date the day of , and payable after date, which is now discounted at the bank, in , and which said note it is contemplated to renew from time to time; and the said A B being desirous to secure and save the said C D and E F against all responsibility as endorsers of the note aforesaid; therefore, this indenture witnesseth, that the said A B, as well for and in consideration of securing the said endorsers upon the payment of the note aforesaid, as the sum of one dollar to him in hand paid by the said C D and E F, at and before the sealing and delivery hereof, the receipt whereof he hereby acknowledges, hath granted, bargained, sold, released, and confirmed, and by these presents doth grant, bargain, sell, release and confirm unto the said C D and E F, their heirs and assigns, that certain lot, piece or parcel of land, situate, lying and being in [here describe the land], together with all and singular the improvements and appurtenances thereto belonging, or in anywise appertaining, and the reversions and remainders, rents, issues and profits thereof: to have and to hold the said lot, piece or parcel of land, with the premises and hereditaments hereby granted or mentioned, or intended so to be, with the appurtenances, unto the said C D and E F, their heirs and assigns, to the only proper use and behoof of them, the said C D and E F, their heirs and assigns forever: Provided always, nevertheless, that if the said A B, his heirs, executors or administrators, shall and do well and truly pay, or cause to be paid unto the said bank, the aforesaid promissory note for dollars, on the day and time hereinbefore mentioned and appointed for payment thereof, or by other lawful means, save, keep harmless and indemnified, the said C D and E F, their heirs, executors and administrators, from the payment of said note, and all costs, damages or charges, as sureties aforesaid, then and from thenceforth, as well this present indenture, and the estate hereby granted, as the said recited obligation, shall cease, determine, and become absolutely null and void, any thing herein contained to the contrary notwithstanding.

In witness whereof, &c. (as before, on page 16).

A B. [Seal.]
C D. [Seal.]
E F. [Seal.]

Mortgage by demise for years.

This indenture, made this day of , in the year , between L W of , of the one part, and H H and and C A of , of the other part: Witnesseth, that for and in considera-tion of the sum of dollars, by the said H H and C A to the said L W in hand, at and before the sealing and delivery of these presents, well and truly paid, the receipt whereof the said L W doth hereby acknowledge, and thereof, and of every part thereof, doth acquit, release and discharge the said H H and C A, their executors and administrators forever, by these presents: he, the said L W, hath granted, bargained, sold and demised, and by these presents doth grant, bargain, sell and demise, unto the said H H and C A, their executors, administrators and assigns, all and singular the lot of gronnd, with the dwelling house thereon, situate, lying and being in [here describe the property], together with all out-houses and appurtenances thereto belonging, or in any wise appertaining, and the reversion and reversions, remainders, rents, issues and profits, of all and singular the said premises: to have and to hold the said lot of ground mentioned to be hereby demised, as aforesaid, with the appurtenances, unto the said H H and C A, their executors, administrators and assigns, from the day next be-fore the day of the date of these presents, for and during, and until the full end and term of years, from thence next ensu-ing, and fully to be complete and ended: Provided, always, and these presents are upon this express condition, that if the said L W, his heirs, executors or administrators, or any of them, do and shall well and truly pay, or cause to be paid, unto the said H H and C A, their executors, administrators or assigns, at , the sum of dollars, lawful money of the United States, with interest for the same, after the rate of six *per centum per annum*, in manner following (that is to say): the sum of dollars, part thereof, being one half-year's interest of the said dollars, after the rate aforesaid, on the day of now next ensuing, and which will be in the year of our Lord , and the further sum of dollars, being the whole principal money, and another half-year's interest thereof; then from and immediately after such payment so made, as aforesaid, these presents and the said term of years, shall cease, determine, and be absolutely null and void, to all intents and purposes whatsoever. And the said L W doth, for himself, his heirs, executors and administrators, covenant, promise and agree, to and with the said H H and C A, their executors, administrators and assigns, by these presents, in manner following (that is to say): that he, the said L W, his heirs, executors and administrators, or some or one of them, shall and will well and truly pay, or cause to be paid, unto the said H H and C A, their executors, administrators and assigns, the sum of dollars, of lawful money, as aforesaid, with interest as above, at the place and times, and in the manner above limited for payment thereof, according to the true intent and meaning of the above written proviso.

In witness, &c. (as before, on page 16).

L W. [Seal.]
H H. [Seal.]
C A. [Seal.]

Deed of mortgage of goods.

This indenture, made this day of , in the year , between A B of , of the one part, and C D of , of the other part: Witnesseth, that the said A B, in consideration of the sum of dollars, by the said C D to the said A B in hand paid, at and before the sealiug and delivery of these presents, the receipt whereof the said A B doth hereby acknowledge, and thereof, and of every part thereof, doth acquit and discharge the said C D, his executors and administrators, forever, by these presents, he, the said A B, hath granted, bargained and sold, and by these presents doth grant, bargain and sell, unto the said C D, his executors, administrators and assigns, all and singular the following goods and chattels—that is to say [here describe the goods]: To have and to hold, all and singular, the said goods and chattels unto the said C D, his executors, administrators and assigns forever: Provided, always, and it is hereby agreed and declared, that if the said A B, his executors, administrators or assigns, or any of them, do or shall well and truly pay, or cause to be paid, unto the said C D, his executors, administrators or assigns, the sum of dollars, of lawful money, with legal interest thereon, then these presents, and every clause, article, condition and thing herein contained, shall cease and be void, any thing contained herein to the contrary notwithstanding. And the said A B, for himself, his heirs, executors and administrators, doth covenant, promise and agree, to and with the said C D, his executors, administrators and assigns, by these presents, in manner following (that is to say): that he, the said A B, his heirs, executors and administrators, or some or one of them, shall and will well and truly pay, or cause to be paid, unto the said C D, his executors, administrators or assigns, the sum of dollars, of lawful money, with interest as aforesaid, on the day of , in the year of our Lord . And further, that he, the said A B, his executors, administrators and assigns, all and singular the said goods and chattels hereby bargained and sold, or so intended to be, unto the said C D, his executors, administrators or assigns, against him, the said A B, his executors, administrators or assigns, and all and every other person or persons whomsoever, shall and will warrant and forever defend by these presents. And the said C D, for himself, his heirs, executors and administrators, doth covenant, promise and agree, to and with A B, his executors, administrators and assigns, that he, the said C D, his executors, &c., shall and will, immediately upon the receipt of the said sum of dollars, lawful money, with the interest thereon, as aforesaid, at the time herein limited and appointed for the payment thereof, deliver, or cause to be delivered, unto the said A B, his executors, &c., all and singular the goods and chattels above bargained and sold, and which at the time of the executing of these presents are received by the said C D, of and from the said A B, in as good plight and condition as the same now are.

In witness, &c. (as before, on page 16).

A B. [Seal.]
C D. [Seal.]

Deed of partition.

This indenture, made this day of , in the year , between A B of , of the one part, and C D of , of the other part: Witnesseth, that whereas the said A B and C D, parties to this indenture, are seized in fee simple of, and have equal shares as tenants in common in and to a certain lot, piece or parcel of land, situate, lying and being in , adjoining the lands of E H and M P, and bounded as follows, to wit: Beginning at [here describe the boundaries of the land]; which lot, piece or parcel of land was conveyed to the said A B and C D, by R T, by deed bearing date the day of , in the year , and of record in the clerk's office of , and to which, for more particular information, reference is hereby made: Now, therefore, to the end and intent that a perfect partition may be had and made between them, the said A B and C D, of all and singular the lot, piece or parcel of land to them conveyed as aforesaid, and that every of them, their, and every of their heirs, executors, administrators or assigns, may from henceforth, severally, have and enjoy in severalty, without any impeachment or disturbance of the other of them, his or their heirs, executors, administrators or assigns, his and their portion and part of the said lot, piece or parcel of land to them conveyed as aforesaid, they, the said A B and C D, by their own mutual consent and agreement, have made partition and division, and by these presents do, for them and their heirs, make partition and division of the said lot, piece or parcel of land to them conveyed as aforesaid, in manner and form as hereinafter is mentioned (that is to say): First, the said A B shall have, for his part and portion of the said lot, piece or parcel of land above mentioned and described, all that part of said land lying and being [here describe A B's portion]: to have and to hold the said part of said lot last described, unto him, the said A B, his heirs and assigns forever, in severalty, and divided from the part and portion of the said C D, his heirs and assigns: And he, the said C D, shall have, for his part and portion of the said lot, piece or parcel of land above mentioned and described, all that part of said land lying and being [here describe C D's portion]: to have and to hold the said part of said lot last described, unto him, the said C D, his heirs and assigns forever, in severalty, and divided from the part and portion of the said A B, as aforesaid. And the said A B, for himself, his heirs, executors and administrators, doth covenant, promise and agree to and with the said C D, his heirs and assigns, in manner following (that is to say): that he, the said C D, his heirs and assigns, shall have, hold and enjoy the said part and portion of the above described lot, situate, lying and being in [here describe C D's portion], with all and singular the appurtenances thereto belonging, or in any wise appertaining, to and for his and their own use and uses, without the let, suit, hindrance, interruption or denial of the said A B, or his heirs or assigns, or of any other persons claiming, or to claim, by, from or under them, or any of them. And the said C D, for himself, his heirs, executors and administrators, doth covenant, promise and agree to and with the said A B, his heirs and assigns, in manner following (that is to say): that he, the said A B, his heirs and assigns, shall have, hold and enjoy the said part and portion of the above described lot, situate, lying and being in [here describe A B's portion], with all and singular the appurtenances thereto belonging, or in any wise appertaining, to and for his and their own use and uses, without the let, suit, hindrance, interruption or denial of the said C D, or his heirs or assigns, or of any other persons claiming or to claim, by, from or under them, or any of them.

In witness, &c. (as before, on page 16).

A B. [Seal.]
C D. [Seal.]

Deed of partition between copartners on dissolution of copartnership—one taking the debts and the other assigning.

This indenture, made this day of , in the year , between R C of the one part, and J F of the other part: Whereas the said parties to these presents have been of late, copartners together in the trade of ; and by reason of the said joint trade and dealings, divers debts became and now are due unto the said R C and J F, for divers goods and wares; and also the said R C and J F are and stand engaged for divers sums of money: And whereas also the said parties, for divers good reasons them moving, have concluded and agreed to put an end to their joint trade and copartnership, and the said R C is contented and hath agreed, for the consideration hereinafter mentioned, to assign unto the said J F all the debts and sums of money which are due and owing unto them, the said R C and J F jointly. And the said J F hath likewise agreed and undertaken to discharge and pay all debts and sums of money which they, the said R C and J F, do jointly owe to any person or persons, for or by reason of their said joint trade or copartnership: Now, this indenture witnesseth, that the said R C and J F have mutually dissolved the said copartnership; and the said R C, for the consideration hereinafter in these presents mentioned, hath granted, assigned and set over, and by these presents doth grant, assign and set over, unto the said J F, his executors, administrators and assigns, all and singular such debts and sums of money as are owing to the said R C, severally or jointly with the said J F, for or concerning the said joint trade, and all his right, title, interest, property, claim and demand whatsoever, in or to the said debts, or any of them, and also all and singular bills, bonds, specialties and securities whatsoever, for and concerning the said debts, and the late copartnership between them, all of which said debts are mentioned or expressed in a certain schedule hereto annexed. To have and to hold all and every the said debts, specialties and securities unto the said J F, his executors, administrators or assigns, to his and their own proper use and benefit, without any manner of account therefor to be given to him, the said R C, his executors, administrators or assigns. And that he, the said R C, his executors or administrators, shall not, at any time or times hereafter, willingly do or suffer any act or thing to hinder, let or disturb him, the said J F, his executors, administrators or assigns, in the recovery, getting in or obtaining the said debts, or any of them. In consideration whereof, the said J F, for himself, his executors and administrators, doth covenant, promise and agree to and with the said R C, his executors and administrators, in manner and form following (that is to say): That he, the said J F, his executors or assigns, shall and will, at or before the day of , procure and obtain to and for the said R C, his executors or administrators, sufficient general release and other discharges in the law, from all the creditors of the copartnership aforesaid; and also that he, the said J F, his executors or administrators, shall and will, at all times forever hereafter, save, and keep harmless and indemnified, the said R C, his executors or administrators, against all and every person and persons whatsoever, to whom they, the said R C and J F, or either of them, are indebted, touching or concerning the said copartnership, and of and from all actions, suits, costs, damages, charges, judgments, executions and demands whatsoever, which shall at any time hereafter arise and come against the said R C, his executors or administrators, or any of his or their lands, tenements, goods and chattels, or any part thereof, for or by reason of any debts or sums of money owing by, or for, or by reason of any bond, specialty, promise or contract touching the said copartnership.

In witness, &c. (as before, on page 16).

R C. [Seal.]
J F. [Seal.]

Deed of release of property conveyed under a deed of trust.

This indenture, made this day of , in the year , between F P of , of the first part, B D of , of the second part, and R D of , of the third part: Whereas, by a certain deed bearing date the day of , in the year , made, or expressed to be made between the said B D (debtor) of the first part, the said F P (trustee) of the second part, and the said R D (creditor) of the third part: It is witnessed, that in consideration of the sum of dollars by the said F P to the said B D in hand paid, he, the said B D, did grant, bargain and sell unto the said F P, his heirs and assigns, al, &c. [here describe the property conveyed in trust]. To have and to hold the same unto the use of the said F P, his heirs and assigns forever. In trust, nevertheless, that he, the said B D, his heirs, executors or administrators, shall, on or before the day of , well and truly pay unto the said R D, his heirs, executors, administrators or assigns, the sum of dollars, with legal interest thereon, as by reference being had to said deed, recorded in the clerk's office of court, will more fully and at large appear: And whereas the said sum of dollars, with the interest thereon as aforesaid, has been fully paid and satisfied within the time stipulated as above, by the said B D; and he, the said B D, hath requested the said F P to reconvey and release the premises so conveyed in trust, as above recited, unto him in manner hereinafter mentioned: Now, this indenture witnesseth, that for and in consideration of the sum of dollars, lawful money of the United States, to him, the said F P, in hand paid by the said B D, at or before the sealing and delivery of these presents, the receipt whereof the said F P doth hereby acknowledge, he, the said F P, the said R D, a party of the third part, consenting thereto, hath bargained, sold, aliened, released and confirmed, and by these presents doth bargain, sell, alien, release and confirm unto the said B D, his heirs and assigns, all that messuage, &c., lying and being in , being the same property that was conveyed by the said B D to the said F P, in trust for the benefit of the said R D, as is above mentioned, with their and every of their appurtenances, freed and absolutely discharged of and from the said trust, and the principal money and interest thereby secured, and every part and parcel thereof, and all the estate, right, title and interest of him, the said F P, trustee, as aforesaid, for R D, in, of, or to the same. To have and to hold the said messuage, &c. and premises mentioned to be hereby released as aforesaid, with their and every of their appurtenances, unto the said B D, his heirs and assigns, to the only proper use and behoof of the said B D, his heirs and assigns forever; so as that neither he, the said F P, nor his heirs, executors, administrators or assigns, shall or may, at any time or times hereafter, have, claim, pretend to, challenge or demand any right, title or interest, claim or demand whatsoever, either in law or equity, in, to, or out of the said premises, or any part or parcel thereof, and all the right, title and interest which he, the said F P, acting as trustee for the said R D, might or could have had, in, to, or out of the said premises, and every part and parcel of the same, is, and by these presents are utterly excluded and forever barred.

In witness whereof, &c. (as before, on page 16).

F P. [Seal.]
B D. [Seal.]
R D. [Seal.]

Deed of trust to secure the payment of money.

Whereas N A of , stands justly indebted to B M of , in the sum of dollars, good and lawful money of the United States, by his bond bearing date the day of , in the year , payable after date, with interest thereon, payable from the date: And whereas N A desires to secure more effectually the payment of the said sum of dollars, with interest as aforesaid: Now, therefore, this deed, made the day of , in the year , between N A of the first part, (trustees) of the second part, and B M of the third part: Witnesseth, that the said N A, for and in consideration of the sum of dollars to him in hand paid by the said , before the sealing and delivery of these presents, the receipt whereof is hereby acknowledged, hath granted, bargained, sold, aliened, enfeoffed, released and confirmed, and by these presents doth grant, bargain, sell, alien, enfeoff, release and confirm unto the said , their heirs and assigns, a certain lot, piece or parcel of land, situate, lying and being in (it being the same property which was conveyed to the said N A, by E T, by deed dated the day of , in the year , and of record in the office of the court of), bounded as follows, to wit [here give the boundaries], together with all the estate, right, title, interest and property, claim and demand whatever, of him, the said N A, in law or equity, or otherwise however, of, in, to or out of the same. To have and to hold the said lot, piece or parcel of land, and every part and parcel thereof, with their appurtenances, unto the said , their heirs and assigns forever, and to the only proper use and behoof of the said , their heirs and assigns forever. And the said N A, for himself, his heirs, executors and administrators, doth covenant, promise, grant and agree to and with the said , their heirs and assigns, by these presents, in manner and form following, to wit: That he, the said N A, his heirs and assigns, the said lot, piece or parcel of land and premises hereby granted or intended so to be, with the appurtenances, unto the said , their heirs and assigns, against him, the said N A, and his heirs, and against all and every person or persons whatever, will warrant and forever defend by these presents. In trust, nevertheless, and for the following use, intent and purposes, and none other, that if the said N A, his heirs, executors or administrators, shall fail or refuse to pay to the said B M as aforesaid, his heirs, executors, administrators or assigns, the said sum of dollars, specified in the said bond, after the date of the said bond, or shall fail or refuse to pay the interest thereon, at the time or times mentioned in the said bond, then the said shall, so soon after such failure or refusal as they or the survivors or survivor of them shall be required so to do by the said B M, his heirs, executors, administrators or assigns, proceed to sell at public auction, upon the premises, for cash, first giving days' notice of the time and place of sale, in one or more of the newspapers printed in , the said lot, piece or parcel of land hereby conveyed, and out of the proceeds of such sale they shall first pay all costs and charges attending the execution of this trust; secondly, they shall pay to the said B M, his heirs, executors, administrators and assigns, the said sum of dollars, with all the interest that shall have accrued thereon and remained unpaid, and the balance, if any, they shall pay to the said N A, his heirs, executors, administrators or assigns; and if the said N A shall well and truly pay and discharge the said bond, then this deed shall be void, else shall remain in full force and virtue.

In witness, &c. (as before, on page 16).

N A. [Seal.]
B M. [Seal.]

Deed of trust of personal estate.

An indenture, made this day of , in the year , between H C of the first part, R S of the second part, and A E of the third part: Whereas the said H C is justly indebted to the said A E in the sum of dollars, lawful money of the United States, to be paid on the day of , in the year , as by a note dated the day of , in the year , more fully appears: which debt, with the legal interest thereon accruing, the said H C is willing to secure: Now, this indenture witnesseth, that for and in consideration of the premises, and also for the further consideration of dollars, lawful money of the United States, to the said H C in hand paid by the said R S, at or before the sealing and delivery of these presents, the receipt whereof is hereby acknowledged, he, the said H C, hath bargained and sold, and doth hereby bargain and sell unto the said R S, his executors, administrators and assigns, the following property, to wit [here describe the property conveyed]: To have and to hold the said property to the said R S, his executors, administrators and assigns, and to the only proper use and behoof of the said R S, his executors, &c. forever. Upon trust, nevertheless, that the said R S, his executors, administrators and assigns, shall permit the said H C to possess and enjoy the use and benefit of the said property, until default be made in the payment of the said sum of dollars, or any part thereof, with interest thereon as aforesaid. And then upon this farther trust, that the said R S, his executors, administrators or assigns, shall and will, so soon after the happening of such default of payment, as he or they may think proper, or said A E, his heirs, executors, administrators or assigns, shall request, sell the said property, or such part thereof as may be deemed necessary, to the highest bidder, for cash, at public auction, after having fixed the time and place of sale, at his or their discretion, and given days' notice thereof, in one of the newspapers published in . And out of the moneys arising from such sale, after satisfying the charges thereof, and all other expenses attending the premises, pay to the said A E, his heirs, executors, administrators or assigns, the sum of dollars, with the interest which may thereon have accrued, or so much of said sum as may then be due and unpaid, and the balance, if any, shall pay to the said H C, his heirs, executors, administrators or assigns. But if the whole of the said sum of dollars, with interest as aforesaid, shall be fully paid and discharged to the said A E, his heirs, executors, administrators or assigns, when the same is payable, so that no default of payment of the said sum, or any part thereof, be made, then this indenture to be void, or else to remain in full force and virtue.

In witness, &c. (as before, on page 16).

H C. [Seal.]
R S. [Seal.]
A E. [Seal.]

Deed of trust to indemnify surety.

An indenture, made this day of , in the year , between T D of , of the first part, M W and C H of the second part, and S R of the third part: Whereas the said party to the third part has become bound with, and as surety for the said T D, for the payment of dollars to N P, to be paid on the day of , in the year , as fully appears by the bond of the said parties to the first and third parts to this indenture, dated day of , in the year : And whereas it is the wish of the said T D to keep indemnified his said surety, and to save him harmless from all actions, suits, charges, payments and damages, by reason of his having become bound as aforesaid: Now, this indenture witnesseth, that for and in consideration of the premises, and also for the farther consideration of dollars, lawful money of the United States, to the said T D in hand paid by the said M W and C H, at and before the sealing and delivery of this indenture, the receipt whereof the said T D hereby acknowledges, he, the said T D, hath given, granted, bargained, sold, aliened, enfeoffed, released, transferred and confirmed, and by these presents doth give, grant, bargain, sell, alien, enfeoff, release, transfer and confirm, to the said M W and C H, their heirs, executors or administrators, all the right, title, interest and estate of him, the said T D, in and to the lot, piece or parcel of land, with the tenements and premises thereon, situate, lying and being in , being the same property that was conveyed to him, the said T D, by J C, by deed bearing date day of , in the year , and of record in the clerk's office of court, to which, for further information, reference is hereby made: To have and to hold said property hereby conveyed, unto the said M W and C H, their heirs, executors or administrators, forever. Upon trust, nevertheless, that the said M W and C H, their heirs, executors or administrators, shall permit the said T D to receive and enjoy the rents of said tenement hereby conveyed, until default be made in the payment of the said sum of dollars, or any part thereof, so that the said party to the third part, or his heirs, executors or administrators, shall be damnified by reason of his having become surety as aforesaid. And then upon this farther trust, that they, the said trustees, or either of them, or the survivor of them, or the heirs, executors or administrators of such survivor, shall and will, so soon after the happening of such default and damnification, as aforesaid, as they or either of them, or the survivor of them, or the heirs, executors or administrators of such survivor may think proper, or the said party to the third part, or his heirs, shall request, sell the said property hereby conveyed, at public auction, to the best bidder, for cash, after having given notice of the time and place of such sale days, in some newspaper published in . And out of the moneys arising from such sale, shall, after satisfying the charges attending such sale, pay to the said surety all damages which he may have been subjected to by having joined in the bond aforesaid, and the balance, if any, pay to the said

T D, his heirs, executors or administrators. But if the whole amount of the debt aforesaid shall be fully paid at the time aforesaid, by him, the said T D, so that his surety aforesaid, or his heirs, executors or administrators, shall not be damnified by reason of his aforesaid undertaking, then this indenture to be void, else to remain in full force and virtue.

In witness, &c. (as before, on page 16).

T D. [Seal.]
M W. [Seal.]
C H. [Seal.]

Deed for land sold under a deed of trust.

This indenture, made this day of , in the year , between A S of , of the one part, and H T of , of the other part: Whereas a certain M N of , by a certain deed, bearing date the day of , in the year , and recorded in the clerk's office of court, did give, grant, bargain and sell unto the said A S, his heirs and assigns, all that certain lot, piece or parcel of land, situate, lying and being in , together with the tenement and premises thereto belonging, or in any wise appertaining, in trust, for the benefit of a certain C L. And by which deed the said A S, his heirs and assigns, and the survivor or survivors of them, was and were empowered, on failure of the said M N to perform certain acts and deeds therein mentioned, to sell the said property, or as much thereof, as shall be found necessary to fulfil the purposes of the said trusts and provisoes therein contained: And whereas the said M N failed to perform the requirements contained in said deed, and the said A S, in execution of the trust as above created, did, on the day of , after giving days' notice of the time and place of sale, by advertising the same in the newspaper called , published in , expose to sale the lot, piece or parcel of land, situate, lying and being in the county of , together with the tenement and premises thereto belonging, or in any wise appertaining, and which property was conveyed to the said M N by R P, by deed bearing date the day of , in the year , and which is recorded in the clerk's office of court, and to which deed reference is hereby made for a more particular description of the said property. At which sale the said H T became the purchaser thereof, being the highest bidder: Now, this indenture witnesseth, that the said A S, in performance of his duties as trustee of and for the said C L, and for and in consideration of the sum of dollars, good and lawful money of the United States, to him, the said A S, in hand paid by the said H T, at or before the sealing and delivery of these presents, and which he, the said A S, doth hereby acknowledge; the said sum of dollars to be applied by the said A S, first to defray all the expenses attending the execution of the trust created by the above part recited deed; and secondly, to pay unto the said C L, his heirs and assigns, all the sum or sums of money due and owing him or them by or from the said M N, and the residue, if any, to refund to the said M N, his heirs and assigns, in accordance with the provisions of the above deed, to which reference is hereby made for further information, hath given, granted, bargained and sold, and by these presents doth give, grant, bargain and sell unto the said H T, his heirs, executors and administrators, the lot, piece or parcel of land, together with the tenement and premises thereto belonging, as above mentioned and described, with all the appurtenances thereto appertaining and belonging: To have and to hold the said lot, with its appurtenances, unto the said H T, his heirs and assigns, and to the only proper use and behoof of the said H T, his heirs and assigns, forever. And the said A S the said lot, piece or parcel of land, with all the premises and appurtenances thereto belonging, or in any wise appertaining, unto the said H T, his heirs, &c., will warrant and forever defend, by these presents, from and against all and every claim or claims, demand or demands of him, the said A S, his heirs, &c., and against all and every person or persons claiming by, through or under him or them.

In witness, &c. (as before, on page 16).

A S. [Seal.]
H T. [Seal.]

XIV.

DEEDS IN VIRGINIA.

Deed conveying grantors' whole interest, without covenants of title.

This deed, made the day of , in the year , between A B and Caroline his wife, of the one part, and C D of the other part: Witnesseth, that in consideration of [here state the consideration], the said A B and Caroline his wife do grant unto the said C D all, &c. [here describe the property].

Witness the following signatures and seals.

A B. [Seal.]
CAROLINE B. [Seal.]

Deed of bargain and sale, with covenant of general warranty.

This deed, made this day of , in the year , between A B and Caroline his wife, of the one part, and C D of the other part: Witnesseth, that in consideration of the sum of dollars, the said A B and Caroline his wife do grant unto the said C D, with *general* warranty [here describe property conveyed].

Witness the following signatures and seals.

A B. [Seal.]
CAROLINE B. [Seal.]

Deed of bargain and sale, with covenant of special warranty.

Follow next preceding Form, inserting the word "special" in lieu of the word "general."

Form of deed of bargain and sale, with general warranty, containing covenants of title, &c.

This deed, made this day of , in the year one thousand eight hundred and , between A B and Jane his wife, of the city of Richmond, parties of the first part, and R S of the county of Hanover, party of the second part: Witnesseth, that in consideration of the sum of dollars, the said A B and Jane his wife do grant unto the said R S, with general warranty, all [here describe property conveyed].

The said A B covenants that he has the right to convey the said land to the grantee; that he has done no act to encumber the said land; that the grantee shall have quiet possession of the said land, free from all encumbrances; and that they, the said parties of the first part, will execute such further assurances of the said land as may be requisite.

Witness the following signatures and seals.

A B. [Seal.]
JANE B. [Seal.]

Note.—The utility of these covenants of title will be seen, on reference to 2 Lomax's Digest, Real Property, 263-277. These covenants are usually inserted in English conveyances, but have been greatly neglected in Virginia. They are beneficial to the grantee, affording a readier remedy, in case of defective title, than can be had under the general warranty alone, and it is therefore better to insert them in every case in which they may be lawfully required by the purchaser. As to measure of relief, and time at which it may be afforded, on covenant for general warranty alone, see 3 Call, 220; 1 H. & M. 202; 2 H. & M. 164; 1 Munf. 500; 4 Munf. 332; 5 Munf. 415; 2 Rand. 132.

Form of lease, with covenants for payment of rent, re-entry, &c.

This deed, made the day of , in the year , between A B of the one part, and C D of the other part: Witnesseth, that the said A B doth demise unto the said C D, his personal representative and assigns, all, &c. [here describe the property], from the day of , for the term of thence ensuing, yielding therefor, during the said term, the rent of [here state the rent, and mode of payment.[1]]

The said A B covenants for the lessee's quiet enjoyment of his term.

The said C D covenants to pay the rent; to pay the taxes; that he will not assign without leave; that he will leave the premises in good repair; and that the lessor may re-enter for default of days in the payment of rent, or for the breach of covenants.(*)

Witness the following signatures and seals.

A B. [Seal.]
C D. [Seal.]

[1] Any of these covenants may be omitted. The insertion of them will be determined by the contract between the parties.

Form of lease, with covenant for renewal.

Follow next preceding Form to (*), and then proceed:

The said A B covenants that he will, on or before the expiration of this present lease, at the request and expense of the said C D, his executors, administrators or assigns, grant and execute to him and them a new lease of the premises hereby demised, with their appurtenances, for the further term of years, to commence from the expiration of the term hereby granted, at the same yearly rent, payable in the like manner, and subject to the like covenants and agreements (except a covenant for further renewal) as are contained in these presents.

Witness the following signatures and seals.

A B. [Seal.]
C D. [Seal.]

A deed of trust to secure the payment of one note or bond.

This deed, made this day of , in the year one thousand eight hundred and , between A B of the city of Richmond, of the one part, and D F of the said city, of the other part: Witnesseth, that the said A B doth grant unto the said D F the following property, to wit [here describe the property]:

In trust, to secure to C E of the city of Richmond, the payment of the sum of a negotiable note, drawn by the said A B, dated the day of , and payable to the said C E, or order, months after its date, being for the sum of dollars [or if a bond, say: of a certain bond executed by the said A B, bearing date on the day of , and being for the payment of dollars, on the day of].

And it is covenanted and agreed between the parties aforesaid, that in case of a sale the same shall be made, after first advertising the time, place and terms thereof, for days[1] in some newspaper

[1] The sixth section of statute requires "reasonable notice." This term is uncertain, and it is therefore advisable that the deed should specify the number of days and manner of advertisement. In the country it is usual, either in addition to, or in exclusion of the advertisement in newspaper, to require a notice to be posted up at the front door of the courthouse, or at some other public place.

published in the city of Richmond, and upon the following terms, to wit: for cash as to so much of the proceeds as may be necessary to defray the expenses of executing this trust, the fees for drawing and recording this deed, if then unpaid, and to discharge the amount of money, principal and interest, then payable upon the said note (or bond); and if there be any residue of said purchase money, the same shall be made payable at such time, and be secured in such manner as the said A B, his executors, administrators or assigns, shall prescribe and direct, or in case of his or their failure to give such direction, at such time and in such manner as the said D F shall think fit. The said A B covenants to pay all taxes, assessments, dues and charges upon the said property hereby conveyed, so long as he or his heirs or assigns shall hold the same.

Witness the following signatures and seals.

A B. [Seal.]
D F. [Seal.]

A deed of trust to secure the payment of two or more notes or bonds.

This deed, made this day of , in the year one thousand eight hundred and , between A B of the city of Richmond, of the one part, and D F (trustee) of the said city, of the other part: Witnesseth, that the said A B doth grant unto the said D F the following property, to wit [here describe the property conveyed]:

In trust, to secure to C E of the city of Richmond, the payment of the sum of two bonds (or notes), the first bearing date on the day of , payable after its date, and the second bearing date on the day of , payable after its date, both executed by the said A B, and payable to the said C E. In the event of default in the payment of either of said bonds (or notes), in whole or in part, at the periods they shall respectively fall due, sale may be made.[1] And it is covenanted and agreed between the parties aforesaid, that in case of a sale, the same shall be made, after first advertising the time, place, and terms thereof, for days,

[1] This provision is inserted for abundant caution. Though it may not be absolutely necessary, yet as doubts may be raised as to the meaning of the term "the debt becoming payable," used in the statute, it is well to avoid such objections. See also note to next preceding form.

in some newspaper published in the city of Richmond, and upon the following terms, to wit: for cash as to so much of the proceeds as may be necessary to defray the expenses of executing this trust, the fees for drawing and recording this deed, if then unpaid, and to discharge the amount of money, principal and interest, then payable upon the said bonds (or notes); and if at the time of such sale, any bond or bonds (or note or notes), shall not have become due and payable, and the purchase money be sufficient, such part or parts of the said purchase money as will be sufficient to pay off and discharge such remaining bond or bonds (or note or notes) shall be made payable at such time or times as the said remaining bond or bonds (or note or notes) will become due; the payment of which part or parts shall be properly secured; and if there be any residue of said purchase money, the same shall be made payable at such time, and be secured in such manner, as the said A B, his executors, administrators or assigns, shall prescribe and direct; or in case of his or their failure to give such direction, at such time and in such manner as the said D F shall think fit. The said A B covenants to pay all taxes, assessments, dues and charges upon the said property hereby conveyed, so long as he or his heirs or assigns shall hold the same.

Witness the following signatures and seals.

A B. [Seal.]
D F. [Seal.]

A deed of trust to indemnify a surety on a bond.

Whereas S R has become bound with, and as surety for T D, for the payment of dollars to N P, to be paid on the day of , in the year , as fully appears by the bond of the said T D and S R, executed to the said N P, dated the day of , in the year : and whereas it is the wish of the said T D to keep indemnified his said surety, and to save him harmless from all damages, by reason of his having become bound as aforesaid: Now, therefore, this deed, made the day of , in the year , between the said T D of the one part, and J K (trustee) of the other part: Witnesseth, that the said T D doth grant unto the said J K the following property [here describe it]:

In trust, to secure the said S R from all loss and damage by reason of the suretyship aforesaid. And it is provided that the said T D shall be in possession of the said property, and receive and enjoy the rents and profits thereof, until default be made in the payment of the said sum of dollars, or any part thereof, for which the said bond was given as aforesaid; and upon such default being made, the said J K shall, after advertisement for days in some newspaper published in the city of Richmond, proceed to sell at public auction, on the premises, for cash to the highest bidder, the said property, the proceeds of which sale to be applied as required in such cases by the sixth section of chapter 117 of the Code of Virginia. The said T D covenants to pay all taxes, assessments, dues and charges upon the said property hereby conveyed, so long as he or his heirs or assigns shall hold the same.

Witness the following signatures and seals.

T D. [Seal.]
J K. [Seal.]

A deed of trust to indemnify an endorser.

This deed, made the day of , in the year , between A B of the city of Richmond, party of the first part, C D of the said city, party of the second part, and E F of the said city, party of the third part: Whereas the said E F, party of the third part, hath endorsed, for the benefit and accommodation of the said A B, party of the first part, four negotiable notes, drawn by the said A B, bearing even date with this deed; the first for the sum of $600, payable four months after its date; the second for the sum of $400, payable eight months after its date; the third for the sum of $300, payable twelve months after its date; and the fourth for the sum of $200, payable sixteen months after its date: And whereas the said E F may, for the like benefit and accommodation of the said A B, endorse other note or notes given in renewal or continuation of the said four notes, or either of them, in whole or in part; and the said A B being desirous of securing the said E F against all loss on account of endorsements already made, or hereafter to be made, for the benefit and accommodation of him, the said A B, as aforesaid, and to effect this purpose hath consented to convey in trust the property hereinafter described: Now, therefore, this deed witnesseth, that the said A B, in consideration of the premises, doth grant unto the said C D all that [here describe the property conveyed]:

In trust, to secure the said E F against all loss and damage by reason of endorsements already made by the said E F, on the said four notes, and of such other endorsement or endorsements which he may hereafter make on other note or notes given in renewal or continuation of the said four notes, or either of them, in whole or in part.

And if the said E F should be compelled to pay, or shall pay at or after maturity, the said four notes, or either of them, in whole or in part, or should the said E F be compelled to pay, or shall pay at or after maturity, any note or notes given in renewal or continuation of the said four notes, or either of them, in whole or in part, then, and in either event, the said E F may require the said C D to advertise and sell the said property so conveyed, in execution of this trust. If sale be required by said E F, or his heirs, personal representatives or assigns, the said C D shall make such sale, after first advertising the time, place and terms thereof, in some newspaper published in the city of Richmond, for days; said sale to be made at public auction, on the premises, to the highest bidder, and upon the following terms, to wit: for cash as to so much of the proceeds as may be necessary to defray the expenses of executing this trust, the fees for drawing and recording this deed, if then unpaid, and to discharge the amount of money then paid by said E F, with interest thereon from the time of such payment; and if at the time of such sale, either one or more of said four notes, or notes given in renewal or continuation of the same, or either of them, in whole or in part, shall not have become due and payable, and the purchase money be sufficient, such part or parts of the said purchase money as will be sufficient to pay off and discharge such remaining note or notes, shall be made payable at such time or times as the said remaining note or notes will become due; the payment of which part or parts shall be properly secured; and if there be any residue of said purchase money, the same shall be made payable at such time, and be secured in such manner, as the said A B, his executors, administrators or assigns, shall prescribe and direct; or in case of his or their failure to give such direction, at such time and in such manner as the said C D shall think fit. The said A B covenants to pay all taxes, assessments, dues and charges upon the said property hereby conveyed, so long as he or his heirs or assigns shall hold the same.

Witness the following signatures and seals.

A B. [Seal.]
C D. [Seal.]

Deed of release.

This deed, made the day of , in the year , between C D (trustee), party of the first part, A B, party of the second part, and E F, party of the third part: Whereas, by a deed dated the day of , in the year , and of record in the clerk's office of county court, the said A B, in order to secure to the said E F the payment of a certain bond executed by the said A B, and payable to the said E F, bearing date on the day of , in the year , and for the payment of the sum of $ on the day of , 18 , did convey in trust to the said C D certain property set forth and described in said deed, as follows [here copy description of property, as contained in trust deed]: and whereas the said bond has been fully paid, and the said A B desires the said property to be released to him: Now, therefore, this deed witnesseth, that the said C D, trustee as aforesaid, in consideration of the premises, and by and with the consent of the said E F, testified to by his becoming a party to this deed and signing and sealing the same, doth grant and release unto the said A B all that [here describe the property released]. The said E F releases to the said A B all his claims upon the said land.

Witness the following signatures and seals.

C D. [Seal.]
E F. [Seal.]

A release of claim to property other than lien of a trust deed.[1]

This deed, made the day of , in the year , between A B of the one part, and C D of the other part: Witnesseth, that in consideration of the sum of dollars, the said A B releases all his claims upon the lands [here describe premises] unto the said C D.

Witness the following signature and seal.

—— —— [Seal.]

[1] This may be effected by Form on p. 111, which conveys all the grantor's interest.

Form of a deed from clerk to purchaser of land sold for delinquent taxes.

This deed, made the day of , in the year 18 , between J E, clerk of the county court of Henrico, of the one part, and of the other part: Whereas a "list of real estate within the county of Henrico, sold in the months of October and November, 1850, for the non-payment of taxes thereon for the years 1845, '46, '47, '48 and '49, with a certificate attached thereto of such oath as is prescribed by the 10th section of chapter 37 of the Code of Virginia, was returned to the court of said county on the 8th day of January, 1851, being the second term next after the completion of the said sales; and the court seeing no cause to doubt the correctness of the list, ordered a copy thereof to be certified to the first auditor: And whereas by the said list it appears that , charged in the column representing the quantity of land charged with the taxes on of land, the local description of which was ; that the amount of taxes due thereon was ; that the quantity of land was ; that said sale was made on 7th October, 18 ; that the entire tract of land was sold; that the name of the purchaser was , and the amount of purchase money ; and the said purchaser had a report made by the surveyor of the county, to the court thereof, according to the 15th section of said chapter 37 of the Code, and the said court seeing no objection to said report, did, on the day of , 18 , order the same to be recorded; and two years having expired since the said sale, the purchaser of the said real estate alleging the same has not been redeemed, has applied for a deed conveying the same: Now, this deed witnesseth, that in consideration of the premises, and pursuant to the 16th section of chapter 37 of the Code, the said J E, clerk of the said county court of Henrico, doth grant unto the said the said real estate so sold to him, and specified in the report made by the surveyor as aforesaid.

Witness the following signature and seal.

J E, Clerk. [Seal.]

Deed from trustee for married woman to purchaser.

To J D, trustee for my benefit in a deed
from M R, dated the day of , 18 :

SIR:

I request you to make sale of the property conveyed by the said deed to Albert A, at the price of dollars, and to convey the same to the said purchaser.

Witness my hand and seal on this day of , 18 .

Witness as to Caroline B:
JOSEPH P.
QUINTUS R.

CAROLINE B. [Seal.]

This deed, made this day of 18 , between J D, trustee, as hereinafter mentioned, party of the first part, and Albert A, party of the second part: Whereas M R, by deed dated on the day of , and recorded in the clerk's office of Henrico county court, conveyed in trust to the said J D, trustee, the land hereinafter mentioned, upon the following among other trusts, to wit, that whenever directed by Caroline B, the wife of Robert B, by a writing under her hand and seal, attested by two witnesses, the said J D, trustee as aforesaid, should sell and convey the land to the purchaser; and the said Caroline B hath, by a writing under her hand and seal, dated the day of 18 , and attested by two witnesses, directed the said J D, trustee as aforesaid, to sell and convey the said land, hereinafter mentioned, unto Albert A, at the price of dollars, which direction in writing is annexed to this deed: Now, therefore, this deed witnesseth, that the said J D, trustee as aforesaid, in consideration of the premises, and of the said sum of dollars, and by the direction in writing as aforesaid of the said Caroline B, under her hand and seal, attested by two witnesses, doth grant, with special warranty, unto the said Albert A all that land lying and being [here describe the location of the property conveyed].

Witness the following signature and seal.

J D, Trustee. [Seal.]

XV.

DEEDS IN THE SEVERAL STATES.

ALABAMA.

Deed of bargain and sale, with general warranty.

This indenture, made this day of , 1856, between William Jarratt and Mary his wife, of the county of Limestone, and State of Alabama, of the one part, and David Ridgway, of the same county and State, of the second part: Witnesseth, that the said William Jarratt and Mary his wife, for and in consideration of the sum of dollars to them in hand paid by the said Ridgway, the receipt whereof is hereby acknowledged, have this day bargained, sold and conveyed, and by these presents do bargain, sell and convey unto the said Ridgway all that tract of land lying in the said county of Limestone, and State aforesaid, known as the northeast quarter of section twenty-five, township six, range four west, containing acres, more or less. To have and to hold the above named tract of land, with all tenements and appurtenances thereto belonging, unto the said Ridgway, his heirs and assigns, forever.

[And the said William Jarratt, and Mary his wife, for themselves, their heirs, administrators and executors, do hereby, and in consideration of the premises, warrant and will forever defend the title to the above described tract of land, and all its tenements and appurtenances, unto the said Ridgway, his heirs and assigns, from and against themselves, and all persons claiming or holding under them, the said Jarratt, and Mary his wife, and also against the lawful claim or demand of all other persons whomsoever.]

In testimony whereof, the parties have hereunto set their hands and affixed their seals the day and year above written.

WILLIAM JARRATT. [Seal.]
MARY JARRATT. [Seal.]
DAVID RIDGWAY. [Seal.]

The following is the short form of the same instrument:

Short form of deed of bargain and sale.

In consideration of dollars, received of , do hereby grant, bargain, sell and convey unto the said , and to heirs and assigns forever, the following tract of land in , to wit [here describe land]: And the said do hereby covenant with the said , that seized of an estate in fee simple in said land; that said land is free from any incumbrance; and that will warrant and defend the title of the said , heirs and assigns, thereunto, forever.

In testimony whereof, have hereunto set hand and seal this day of , A. D. 18 .

Executed in presence of } ——— ——— [Seal.]
——— ——— [Seal.]

The following is a short form of a quit-claim deed in Alabama:

Form of quit-claim deed.

In consideration of dollars, received of L S, we A B, and Caroline his wife, hereby remise, release, and forever quit-claim unto the said L S, and to his heirs and assigns, all the right, title and claim which we have, in and to the following tract of land, in the county of , to wit [here describe land]:

In testimony whereof, we have hereunto set our hands and seals this day of , A. D. 18 .

Executed in presence of } A B. [Seal.]
CAROLINE B. [Seal.]

Deed of trust.

This indenture, made and entered into this the day of , 18 , by and between A B of the first part, C D of the second part, and E F of the third part, all of the county of , in the State of Alabama: Whereas the said party of the first part is justly indebted to the said party of the third part, in the sum of dollars, due [here specify the nature of the debt], on the day of , 18 , as will more fully appear by his note under seal for that sum, to the said party of the third part (E F), bearing date on the day of , 18 , and due as above set forth;

which indebtedness the said party of the first part (A B) is desirous to secure:

Now, this indenture witnesseth, that for and in consideration of the premises, and for the further consideration of [any small amount, say, *one* or *five* dollars], paid by the party of the second part to the party of the first part, the receipt of which is hereby acknowledged, the said parties of the first part have bargained, sold and transferred, and by these presents do bargain, sell and transfer to the said party of the second part, the following described property, to wit [here set forth the property, if real, give a description of the land; if personal, give description also]:

To have and to hold the said property [of whatever kind it may be], to the said party of the second part, his executors, &c. forever: Upon trust, nevertheless, that the said party of the second part will permit [the said named property] to remain in the quiet and peaceable possession and use of the party of the first part, until default be made in the payment by him of said dollars, in whole or in part. If default be made as aforesaid, the said C D shall, as soon as he may think proper thereafter, or as soon as the said E F shall direct, sell the said [property] hereby intended to be conveyed [at any named place], at public sale for [cash or credit, as the case may be], he first fixing the time of said sale, and giving at least [any number of days' notice that may be required by the parties, by posting up advertisements, or publication in a paper, as may be required], and out of the proceeds of said sale, he shall first pay all costs incident to, and properly arising out of the execution of this deed; out of the balance, if there be a sufficiency for the purpose, he shall pay off and discharge the said debt hereby secured, and the interest thereon; if there be not enough for that purpose, he shall pay all of said balance upon said debt, after paying the expenses as aforesaid; and if there be any surplus after paying as aforesaid, it shall be paid over to the said party of the first part. But if the said party of the first part pay off this indebtedness and expenses, so that no default be made in the same, then this deed to be of no force or effect.

In testimony whereof, the said parties hereto have set their hands and seals the day and date above written.

——— ——— [Seal.]
——— ——— [Seal.]
——— ——— [Seal.]

Arkansas.

The following form conveys nothing more than the naked interest of the grantor of land in this State. It has not the effect of a general warranty deed:

Form of deed to convey grantor's interest.

This deed, made the fifth day of December, in the year 1866, between A B of the city of , of the first part, and L M of the same place, of the second part: Witnesseth, that the said A B, for and in consideration of one thousand dollars, lawful money of the United States, to him in hand paid by the said L M, the receipt whereof is hereby acknowledged, hath granted, bargained and sold, and by these presents doth grant, bargain, sell, convey and confirm unto the said L M, his heirs, executors, administrators and assigns, forever, all and singular, that certain piece or parcel of land, situated in the city of [here describe the land], together with all and singular the tenements, hereditaments and appurtenances thereunto belonging, and the reversions, remainders, rents, issues and profits thereof, and all the estate, title and interest of the said A B to the said premises, or any part thereof.

In testimony whereof, the parties hereto have hereunto set their hands and affixed their seals on the day and year above written.

——— ——— [Seal.]
——— ——— [Seal.]

The following is the form of a deed with general warranty:

Form of deed of bargain and sale with general warranty.

This deed, made the day of , 1866, between A B and Caroline his wife, of the , parties of the first part, and N M of the , party of the second part: Witnesseth, that the said parties of the first part, for and in consideration of the sum of one thousand dollars, lawful money of the United States, to them in hand paid by the said party of the second part, at and before the sealing and delivery of these presents, the receipt whereof is hereby acknowledged, have granted, bargained and sold, and by these presents do grant, bargain, sell and convey unto the said party of the second part, and to his heirs and assigns, forever, all that certain piece or parcel of land, situate, lying and being in the city of , together with all and singular the tenements, hereditaments and appurtenances thereunto belonging or in any way appertaining, and the reversion and reversions, remainder and remainders, rents, issues and profits thereof; and also all the estate, right, title, interest, property, possession, claim and demand whatsoever, as well in law as in equity, of the said parties of the first part, of, in or to the above described premises, and every part and parcel thereof, with the appurtenances. To have and to hold all and singular the above mentioned and described premises, together with the appurtenances, unto the said party of the second part, his heirs and assigns, forever. And they, the said A B and Caroline his wife, parties of the first part, promise and agree with the said N M, the party of the second part, that they will forever warrant and defend the title to the said granted lands and premises, against the claims of all and every person or persons whatsoever.

In testimony whereof, the parties hereto have hereunto set their hands and affixed their seals on the day and year above written.

——— ——— [Seal.]
——— ——— [Seal.]

Form of deed of trust.

The deed of trust given under the title "Alabama," may be used in this State.

CALIFORNIA.

Form of deed of bargain and sale.

Adopt the form under title "Alabama."

Form of deed of trust.

Adopt the form under title "Alabama."

CONNECTICUT.

The following is the form of a deed of bargain and sale, with a covenant of general warranty:

Form of deed of bargain and sale, with covenant of general warranty.

To all people to whom these presents shall come—Greeting:

Know ye, that we, A B, and Caroline B his wife, of the , for the consideration of seven hundred dollars, received to the full satisfaction of the purchase money of the property hereinafter described, purchased by J M, do give, grant, bargain, sell, convey and confirm unto the said J M, his heirs and assigns, forever, all that certain [here describe property].

To have and to hold the above granted and bargained premises, with the appurtenances thereof, unto him, the said J M, his heirs and assigns, forever, to his and their own proper use and behoof. And also we, the said A B, and Caroline B his wife, do, for ourselves, our heirs, executors and administrators, covenant with the said J M, his heirs and assigns, that at and until the ensealing of these presents, we, the said A B, and Caroline B his wife, are well seized of the premises, as a good, indefeasible estate in fee simple, and have good right to bargain and sell the same, in manner and form as is above written, and that the same is free of all incumbrance whatsoever.

And furthermore, we, the said A B, and Caroline B his wife, do by these presents bind ourselves, and our heirs, forever, to warrant and defend the above granted and bargained premises unto him, the said J M, his heirs and assigns, against all claims and demands whatsoever.

In witness whereof, we have hereunto set our hands and seals this day of , in the year of our Lord 18 .

Signed, sealed and delivered in the presence of

———— ———— [Seal.]
———— ———— [Seal.]

The following is the form of a mortgage deed:

Form of a mortgage deed.

To all people to whom these presents shall come—Greeting:

Know ye, that we, A B, and Caroline B his wife, of the , for the consideration of five dollars paid by L M, received to the full satisfaction of the said A B and Caroline B, do give, grant, bargain, sell and confirm unto the said L M all that certain [here describe property].

To have and to hold the above granted and bargained premises, with the appurtenances thereof, unto him the said L M, his heirs and assigns, forever, to his and their own proper use and behoof. And also we, the said A B, and Caroline B his wife, do, for ourselves, our heirs, executors and administrators, covenant with the said L M, his heirs and assigns, that at and until the ensealing of these presents, we are well seized of the premises as a good, indefeasible estate in fee simple, and have good right to bargain and sell the same, in manner and form as is above written; and the same is free of all incumbrance whatsoever.

And furthermore, we, the said A B, and Caroline B his wife; do by these presents bind ourselves and our heirs, forever, to warrant and defend the above granted and bargained premises to him, the said L M, his heirs and assigns, against all claims and demands whatsoever: Always provided, that these presents are on condition that whereas if the said A B shall well and truly pay at maturity, to the said L M, a certain debt of five hundred dollars, evidenced by a single bill executed to the said L M by the said A B, bearing even date with this deed, and payable one year after date, then this present deed to be void and of no effect, otherwise to remain in full force, power and virtue in the law.

In witness whereof, we have hereunto set our hands and seals this day of , in the year of our Lord 18 .

Signed, sealed and delivered in presence of ——— ——— [Seal.]
——— ——— [Seal.]

Delaware.

In this State, when there is no express covenant in a deed, the words "grant, bargain and sell" will, unless specially restrained, imply a special warranty against a grantor and his heirs, and all persons claiming under him. Del. Rev. Laws (1852), ch. 83, § 2.

The common law distinctions between "indenture" and "deed poll" should also be observed in the preparation and authentication of conveyances. See Del. Rev. Laws, p. 268, ch. 83, § 9.

Form of indenture of bargain and sale.

This indenture, made the day of , in the year of our Lord one thousand eight hundred and , between A B (of, &c.), party of the first part, and C D (of, &c.), party of the second part: [Whereas, &c.[1]]

Now, this indenture witnesseth, that the said A B, for and in consideration of the sum of dollars ($), good and lawful money of the United States of America, unto him well and truly paid by the said C D, at and before the sealing and delivery of these presents, the receipt whereof the said A B doth hereby acknowledge, and thereof acquit and forever discharge the said C D, the said A B hath granted, bargained and sold, and by these presents doth grant, bargain, sell, alien, enfeoff, release, convey and confirm, unto the said C D, and to his heirs and assigns, all [here describe premises]:

Together with all and singular the ways, waters, water courses, rights, liberties, privileges, hereditaments and appurtenances whatsoever, thereunto belonging, or in any wise appertaining, and the reversions, remainders, rents, issues and profits thereof: And also, all the estate, right, title, interest, property, claim and demand whatsoever, of the said A B, and his heirs in law, equity or otherwise, howsoever, of, in, to, or out of the same, or any part thereof:

To have and to hold the said land (&c. &c.), and the improvements, hereditaments and premises hereby granted or mentioned, or intended so to be, with the appurtenances thereunto appertaining, or in any wise belonging, unto the said C D, his heirs and assigns, to the only proper use and behoof of the said C D, his heirs and assigns, forever.

And the said A B, for himself, his heirs, executors and administrators, doth by these presents covenant, grant and agree, to and

[1] The attorney who enclosed this form to the writer, makes the following remarks in regard to this part of the form:

"We generally recite here the title by deed in same manner as a title by patent (or recite the title immediately after description of the premises).

"A receipt for the purchase money is considered the safest manner of completing a deed here. There are two forms, this and another, in which the recital follows the description."

with the said C D, and his heirs and assigns, that he, the said A B, and his heirs, all and singular the hereditaments and premises herein above described and granted, or mentioned and intended so to be, with the appurtenances, unto the said C D, his heirs and assigns, against him, the said A B, and his heirs, and against all and every other person or persons whomsoever, lawfully claiming or to claim the same, or any part thereof, through, by, from or under him, them, or any of them, shall and will warrant and forever defend.

In witness whereof, the said party of the first part hath hereunto set his hand and seal, dated the day and year first above written.

Signed, sealed and delivered in the presence of } A B. [Seal.]

Received, the day of the date of this indenture, from the said A B, five hundred dollars, the full consideration money hereinbefore mentioned.

Witness:—L M. } A B.

Form of indenture of mortgage.

This indenture, made the day of , in the year of our Lord one thousand eight hundred and , between A B of [place of residence], of the first part, and C D of [place of residence], of the second part: Whereas the said A B, of the first part, in and by his certain obligation, or writing obligatory, under his hand and seal, bearing even date herewith, stands bound unto the said C D, of the second part, in the sum of one thousand dollars, lawful money of the United States, conditioned for the payment of five hundred dollars, lawful money as aforesaid, at or before the expiration of one year from and after the day of said date, with lawful interest for the same, to be paid semi-annually, as by reference to the said obligation and condition thereof will appear:

Now, this indenture witnesseth, that the said A B, as well for and in consideration of the aforesaid debt or sum of five hundred dollars, and for the better securing the payment of the same, with interest as aforesaid, unto the said C D, his heirs and assigns, in discharge of the said recited obligation, as also of the further sum of one dollar, to the said party of the first part, now paid by the said party of the second part, the receipt whereof is hereby acknowledged, hath granted, bargained, sold, released and confirmed, and by these presents doth grant, bargain, sell, release and confirm, unto the said party of the second part, all that [here describe premises conveyed].

Together with all and singular the improvements, ways, waters, water courses, rights, liberties, privileges, hereditaments and appurtenances whatsoever, thereunto belonging, or in any wise appertaining, and the reversions and remainders, rents, issues and profits thereof: To have and to hold the said lot of land [or as the case may be], its improvements, hereditaments and premises, hereby granted or mentioned, or intended so to be, with the appurtenances, unto the said party of the second part, his heirs and assigns, to the only proper use and behoof of the said C D, his heirs and assigns, forever:

Provided, always, nevertheless, that if the said A B, party of the first part, his heirs, executors, administrators or assigns, shall and do well and truly pay, or cause to be paid unto the said party of the second part, his heirs or assigns, the aforesaid debt or sum of five hundred dollars, on the day and time hereinbefore mentioned and appointed for the payment thereof, with interest, according to the condition of the said recited obligation, without any fraud or further delay, and without any deduction, defalcation or abatement to be made of any thing for or in respect of any taxes, charges or assessments whatsoever, then and from thenceforth, as well this present indenture, and the estate hereby granted, as the said recited obligation, shall cease, determine, and become absolutely void and of no effect, any thing herein before contained to the contrary in any wise notwithstanding.

In witness whereof, the said party of the first part hath hereunto set his hand and seal, dated the day and year first above written.

Signed, sealed and delivered in presence of us: A B. [Seal.]

State of Delaware—New Castle County, ss:

Be it remembered, that on this day of , A. D, 18 , personally came before me, H A, notary public for the State of Delaware, A B, party to this indenture, personally known to me to be such, and he, the said A B, acknowledged this indenture to be his deed.

H A, Notary Public.

Form of assignment of indenture of mortgage.

Know all men by these presents, that I, C D, mortgagee named in the foregoing indenture of mortgage (executed by A B), for and in consideration of the sum of   dollars, to him in hand now paid by R L, the receipt whereof is hereby acknowledged, have granted, bargained, sold, assigned and set over, and by these presents do grant, bargain, sell, assign and set over, unto the said R L, his heirs and assigns, the said foregoing indenture of mortgage, and all the said [here describe premises], therein mentioned and described, together with all the rights, members and appurtenances thereunto belonging, and all the estate, right, title and interest therein: To have and to hold, all and singular, the premises hereby granted and assigned, or mentioned, or intended so to be, unto the said R L, his heirs and assigns, forever: Subject, nevertheless, to the right and equity of redemption of the said mortgagor, his heirs and assigns (if any they have), in the same.

Witness my hand and seal, dated the   day of   , in the year of our Lord one thousand eight hundred and   .

Sealed and delivered in presence of us: A. B. [Seal.]

DISTRICT OF COLUMBIA.

The following is the form of a deed of bargain and sale, with general warranty:

Deed of bargain and sale, with general warranty.

This indenture, made this   day of   , in the year of our Lord one thousand eight hundred and fifty   , by and between A B, and Caroline B his wife, of the county of Washington, in the District of Columbia, of the first part, and N M, of the same county, of the second part: Witnesseth, that the said A B, and Caroline B his wife, for and in consideration of the sum of five hundred dollars, current money of the United States, to them in hand paid at and before the ensealing and delivery of these presents, by the said N M, the receipt whereof is hereby acknowledged, have given, granted, bargained and sold, aliened, enfeoffed, conveyed and confirmed, and by these presents do give, grant, bargain and sell, alien, enfeoff, convey and confirm unto him, the said N M, and his heirs and assigns, forever, all those certain [here describe property conveyed], together with all and singular the buildings, improvements, rights, ways, privileges and appurtenances to the same belonging or in any manner appertaining, and the remainders, reversions, rents, issues and profits of the same, and all the right, title, interest and estate of them, the said parties of the first part, in and to the same. To have and to hold the said lots, pieces or parcels of ground and premises, with the appurtenances, as aforesaid, unto him, the said N M, and to his heirs and assigns, to his and their only use, benefit and behoof, forever. And the said parties of the first part, for themselves, and their heirs, executors and administrators, hereby covenant, promise and agree, to and with the said party of the second part, and his heirs, executors, administrators and assigns, in the manner and form following, that is to say: That they, the said parties of the first part, and their heirs, shall and will warrant and forever defend the said lots, pieces or parcels of ground and premises, with the appurtenances, as aforesaid, hereby conveyed or intended to be conveyed unto him, the said party of the second part, his heirs and assigns, from and against them, the said parties of the first part, their heirs and assigns, and against all persons claiming or to claim the said described premises, or any part thereof, by, through or under them, or any and every of them.

And further, that they, the said parties of the first part, and their heirs, shall and will, at any and all times hereafter, at the cost and request of the said party of the second part, his heirs and assigns, make, execute and deliver such other and further assurances in law, for the more perfect conveyance of the premises as afore described, unto him, the said party of the second part, and his heirs and assigns, as he or they, or his or their counsel learned in the law, shall or may devise, advise and require.

In testimony whereof, the said parties of the first part have hereunto set their hands and seals the day and year first hereinbefore written.

Signed, sealed and delivered in presence of } ——— ——— [Seal.]
——— ——— [Seal.]

The following is the form of a deed of trust:

Form of deed of trust.

This indenture, made this day of , in the year of our Lord one thousand eight hundred and , by and between A B of the first part, and J M of the second part: Whereas the said party of the first part is justly indebted to N R in the sum of five hundred dollars, for which amount said N R holds the promissory note of said A B, bearing even date herewith, and being for the payment of the said sum of five hundred dollars on the day of : And whereas the said party of the first part is desirous to secure the full and punctual payment of said sum, and all interest, costs and expenses that may accrue thereon, according to the true intent and meaning of the aforesaid promissory note: Now, therefore, this indenture witnesseth, that the said party of the first part, in consideration of the premises, and of the sum of one dollar to him in hand paid by the said party of the second part, at and before the ensealing and delivery of these presents, the receipt whereof is hereby acknowledged, hath given, granted, bargained and sold, aliened, enfeoffed, conveyed and confirmed, and by these presents doth give, grant, bargain and sell, alien, enfeoff, convey and confirm unto the said J M, party of the second part, all those [here describe property conveyed], together with all and singular the improvements, privileges, hereditaments and appurtenances to the same belonging or in any manner appertaining. To have and to hold the same unto and to the use of the said J M.

In trust, nevertheless, for the uses and purposes following, and none other; that is to say, to suffer and permit the said party of the first part, his heirs and assigns, to have, hold, use, occupy, possess and enjoy the said premises, with the appurtenances, as afore described, and the rents, issues and profits of the same to take, receive and apply to his own use until some default or failure shall have been made in the payment of the said debt due as aforesaid to the said N R, or in any part thereof, or of any proper interest, costs and charges thereon, or which may accrue thereon; and upon any and every such default or failure being made in the payment as aforesaid, the said party of the second part shall, at the request in writing of the said N R, proceed to sell and dispose of the said premises as afore described, or so much thereof as he may deem necessary, at public sale, to the highest bidder, upon such terms and conditions as he, the said party of the second part, may deem most for the interest of all parties concerned in said sale, first giving days' notice of the time, place and terms of such sale, by advertisement in some newspaper printed and published in the city of Washington, and such sale to repeat or postpone from time to time, as he, the said party of the second part, may deem expedient, and out of the proceeds arising from such sale or sales (after paying the proper expenses thereof, and other expenses of this trust, including per centum on the gross amount of said sale or sales, as compensation to said trustee for his trouble and diligence in executing this trust), to pay, in the first place, whatever of said debt, interest, costs and expenses may be due and unpaid at time of such sale or sales; secondly, to pay whatever of said debt, interest, costs and expenses may then remain unpaid, although the same may not then have become due and payable; and lastly, the surplus, if any, to pay over to the said A B, his heirs, executors, administrators or assigns; and in the event of any such sale or sales, under the provisions of this trust, to convey to the purchaser or purchasers all the right, title and estate, legal and equitable, of the said party of the first part, in and to the premises sold; and on any sale being hereafter made under the provisions of this trust, and the terms thereof being complied with to the satisfaction of said trustee so selling, to surrender to such purchaser or purchasers, his, her or their proper representative, the full and peaceable possession of the premises sold.

In testimony whereof, the said party of the first part hath hereunto set his hand and seal the day and year first before written.

Signed, sealed and delivered in presence of — — [Seal.]

The following is the form of a deed of release:

Form of deed of release.

This indenture, made this day of , in the year eighteen hundred and fifty , by and between J M, of the first part, and A B, of the second part, witnesseth: Whereas the said A B, by his deed of indenture, duly made and executed, bearing date on or about the day of , in the year eighteen hundred and , did grant and convey to the said J M, and to his heirs and assigns, "all [here describe property in the same manner as described in trust deed]:"

And whereas the debt, with the interest and costs mentioned in said conveyance, has been fully paid and discharged to N R, and the purposes for which said trust was created, have therefore ceased and determined, the said A B is entitled in law to a conveyance of the premises, free and discharged of and from the said trusts as aforesaid, and as fully as if said deed had not been made: Now, this indenture witnesseth, that for and in consideration of the premises, and of the further sum of one dollar, to him the said party of the first part, in hand paid by the said party of the second part, at and before the ensealing and delivery of these presents, the receipt whereof is hereby acknowledged, he, the said party of the first part, hath given, granted, bargained, sold, conveyed, released and assigned, and by these presents doth give, grant, bargain, sell, convey, release and assign all and singular the aforementioned premises, with the appurtenances, and every part and parcel thereof, as fully and entirely as the same now are in law or equity vested and standing in the said party of the first part, by or under the said in part recited deed, unto A B, the party of the second part, his heirs and assigns, forever, to have and to hold the same, and every part and parcel thereof, with the appurtenances, unto him, the said party of the second part, his heirs and assigns, forever, to his and their only proper use, benefit and behoof, forever, free, clear and forever discharged of and from all and every right, title, interest and trust now existing in said party of the first part, by or under the said conveyance as aforesaid.

In witness whereof, the said party of the first part hath hereunto set his hand and seal the day and year first above written.

Signed, sealed and delivered in presence of } ——— ——— [Seal.]

FLORIDA.

Form of deed of bargain and sale.

Adopt the form under title "Alabama," page 121, ante. The deed should be sealed and delivered in the presence of two witnesses. Thompson's Digest, p. 167. The witnesses should also attest the conveyance. Ibid. 180, § 4.

Form of deed of trust.

Adopt the form under title "Alabama," page 122, ante. Let the sealing and delivery be attested by two witnesses.

Georgia.

Form of deed of bargain and sale.

Adopt the form under title "Alabama," page 121, ante.

Form of deed of trust.

Adopt the form under title "Alabama," page 122, ante.

Illinois.

Form of deed of bargain and sale, having the effect of deed with general warranty, &c.[1]

This deed, made this day of , in the year 18 , between A B, and Caroline his wife, parties of the first part, and James Richards, party of the second part: Witnesseth, that the said parties of the first part, for and in consideration of the sum of dollars, to them in hand paid by the said party of the second part, the receipt whereof is hereby acknowledged, do grant, bargain and sell, unto the said James Richards, and to his heirs and assigns, forever, all, &c. [here describe the premises], together with all and singular the hereditaments and appurtenances thereunto belonging, or in any wise appertaining: To have and to hold

[1] By the Rev. Stat. 1845, ch. 24, § 11, "all deeds, whereby any estate of inheritance, in fee simple, shall hereafter be limited to the grantee and his heirs, or other legal representative, the words "grant," "bargain," "sell," shall be judged an express covenant to the grantee, his heirs and other legal representatives, to wit: that the grantor was seized of an indefeasible estate in fee simple, free from incumbrances done or suffered from the grantor, except the rents and services that may be reserved; as also for quiet enjoyment against the grantor, his heirs and assigns, unless limited by express words contained in such deed, &c."

the said premises hereby granted, unto the said James Richards, his heirs and assigns, forever.

In witness whereof, the said parties of the first part have hereunto set their hands and seals the day and year first herein written.

A B. [Seal.]
CAROLINE B. [Seal.]

Form of quit-claim deed.

Know all men by these presents, that we, A B, and Caroline B (wife of the said A B), in consideration of the sum of dollars, to us in hand paid by C D, the receipt whereof is hereby acknowledged, do hereby quit-claim unto the said C D, all and each of our right, title and interest in and to all, &c. [here describe premises], with all and singular the hereditaments and appurtenances thereunto belonging, or in any wise appertaining.

In witness whereof, we have hereunto set our hands and seals on this day of , in the year 18 .

——— ——— [Seal.]
——— ——— [Seal.]

Form of power of attorney to sell and convey land.

Know all men by these presents, that I, A B, of the county of , in the State of Illinois, have made, constituted and appointed, and by these presents do make, constitute and appoint C D of the county of , in the State aforesaid, my true and lawful attorney, for me and in my name, to grant, bargain, sell and convey, to any person or persons, who may desire to purchase the same, the northwest quarter of section number five, in township number one, north of the base line, in range number three, east of the fourth principal meridian, in the State of Illinois: Hereby giving and granting to my said attorney full power and authority in the premises, to do all acts necessary and proper to be done in the promises, in as full and ample a manner as I myself might or could do, if personally present. And I do hereby ratify and confirm all the acts of my said attorney, lawfully done in the premises.

Witness my hand and seal, at the county aforesaid, this day of , A. D. 18 . A B. [Seal.]

Note.—This form may be used for any purpose, by inserting the particular acts which the attorney is authorized to perform.

INDIANA.

The latest revisal in this State sanctions the following forms:

Form of deed with general warranty.

By Rev. Stat. Ind. 1852, ch. 23, § 12, "Any conveyance of lands, worded in substance, as follows: 'A B conveys and warrants to C D' [here describe the premises], 'for the sum of' [here insert the consideration], the said conveyance being dated and duly signed, sealed and acknowledged by the grantor, shall be deemed and held to be a conveyance in fee simple to the grantee, his heirs and assigns, with covenant from the grantor, for himself, and his heirs and personal representatives, that he is lawfully seized of the premises, has a good right to convey the same, and guarantees the quiet possession thereof; that the same are free from all incumbrances, and that he will warrant and defend the title to the same against all lawful claims." In conformity to this statute, the following form would seem to be sufficient as a conveyance, with general warranty, &c.

This deed, made this day of , 18 , between A B, of the one part, and C D, of the other part: Witnesseth, that the said A B conveys and warrants to C D [here describe the premises], for the sum of [here insert the consideration].

In witness whereof, the said A B hath hereunto set his hand and seal on the day and year first herein written as the date hereof.

A B. [Seal.]

Form of quit-claim deed.

By Rev. Stat. Ind. 1852, ch. 23, § 13, "Any conveyance of lands, worded in substance, as follows: 'A B quit-claims to C D' [here describe the premises], 'for the sum of' [here insert the consideration], 'the said conveyance being duly signed, sealed and acknowledged by the grantor, shall be deemed a good and sufficient conveyance, &c.'" The following form complies with this statute:]

This deed, made this day of , 18 , between A B, of the one part, and C D, of the other part: Witnesseth, that the said

A B quit-claims to C D [here describe the premises], for the sum of [here insert the consideration].

In witness whereof, the said A B hath hereunto set his hand and seal on the day and year first herein written as the date hereof.

A B. [Seal.]

Form of mortgage deed.

By Rev. Stat. Ind. ch. 23, § 15, a mortgage may be in these words: "A B mortgages to C D [describe the premises], to secure [describe the debt]. If it be designed to warrant the title, a warranty of title ought to be inserted. The following form contains the warranty of title between parentheses:

This deed, made on this day of , 18 , between A B, of the one part, and C D, of the other part: Witnesseth, that the said A B mortgages to C D [here describe the premises], to secure [here describe the debt]. (And the said A B, for himself, his heirs and personal representatives, covenants with the said C D, his heirs and personal representatives, that he, the said A B, is lawfully seized of the premises hereby mortgaged, and that the same are free from all incumbrances; and that he, the said A B, will warrant and defend the title to the same against all lawful claims.)

In witness whereof, the said A B hath hereunto set his hand and seal on the day and year first herein written as the date hereof.

A B. [Seal.]

Iowa.

The following forms are prescribed by the Code of Iowa of 1851, § 1232:

Form of a quit-claim deed.

"For the consideration of dollars, I hereby quit-claim to A B, all my interest in the following tract of land [describing it]."

Form of a deed in fee simple without warranty.

"For the consideration of dollars, I hereby convey to A B the following tract of land [describing it].

Form of a deed in fee simple with warranty.

The same as in the last preceding form, adding the words, "and I warrant the title against all persons whatsoever."

Form of a mortgage.

The same as a deed of conveyance, adding the words, "to be upon consideration I pay," etc.

Form of a deed of trust.

"For the purpose of securing to A B the sum of dollars, with interest from date, at the rate of per centum per annum (as the case may be), I hereby convey to C D [describe the property], and if the sum secured to A B is not paid to him by [stating the time of payment], I hereby authorize the said C D to sell the property herein conveyed [stating the manner, place of sale, notice to be given, etc.], to execute a deed to the purchasers, to pay off the amount herein secured, with interest and costs, and to hold the remainder subject to my order."

From the language of the statute, these *deeds* would probably be sustained, if the exact words above cited were all that were used in them, the term "deed" in Iowa not necessarily importing a *sealed* instrument (Code of Iowa, part 1, title 1, ch. 3, p. 7, def. 20); yet, for abundant caution, it would be wise to preface and conclude all the foregoing forms thus:

General form of commencement and conclusion.

This deed, made this day of , 18 , between A B of the one part, and C D of the other part: Witnesseth, &c. &c. (as in the several foregoing forms; then conclude):

In witness whereof, the said A B hath hereunto set his hand and seal on the day and year first herein written as the date hereof.

A B. [Seal.]

Kentucky.

Form of deed of bargain and sale.

The form under title "Alabama," p. 121, ante, may be adopted. It seems not to be necessary that the conveyance of land by any other than a State or corporation, should be a sealed instrument; yet it is better, for abundant caution, always to annex a scroll or seal.

Form of deed of trust.

Follow form under title "Alabama," p. 122, ante.

Louisiana.

The form of an "authentic act," or "act of sale," which in this State supplies the place of the deed, is as follows:

Form of act of sale.

State of Louisiana—City of New Orleans:

Be it known, that on this day of , before me, R S, a notary public in and for the city and parish of New Orleans, State of Louisiana aforesaid, duly commissioned and sworn, personally came and appeared Robert J of this city, *who is unmarried,* who declared, that for the consideration hereinafter expressed, he doth, by these presents, grant, bargain, sell, convey, transfer, assign and set over, with all legal warranties, unto the said J M of this city, *who is also unmarried,* here present, accepting and purchasing for himself, his heirs and assigns, and acknowledging delivery and possession thereof, a certain lot, &c. [here describe premises, &c.]: to have and to hold the said lot of ground and buildings, unto the said J M, his heirs and assigns, to their proper use and behoof, forever. And the said Robert J, for himself and his heirs, the said property to the said J M, his heirs and assigns, shall and will warrant and forever defend, against the lawful claims of all persons whomsoever, by these presents. And the said Robert J doth moreover subrogate the said purchaser to all the rights and actions of warranty, which he now has or may have against his own vendor, or against the vendors of his vendor, fully authorizing the said purchaser to exercise the said rights and actions, in the same manner as he himself might or could have done. This sale is made and accepted for and in consideration of the sum of dollars, in ready current money, which the said vendor acknowledges to have received from the said purchaser, delivered in the presence of the undersigned, notary and witnesses, for which a full acquittance is hereby granted. By reference to the annexed certificates of the recorder of mortgages and register of conveyances for this city, dated this day, it appears that there is no mortgage recorded in the name of said Robert J, on the property herein above conveyed, and that the same has not been alienated by the vendor, and that all the State and city taxes on the said property have been paid.(*)

Thus done and passed, in my office, in the city of New Orleans aforesaid, in the presence of A B and C D, witnesses of lawful age (i. e. 14 years of age), and domiciliated in this city, who hereunto sign their names, together with the said parties, and me, the said notary, on this day of , in the year one thousand eight hundred and fifty .

ROBERT J.
J M.
[Seal of Notary.] A B, C D, } Witnesses.
N O, Notary Public.

Form of wife's renunciation.

Follow preceding form to the (*), omitting italics; then proceed:

"And next personally appeared Mrs. Delia Beckwith (i. e., the maiden name), of lawful age, wife of said Robert J, who, after undersigned notary (or other) had explained to her verbally the nature and purport of the foregoing act of [sale, mortgage, or other], from her said husband to said J M, declared that she was desirous of releasing in favor of said J M, the property hereinbefore [sold, or other] from the matrimonial, dotal, paraphernal and other rights, and from all claims, mortgages and privileges to which she may be entitled, whether by virtue of her marriage with said Robert J, or otherwise. Whereupon the undersigned notary (or other) did verbally explain to said Mrs. D B J, out of the presence of her said husband, the nature and extent of her rights, which are here detailed, to wit:"

[The wife has a legal mortgage on the property of her husband in the following cases: 1st. For restitution of her dowry and for the reinvestment of the dotal property sold by her husband, and which she brought in marriage, reckoning from the celebration of marriage. 2d. For restitution and reinvestment of dotal property which came to her after marriage either by succession or donation from day succession opened or was perfected. 3d. For reimbursing amount of paraphernal property alienated by her and received by her husband or otherwise disposed of for his interest. 4th. To indemnify her for debts contracted with her husband. 5th. For donations made to her by her husband on account of marriage:]

And that, by renouncing said rights on the property hereinbefore [sold, or other] she would deprive herself and heirs irrevocably of all recourse thereon. And said Mrs. D B J did thereupon declare to me [notary or other] that she fully understood the nature and extent of her said rights on the property of her said husband, and that she nevertheless did persist in her intention of renouncing the same in favor of said J M, on property hereinbefore [sold or .]

And said husband being now present, assisting and authorizing his wife in the execution of these presents, and consenting thereto, said Mrs. D B J did again declare that she did and does hereby make a formal renunciation and relinquishment of all her said rights and mortgages on the property hereinbefore [sold or] in favor of said J M, binding herself and her heirs at all times to sustain and acknowledge the validity of this renunciation.

Thus done and passed, &c. (as before, to the conclusion; husband, wife, grantor, witnesses and notary signing it, and notary affixing the seal).

MAINE.

Form of deed of bargain and sale, with general warranty.

Know all men by these presents, that we, Alfred B and Caroline B his wife, in consideration of the sum of five hundred dollars paid by L M (the receipt whereof we do hereby acknowledge), do hereby give, grant, bargain, sell and convey unto the said L M, his heirs and assigns, forever, all that [here describe the property]. To have and to hold the afore granted and bargained premises, with all the privileges and appurtenances thereof, to the said L M, his heirs and assigns, to his and their use and benefit forever. And we do covenant with the said L M, his heirs and assigns, that we are lawfully seized in fee of the premises; that they are free of all incumbrances; that we have good right to sell and convey the same to the said L M; and that we will warrant and defend the same to the said L M, his heirs and assigns, forever, against the lawful claims and demands of all persons.

In witness whereof, I, the said Alfred B, and I, the said Caroline B, wife of said Alfred B, in consideration of one dollar to me paid by the said L M, in token of a full relinqnishment of all my right to dower in the premises, have hereunto set our hands and seals this day of , in the year of our Lord one thousand eight hundred and .

Signed, sealed and delivered in presence of

——— ——— [Seal.]
——— ——— [Seal.]

Form of quit-claim deed.

Know all men by these presents, that we, Alfred B and Caroline B his wife, in consideration of five hundred dollars to us paid by L M (the receipt whereof we do hereby acknowledge), have remised, released and forever quit-claimed, and do for ourselves and our heirs, by these presents, remise, release and forever quit-claim unto the said L M, his heirs and assigns, all that [here describe the property].

To have and to hold the aforementioned premises, with all the privileges and appurtenances thereto belonging, to him, the said L M, his heirs and assigns, forever; so that neither they, the said Alfred B, and Caroline B his wife, nor their heirs, nor any other person or persons claiming from or under them or either of them or in the name, right or stead of them or either of them, shall or will, by any way or means, have, claim or demand any right or title to the aforesaid premises, or their appurtenances, or to any part or parcel thereof, forever.

In witness whereof, I, the said Alfred B, and I, the said Caroline B, wife of said Alfred B, in consideration of one dollar to me paid by the said L M, in token of a full relinquishment of all my right to dower in the premises, have hereunto set our hands and seals this day of , in the year of our Lord one thousand eight hundred and fifty .

Signed, sealed and delivered in presence of us: ——— ——— [Seal.]
——— ——— [Seal.]

MARYLAND.

Form of deed of bargain and sale.

This indenture, made this fifth day of May, in the year of our Lord one thousand eight hundred and twenty-six, between Benjamin Bargainor of Baltimore county, in the State of Maryland, of the one part, and Peter Purchaser of the said county and State, of the other part: Witnesseth, that for and in consideration of the sum of twenty dollars, current money, by the said Peter Purchaser to the said Benjamin Bargainor in hand paid, at and before the sealing and delivery of these presents, the receipt of which he doth hereby acknowledge, and himself to be therewith fully satisfied, contented and paid, the said Benjamin Bargainor hath bargained and sold, aliened and enfeoffed, and by these presents doth give, grant, bargain and sell, alien, enfeoff, release, convey and confirm unto the said Peter Purchaser, his heirs and assigns, all the tract or parcel of land called "Old Nick's Fancy," situate and lying in Baltimore county aforesaid, and contained within the following metes and bounds, courses and distances, to wit: Beginning, &c. [to the end of the description], together with all and singular the buildings, improvements, ways, waters, water courses, rights, members, privileges, advantages and appurtenances thereto belonging, or in any wise appertaining, and all the estate, right, title and interest, trust, property, claim and demand whatsoever, at law and in equity, of him, the said Benjamin Bargainor, of, in and to the same.

To have and to hold the said herein described premises, with the appurtenances thereunto belonging, unto the said Peter Purchaser, his heirs and assigns, to the only proper use of the said Peter Purchaser, his heirs and assigns, forever.

In testimony whereof, the said Benjamin Bargainor has hereunto set his hand and seal on the day and year first above written.

Signed, sealed and delivered in presence of A B. C D. BENJAMIN BARGAINOR. [Seal.]

In this deed may be introduced the following covenants:

Covenant for further assurance.

And the said Benjamin Bargainor, for himself and his heirs, doth hereby covenant, promise and agree, to and with the said Peter Purchaser, his heirs and assigns, that he, the said Benjamin Bargainor, his heirs, and all persons claiming under them, shall and will, from time to time, and at all times hereafter, at the reasonable request, cost and charge of the said Peter Purchaser, or any of his heirs or assigns, make and lawfully execute, acknowledge and deliver, all and every such further and other deed, conveyance and assurance in the law whatsoever, for the better and more fully conveying and assuring to the said Peter Purchaser, his heirs and assigns, the said premises, with the appurtenances heretofore described and mentioned to be bargained and sold, according to the true intent and meaning of the parties to these presents, as by the said Peter Purchaser, or his heirs or assigns, or by any of their counsel learned in the law, shall be reasonably devised, or advised and required.

Covenant of general warranty.

And also, that he, the said Benjamin Bargainor, his heirs and assigns, the tract and parcel of land and premises above described, and herein mentioned to be granted, bargained and sold, with the appurtenances, unto the said Peter Purchaser, his heirs and assigns, shall and will warrant and forever defend, by these premises, against the claims of all persons whomsoever.

Covenant of special warranty.

The last form is converted into a special warranty, by adding to it the words, "claiming in any manner by, from, under, or in trust for, the said Benjamin Bargainor, or his heirs."

Form of mortgage for securing debt, &c.

This indenture, made this day of , in the year of our Lord one thousand eight hundred and , between Moses Mortgagor of Baltimore county, in the State of Maryland, of the one part, and Matthew Mortgagee of Harford county, in the State aforesaid, of the other part: Whereas the said Moses Mortgagor, by his bond or obligation duly executed, bearing date on the day of , in the year of our Lord one thousand eight hundred and , stands bound unto the said Matthew Mortgagee, his executors, administrators and assigns, in the sum of dollars, current money, with a condition thereunder written, for the payment of the sum of dollars, current money, with the legal interest for the same, on or before the day of , as by the said bond and condition may more fully appear: Now, this indenture witnesseth, that the said Moses Mortgagor, in consideration of the said debt or sum of dollars, owing to the said Matthew Mortgagee, as aforesaid, and for the better securing the payment thereof, with interest, to the said Matthew Mortgagee, his executors, administrators or assigns, according to the condition of the said bond, and also in consideration of the further sum of five dollars, current money, to him the said Moses Mortgagor, by the said Matthew Mortgagee, in hand well and truly paid, at and before the sealing and delivery of these presents, the receipt whereof is hereby acknowledged by the said Moses Mortgagor, hath granted, bargained and sold, released and confirmed, and by these presents doth grant, bargain and sell, release and confirm, unto the said Matthew Mortgagee, his heirs and assigns, all that tract of land, lying and being in Baltimore county [here describe the premises]: To have and to hold the said tract of land, and every part and parcel thereof, with the appurtenances thereunto belonging, to the said Matthew Mortgagee, his heirs and assigns, forever, to his and their own use and behoof: provided, always, and it is the true intent and meaning of these presents, and of the said parties hereunto, that if the said Moses Mortgagor, his heirs, executors or administrators, do and shall well and truly pay, or cause to be paid, unto the said Matthew Mortgagee, his executors, administrators or assigns, the said full sum of dollars, current money, with legal interest for the same, on or before the day of , in the year , without any deduction or abatement whatsoever, then and from thenceforth, these presents, and every matter and thing therein contained, shall cease and be utterly null and void; any thing therein to the contrary thereof, in any wise, notwithstanding.

In witness whereof, the said Moses Mortgagor has hereunto set his hand and seal on the day and year first above written.

MOSES MORTGAGOR. [Seal.]

MASSACHUSETTS.

Form of deed of bargain and sale, with general warranty.

Know all men by these presents, that I, A B of , in the county of , and State of , in consideration of one dollar to me paid by G F of, &c., the receipt of which is hereby acknowledged, do give, grant, sell and convey unto the said G F, his heirs and assigns, a certain tract of land [description].

To have and to hold the aforegranted premises, to the said G F, his heirs and assigns, to his and their use and behoof forever.

And I do, for myself, my heirs, executors and administrators, covenant with the said G F, his heirs and assigns, that I am lawfully seized in fee of the aforegranted premises; that they are free of all incumbrances; that I have good right to sell and convey the same to the said G F, and that I will warrant and defend the same to the said G F, his heirs and assigns, forever, against the lawful claims and demands of all persons.

In witness whereof, I have hereunto set my hand and seal this day of , in the year, &c.

Signed, sealed and delivered in presence of } ——— ——— [Seal.]

The effect of the above deed is clearly expressed in the covenant. It gives to the grantee all the estate, and the grantor warrants against every lawful claimant. It is the highest title provided for by deed in this State.

The form of the quit-claim deed differs from the above as follows: In lieu of the language as above used, "grant, sell and convey," say "grant, sell and quit-claim;" and in lieu of the covenant in the above, use the following:

"And I covenant with the said G F, his heirs and assigns, to warrant and defend said premises against the lawful claims and demands of all persons claiming by or under me."

The following is the form of a quit-claim deed *in extenso.*

Form of quit-claim deed.

Know all men by these presents, that I, A B, of , in the county of , in the State of , in consideration of one dollar to me paid by G W of, &c., the receipt of which is hereby acknowledged, do grant, sell and quit-claim unto the said G W, his heirs and assigns, a certain tract of land, &c. [describing it].

To have and to hold the aforementioned premises to the said G W, his heirs and assigns, to his and their use and behoof, forever.

And I covenant with the said G W, his heirs and assigns, to warrant and defend said premises against the lawful claims and demands of all persons claiming by or under me.

In witness whereof, I have hereunto set my hand and seal this day of , in the year, &c.

——— ——— [Seal.]

The following is the form of these deeds, when a married woman unites in order to release her dower:

Form of deed, wife uniting to release dower.

Follow preceding forms, *not* inserting the name of the wife in the body of the instrument, or making any other modifications, until you arrive at the attesting clause, when you should proceed thus:

In witness whereof, I, the said Alfred B, together with Caroline B my wife, in token of her relinquishment of dower in the premises, have hereunto set our hands and seals this day of .

——— ——— [Seal.]
——— ——— [Seal.]

When property conveyed belongs to wife.

When the property conveyed belongs to the wife, the husband and wife join in the conveyance, and in such case the name of the wife is inserted in the body of the instrument. The foregoing forms may be readily adapted to such case.

Michigan.

Form of deed of bargain and sale, with general warranty.

This indenture, made the day of , in the year of our Lord one thousand eight hundred and fifty , between A B, and B B his wife, parties of the first part, and C D, party of the second part: Witnesseth, that the said parties of the first part, for the sum of dollars to them paid by the said party of the second part, do by these presents grant, bargain, sell, remise, release, alien and confirm unto the said party of the second part, and to his heirs and assigns, forever [here describe property conveyed], with all the hereditaments and appurtenances thereunto belonging. To have and to hold the said premises unto the said party of the second part, and to his heirs and assigns, forever. And the said parties of the first part, for themselves and their heirs, executors, administrators and assigns, do covenant with the said party of the second part, his heirs and assigns, that at the time of the delivery of these presents, they are seized of the above granted premises in fee simple; that they are free from all incumbrances, and that they will, and their heirs, executors, administrators and assigns, shall warrant and defend the same against all lawful claims whatever.

In witness whereof, the said parties of the first part have hereunto set their hands and seals the day and year first above written.

Signed, sealed and delivered in presence of JOHN JONES, PETER PARLEY.

A B. [Seal.]
B B. [Seal.]

Form of quit-claim deed.

This indenture, made the day of 18 , between A B, and B B his wife, parties of the first part, and C D, party of the second part: Witnesseth, that the said parties of the first part, for the sum of dollars to them paid by the said party of the second part, do, by these presents, grant, bargain, sell, remise, release, alien and quit-claim unto the said party of the second part, and to his heirs and assigns, forever [here describe property conveyed], with all the hereditaments and appurtenances thereunto belonging. To have and to hold said premises unto the said party of the second part, and to his heirs and assigns, forever.

In witness whereof, the said parties of the first part have hereunto set their hands and seals the day and year first above written.

Signed, sealed and delivered in presence of JOHN JONES, PETER PARLEY.

A B. [Seal.]
B B. [Seal.]

MINESOTA.

Form of deed of bargain and sale, with general warranty.

This indenture, made this day of , in the year , between J C of , and E (formerly E N), his wife, of the first part, and H M of , of the second part: Witnesseth, that the said J C, and E his wife, for and in consideration of the sum of dollars, good and lawful money of the United States, to them in hand paid by the said H M, at or before the sealing and delivery of these presents, the receipt whereof they do hereby acknowledge, and thereof acquit and forever discharge the said H M, his heirs, executors and administrators, by these presents have granted, bargained, sold, aliened, enfeoffed, released and confirmed, and by these presents do grant, bargain, sell, alien, enfeoff, release and confirm unto the said H M, and unto his heirs and assigns, forever, a certain lot, piece or parcel of land, situate, lying and being in [here describe the land], together with all the estate, right, title, interest and property, claim and demand whatever, of them, the said J C, and E his wife, in law or equity, or otherwise however, of, in, to or out of the same. To have and to hold the said lot, piece or parcel of land, and every part and parcel thereof, with their appurtenances, unto the said H M, his heirs and assigns, forever, and unto the only proper use and behoof of him, the said H M, his heirs and assigns, forever. And the said J C, for himself, his heirs, executors and administrators, and for and in behalf of the said E his wife, and her heirs, doth covenant, promise, grant and agree, to and with the said H M, his heirs and assigns, by these presents, in manner and form following, to wit: That he, the said J C, and his heirs, the said lot, piece or parcel of land and premises hereby granted, or intended so to be, with the appurtenances, unto the said H M, his heirs and assigns, against him, the said J C, and his heirs, and against the heirs of the said E his wife, and against all and every person or persons whatever, will warrant and forever defend by these presents.

In witness whereof, the parties hereto have hereunto set their hands and seals on the day and year first herein mentioned.

Signed, sealed and delivered in presence of us:—M N.
P O.

J C. [Seal.]
E C. [Seal.]

Form of quit-claim deed.

Follow form of quit-claim deed, under title "Michigan."

MISSISSIPPI.

Form of deed of bargain and sale, with general warranty, &c.

Follow form of deed under title "Minnesota."

The statute requires that the deed, in order to affect purchasers, &c., "should be acknowledged by the party or parties who shall have executed it, or be proved by one or more of the subscribing witnesses." Hutch. Code, p. 605. This seems to contemplate the execution of the deed in the presence of two witnesses at the least; and it is therefore safer in all cases so to execute it. It is said, however, that in Wilkens v. Wills, 9 S. & M. 325, it was decided that a deed attested by a single witness might rightfully be admitted to record, upon his proving the execution of the deed. See the Agricultural Bank of Mississippi et als. v. Rice et als., 4 How. 228. In this case, it was not objected in argument that the deed was only attested by one witness.

Form of quit-claim deed.

Follow the form of quit-claim under title "Michigan."

MISSOURI.

Form of deed of bargain and sale, &c.

Follow form under title "Illinois." In Missouri, the term "heirs," or other words of inheritance, are not necessary in order to create or convey an estate in fee simple.

"The words 'grant, bargain and sell,' in all conveyances in which an estate of inheritance in fee simple is limited," it is declared by statute, "shall, unless restrained by express terms contained in such conveyances, be construed to be the following express covenants on the part of the grantor, for himself and his heirs, to the grantee, his heirs and assigns. First, that the grantor was, at the time of the execution of such conveyance, seized of an indefeasible estate in fee simple, in the real estate thereby granted. Second, that such real estate was, at the time of the execution of such conveyance, free from incumbrance done or suffered by the grantor, or any person claiming under him. Third, for further assurances of such real estate to be made by the grantor and his heirs, to the grantee, and his heirs and assigns, and may be sued upon in the same manner as if such covenants were expressly inserted in the conveyance." Miss. Rev. Stat., ch. 32, § 14.

Form of quit-claim deed.

Follow form of quit-claim deed, under title "Illinois."

NEW HAMPSHIRE.

Form of deed of bargain and sale.

Follow form under title "Minesota."

Form of quit-claim deed.

Follow form under title "Michigan." The New Hampshire statute requires the attestation of witnesses, and that the deed be signed and sealed by the party executing.

NEW JERSEY.

Form of deed of bargain and sale, with general warranty.

This indenture, made the day of , in the year of our Lord one thousand eight hundred and , between John Doe, and Mary his wife, of the city of Newark, in the county of Essex, and State of New Jersey, of the first part, and Richard Roe of the same place, of the second part: Witnesseth, that the said party of the first part, for and in consideration of the sum of one thousand dollars, lawful money of the United States of America, to them in hand well and truly paid by the said party of the second part, at and before the sealing and delivery of these presents, the receipt whereof is hereby acknowledged, and the said party of the first part therewith fully satisfied, contented and paid, have given, granted, bargained, sold, aliened, released, enfeoffed, conveyed and confirmed, and by these presents do give, grant, bargain, sell, alien, release, enfeoff, convey and confirm, to the said party of the second part, and to his heirs and assigns, forever, all that lot, tract or parcel of land and premises, hereinafter particularly described, situate, lying and being in the city of Newark, in the county of Essex, and State of New Jersey, beginning, &c. &c. Together with all and singular the houses, buildings, trees, ways, waters, profits, privileges and advantages, with the appurtenances to the same belonging, or in any wise appertaining. Also, all the estate, right, title, interest, property, claim and demand whatsoever, of the said party of the first part, of, in, and to the same, and of, in and to every part and parcel thereof. To have and to hold, all and singular the above described tract or lot of land and premises, with the appurtenances, unto the said party of the second part, his heirs and assigns, to the only proper use, benefit and behoof of the said party of the second part, his heirs and assigns, forever.

And the said John Doe does, for himself, his heirs, executors and administrators, covenant and grant to and with the said party of the second part, his heirs and assigns, that he, the said John Doe, is the true, lawful and right owner of all and singular the above described land and premises, and of every part and parcel thereof, with the appurtenances thereunto belonging: and that the said land and premises, or any part thereof, at the time of sealing and delivery of these presents, are not incumbered by any mortgage, judgment or limitation, or by any incumbrance whatsoever, by which the title of the said party of the second part, hereby made, or intended to be made, for the above described land and premises, can or may be changed, charged, altered or defeated in any way whatsoever. And also, that the said party of the first part now hath good right, full power, and lawful authority to grant, bargain, sell and convey the said land and premises, in manner aforesaid. And also, that the said John Doe, and his heirs, will warrant, secure, and forever defend the said land and premises, unto the said Richard Roe, his heirs and assigns, forever, against the lawful claims and demands of all and every person and persons, freely and clearly freed and discharged of and from all manner of incumbrances whatsoever.

In witness whereof, the said John Doe, and Mary his wife, have hereto set their hands and seals the day and year first above written.

Signed, sealed and delivered in presence of } ——— ——— [Seal.]
——— ——— [Seal.]

Form of deed of bargain and sale, without warranty.

This indenture, made the day of , in the year 18 , between A B of the city of , of the first part, and L M of the same place, of the second part: Witnesseth, that the said A B, for and in consideration of one thousand dollars, lawful money of the United States, to him in hand paid by the said L M, the receipt whereof is hereby acknowledged, hath granted, bargained and sold, and by these presents doth grant, bargain, sell, convey and confirm, unto the said L M, his heirs, executors, administrators and assigns, forever, all and singular that certain piece or parcel of land, situated in the city of [here describe the land], together with all and singular the tenements, hereditaments and appurtenances thereunto belonging, and the reversions, remainders, rents, issues and profits thereof, and all the estate, title and interest of the said A B, to the said premises, or any part thereof. To have and to hold the above granted premises, to him, the said L M, his heirs and assigns, to his and their only benefit, use and behoof, forever.

In witness whereof, the said A B has hereto set his hand and seal the day and year first above written.

Signed, sealed and delivered in presence of } A. B. [Seal.]

New York.

Form of deed of bargain and sale.

This indenture, made the day of , in the year of our Lord one thousand eight hundred and , between A B, of, &c., of the first part, and C D, of, &c., of the second part: Witnesseth, that the said party of the first part, for and in consideration of the sum of dollars, to him in hand paid by the said party of the second part, the receipt whereof is hereby acknowledged, hath bargained and sold, and by these presents doth bargain and sell, unto the said party of the second part, and to his heirs and assigns, forever, all, &c. [here describe the premises], together with all and singular the hereditaments and appurtenances thereunto belonging, or in any wise appertaining, and the reversion and reversions, remainder and remainders, rents, issues and profits thereof; and also, all the estate, right, title, interest, claim or demand whatsoever, of him, the said party of the first part, either in law or equity, of, in and to, the above bargained premises, and every part and parcel thereof.(*)

In witness whereof, the said party of the first part has hereunto set his hand and seal the day and year first above written.

Sealed and delivered in presence of G H. A B. [Seal.]

Form of deed of bargain and sale, with general warranty.

This indenture, made the day of , in the year one thousand eight hundred and , between A B, of, &c., of the first part, and C D, of, &c., of the second part: Witnesseth, that the said party of the first part, for and in consideration of the sum of dollars, lawful money of the United States, to him in hand paid by the said party of the second part, at or before the ensealing and delivery of these presents, the receipt whereof is hereby acknowledged, hath granted, bargained, sold, aliened, remised, released, conveyed and confirmed, and by these presents doth grant, bargain, sell, alien, remise, release, convey and confirm, unto the said party of the second part, and to his heirs and assigns, forever, all [description]; together with all and singular the tenements, hereditaments and appurtenances thereunto belonging, or in any wise appertaining, and the reversion and reversions, remainder and remainders, rents, issues and profits thereof: And also, all the estate, right, title, interest [insert here, dower and right of dower, if necessary], property, possession, claim and demand, whatsoever, as well at law as in equity, of the said party of the first part, of, in or to, the above described premises, and every part and parcel thereof, with the appurtenances. To have and to hold, all and singular the above mentioned and described premises, together with the appurtenances, unto the said party of the second part, his heirs and assigns, forever. And the said A B, for himself, and his heirs, the said premises in the quiet and peaceable possession of the said party of the second part, his heirs and assigns, against the said party of the first part, and his heirs, and against all and every person whomsoever, lawfully claiming, or to claim the same, shall and will warrant and by these presents forever defend.

In witness whereof, the said party of the first part has hereunto set his hand and seal the day and year first above written.

Sealed and delivered in presence of G H. A B. [Seal.]

Form of deed of bargain and sale, with covenants of title, &c.

This indenture, &c. [follow the form of deed of bargain and sale, to the (*), on page 156, and then add]: To have and to hold the above granted, bargained and described premises, with the appurtenances, unto the said party of the second part, his heirs and assigns, to his and their own proper use, benefit and behoof, forever. And the said A B, for himself and his heirs, executors and administrators, doth covenant, grant and agree, to and with the said party of the second part, his heirs and assigns, that the said party of the first part, at the time of the sealing and delivery of these presents, is lawfully seized in his own right [or, as the case may be], of a good, absolute and indefeasible estate of inheritance, in fee simple, of and in all and singular the above granted and described premises, with the appurtenances, and hath good right, full power, and lawful authority, to grant, bargain, sell and convey the same, in manner aforesaid; and that the said party of the second part, his heirs and assigns, shall and may, at all times hereafter, peaceably and quietly have, hold, use, occupy, possess and enjoy, the above granted premises, and every part and parcel thereof, with the appurtenances, without any let, suit, trouble, molestation, eviction or disturbance, of the said party of the first part, his heirs or assigns, or of any other person or persons, lawfully claiming, or to claim the same; and that the same now are free, clear, discharged and unincumbered, of and from all former and other grants, titles, charges, estates, judgments, taxes, assignments and incumbrances, of what nature or kind soever. And also, that the said party of the first part, and his heirs, and all and every person or persons whomsoever, lawfully or equitably deriving any estate, right, title or interest, of, in or to, the herein granted premises, by, from, under, or in trust for him or them, shall and will, at all time or times hereafter, upon the reasonable request, and at the proper costs and charges in the law of the said party of the second part, his heirs and assigns, make, do and execute, or cause to be made, done and executed, all and every such further and other lawful and reasonable acts, conveyances and assurances in the law, for the better and more effectually vesting and confirming the premises hereby granted, or so intended to be, in and to the said party of the second part, his heirs and assigns, forever, as by the said party of the second part, his heirs or assigns, or his or their counsel, learned in the law, shall be reasonably advised, devised or required. And the said A B, for himself and his heirs, the above described and hereby granted and released premises, and every part and parcel thereof, with the appurtenances, unto the said party of the second part, his heirs and assigns, against the said party of the first part, and his heirs, and against all and every person and persons whomsoever, lawfully claiming, or to claim the same, shall and will warrant, and by these presents forever defend.

In witness whereof, the said party of the first part has hereunto set his hand and seal the day and year first above written.

Sealed and delivered in presence of G H. — A B. [Seal.]

Form of quit-claim deed.

Know all men by these presents, that we, A B, of, &c., and E his wife, in consideration of the sum of dollars, to us in hand paid by C D, of, &c., the receipt whereof we do hereby acknowledge, have bargained, sold and quit-claimed, and by these presents do bargain, sell and quit-claim, unto the said C D, and to his heirs and assigns, forever, all our and each of our right, title, interest, estate, claim and demand, both at law and in equity, and as well in possession as in expectancy, of, in and to, all that certain piece or parcel of land, situate, &c. [description], with all and singular the hereditaments and appurtenances thereunto belonging.

In witness whereof, we have hereunto set our hands and seals the day and year first above written.

Sealed and delivered in presence of G H. — A B. [Seal.]
E B. [Seal.]

Form of mortgage by husband and wife.

This indenture, made, &c. between A B, and M his wife, of, &c. of the first part, and C D of, &c. of the second part: Witnesseth, that the party of the first part, for and in consideration of the sum of dollars to them in hand paid, the receipt whereof is hereby acknowledged, have bargained, sold, aliened, released, conveyed and confirmed, and by these presents do bargain, sell, alien, release, convey and confirm unto the said party of the second part, his heirs and assigns, forever, all [description], together with the tenements, hereditaments, and appurtenances thereunto belonging, or in any wise appertaining; and also all the estate, right, title, interest, dower and right of dower, property, possession, claim and demand whatsoever of the said party of the first part, of, in and to the same, and the reversion and reversions, remainder and remainders, rents, issues and profits thereof. To have and to hold the herein-before granted, bargained and described premises, with the appurtenances, unto the said party of the second part, his heirs and assigns, to his and their own proper use, benefit and behoof, forever. This conveyance is intended as a mortgage to secure the payment of the sum of dollars in five years from the day of the date hereof, with semi-annual interest, payable on the second day of January and the first day of July; in each and every year, according to the condition of a certain bond, bearing even date herewith, executed by the said A B to the said party of the second part; and these presents shall be void if such payment be made. But in case default shall be made in the payment of the principal, or interest, as above provided, then the party of the second part, his executors, administrators and assigns, are hereby empowered to sell the premises above described, with all and every of the appurtenances, or any part thereof, in the manner prescribed by law, and out of the money arising from such sale, to retain the said principal and interest, together with the costs and charges of making such sale; and the overplus, if any there be, shall be paid by the party making such sale, on demand, to the parties of the first part, their heirs or assigns. And the said A B, for himself, his heirs, executors and administrators, doth covenant and agree to pay unto the said party of the second part, his executors, administrators or assigns, the said sum of money and interest, as above mentioned, and as expressed in the condition of the said bond.

In witness whereof, the said parties of the first part have hereunto set their hands and seals the day and year first above written.

Signed, sealed and delivered in presence of G. H.

A B. [Seal.]
M B. [Seal.]

NORTH CAROLINA.

Form of deed of bargain and sale.

The form under title "Alabama, p. 121, ante, may be followed. To convey the wife's land, she must unite in the deed with her husband, and acknowledge it. Widows are entitled to dower in such lands only as their husbands die seized and possessed of. 1 R. S. 612, ch. 121. It would seem, therefore, unnecessary for the wife to unite in the deed merely to relinquish her right of dower.

Form of deed of trust.

Follow form of trust deed under title "Alabama," p. 122.

OHIO.

Form of deed of bargain and sale, with warranty.

Know all men, that G W of the city of , State of Ohio, for and in consideration of one thousand dollars to him paid by B F of the same place, the receipt whereof is hereby acknowledged, doth hereby grant, bargain, sell and convey to the said B F, his heirs and assigns, forever, the following real estate [here describe land], together with all the privileges and appurtenances to the same belonging. To have and to hold the same to the said B F, his heirs and assigns, forever—the grantor hereby covenanting with the grantee, his heirs and assigns, that the title so conveyed is clear, free and unincumbered; and that he will warrant and forever defend the same against all claims whatsoever.

In witness whereof, the said G W hath hereunto set his hand and seal this day of , in the year 18 .

Signed, sealed and delivered in presence of J D. R R.

G W. [Seal.]

Form of same, with covenants of title, &c.

Know all men by these presents, that A B, and Sarah B his wife, of the city of , State of , parties of the first part, for and in consideration of the sum of three thousand dollars, lawful money of the United States, to them in hand paid by A R of the city of , in said State, party of the second part, at or before the ensealing and delivery of these presents, the receipt whereof is hereby acknowledged, and the said party of the second part, his heirs, executors and administrators, forever, released and discharged from the same, by these presents have granted, bargained, sold, aliened, remised, released, conveyed and confirmed, and by these presents do grant, bargain, sell, alien, remise, release, convey and confirm unto the said party of the second part, and to his heirs and assigns, forever, all that [here describe land], together with all and singular the tenements, hereditaments, and appurtenances thereunto belonging, or in any wise appertaining, and the reversion and reversions, remainder and remainders, rents, issues and profits thereof; and also all the estate, right, title, interest, dower and right of dower, property, possession, claim and demand whatsoever, as well in law as in equity, of the said parties of the first part, of, in and to the same, and every part and parcel thereof, with the appurtenances. To have and to hold the above granted, bargained and described premises, with the appurtenances, unto the said party of the second part, his heirs and assigns, to his and their own proper use, benefit and behoof, forever.

And the said A B, for himself, his heirs, executors and administrators, doth covenant, grant and agree to and with the said party of the second part, his heirs and assigns, that the said A B, at the time of the sealing and delivery of these presents, was lawfully seized, in his own right, of a good, absolute and indefeasible estate of inheritance, in fee simple, of and in all and singular the above granted and described premises, with the appurtenances; and has good right, full power and lawful authority to grant, bargain, sell and convey the same in manner aforesaid; and that the said party of the second part, his heirs and assigns, shall and may, at all times hereafter, peaceably and quietly have, hold, use, occupy, possess and enjoy the above granted premises, and every part and parcel thereof, with the appurtenances, without any let, suit, trouble, molestation, eviction or disturbance of the said parties of the first part, their heirs or assigns, or of any other person or persons lawfully claiming or to claim the same; and that the same now are free, clear, discharged and unencumbered of and from all former and other grants, titles, charges, estates, judgments, taxes, assessments and incumbrances of what nature or kind soever; and also that the said parties of the first part, and their heirs, and all and every person or persons whomsoever, lawfully or equitably deriving any estate, right, title or interest of, in or to the hereinbefore granted premises, by, from, under, or in trust for them, or either of them, shall and will, at any time or times hereafter, upon the reasonable request, and at the proper costs and charges in the law, of the said party of the second part, his heirs and assigns, make, do and execute, or cause to be made, done and executed, all and every such further and other lawful and reasonable acts, conveyances and assurances in the law, for the better and more effectually vesting and confirming the premises hereby granted, or so intended to be, in and to the said party of the second part, his heirs and assigns, forever, as by the said party of the second part, his heirs or assigns, his or their counsel learned in the law, shall be reasonably advised or required. And the said A B, his heirs, the above described and hereby granted and released premises, and every part and parcel thereof, with the appurtenances, unto the said party of the second part, his heirs and assigns, against the said parties of the first part, and their heirs, and against all and every person and persons whomsoever, lawfully claiming or to claim the same, shall and will warrant, and by these presents forever defend.

In witness whereof, the said parties of the first part have hereunto set their hands and seals this day of , 18 .

Signed, sealed and delivered in presence of J B. B. B.	A B. [Seal.] SARAH B. [Seal.]

Form of quit-claim deed.

Know all men, that W S, and Ann S his wife, of county, State of , in consideration of twelve hundred and fifty dollars to them paid by C B of county, State of , the receipt whereof is hereby acknowledged, do hereby remise, release and forever quit-claim unto the said C B, his heirs and assigns, forever, the following real estate [here describe land], together with all the privileges and appurtenances thereto belonging. To have and to hold the same to the said C B, his heirs and assigns, forever.

In witness whereof, the said W S, together with Ann S his wife, who hereby forever releases and relinquishes all title and claim of dower in and to the premises aforesaid, have hereunto set their hands and seals this day of , in the year 18 .

Signed, sealed and delivered in presence of M F. D W.

W S. [Seal.]
ANN S. [Seal.]

Form of deed of trust creating special estate for wife.

This indenture, made this day of , eighteen hundred and , between C S of county, State of , of the first part, and G G of the city of , in said county, of the second part: Whereas the said C S is desirous to make provision for his daughter, Caroline S, now of the age of twenty-one years, against future contingencies, and for her maintenance and support: and whereas the said C S is desirous that his said daughter should enjoy the proceeds, rents, issues and income of the real estate hereinafter more particularly described, during the term of her natural life, free from the control, liabilities or interference of any husband that she may hereafter have: Now, therefore, this indenture witnesseth, that the said C S, in consideration of the premises, and of the sum of one dollar, lawful money of the United States, to him in hand paid by the said party of the second part, the receipt whereof is hereby acknowledged, hath bargained, sold, aliened, remised, released, conveyed and confirmed, and by these presents doth bargain, sell, alien, remise, release, convey and confirm unto the said party of the second part, all that certain lot [here describe land], together with all and singular the tenements, hereditaments, and appurtenances thereunto belonging or in any wise appertaining; and the reversion and reversions, remainder and remainders, rents, issues and profits thereof; and also all the estate, right, title, interest, property, possession, claim and demand whatsoever, as well at law as in equity, of the said party of the first part, of, in or to the above described premises, and every part and parcel thereof, with the appurtenances. To have and to hold all and singular the above mentioned and described premises, together with the appurtenances, unto the said G G, his successors and assigns:

In trust, and to and for the several uses, intents and purposes hereinafter mentioned, namely:

First. In trust, to lease the same, and to take, collect and receive the rents, issues and profits thereof; and out of the same to keep the said premises in good order and repair, and properly insured, and pay all taxes, assessments and charges that may be imposed thereon.

Secondly. In trust, to pay the residue of such rents, issues and income to my daughter, Caroline S, upon her sole and separate receipt, to the intent and purpose that she may enjoy, possess and have the same, free from the control, interference or liabilities of any husband she may hereafter have, during the term of her natural life.

Thirdly. In trust, to convey the said land and premises to such person or persons as she, the said Caroline S, by her last will and testament, or by an instrument in the nature of a last will and testament, subscribed by her in the presence of two credible witnesses, notwithstanding her coverture, may direct and appoint.

And the said C S hereby declares, that upon the decease of his said daughter, Caroline S, the said trusts shall cease and determine, and the land and premises above described shall belong, in fee simple absolute, to such person or persons as the said Caroline S shall as aforesaid direct and appoint, and in default of such appointment, shall revert to the said C S, the grantor herein named, and to his heirs, to his and their sole use, benefit and behoof, forever.

And the said party of the second part doth hereby signify his acceptance of this trust, and doth hereby covenant and agree to and with the said party of the first part, faithfully to discharge and execute the same according to the true intent and meaning of these presents.

In witness whereof, the said parties have hereunto set their hands and seals the day and year first above written.

Signed, sealed and delivered in presence of J D. J A.

C S. [Seal.]
G G. [Seal.]

Form of a mortgage.

Know all men by these presents, that J P of , county of , for and in consideration of the sum of five dollars, to him in hand paid by M L, of , county of , the receipt whereof is hereby acknowledged, doth hereby bargain, sell and convey to the said M L, his heirs and assigns, forever, the following real estate [here describe it], together with all the privileges and appurtenances to the same belonging.

To have and to hold the same to the said M L, his heirs and assigns, forever.

Provided always, that if the said J P shall cause to be paid unto the said M L, his five certain promissory notes, of even date herewith, for one thousand dollars each, with interest, payable to the said M L, or order, in one, two, three, four and five years, respectively, from the date, then these presents shall be void.

In witness whereof, the said J P hath hereunto set his hand and seal this day of , in the year 18 .

Signed, sealed and acknowledged in presence of HENRY TAPPAN, JOSEPH DENNING. — J P. [Seal.]

Note.—When the notes (to secure which mortgage is given) have been paid, an entry of satisfaction should be made. The following form may be used:

I, M L, of , do hereby certify, that a certain deed of mortgage, dated the day of , in the year 18 , executed by J P of , to secure the payment of five promissory notes, for one thousand dollars each, with interest, to me, and recorded in vol. , page , in the recorder's office in county, is paid.

Given under my hand and seal this day of , in the year 18 .

Attest:—S T. N V. — M L. [Seal.]

PENNSYLVANIA.

Form of deed of bargain and sale.

This indenture, made the day of June, in the year of our Lord one thousand eight hundred and , between A M, of the city of Philadelphia, in the State of Pennsylvania, merchant, and M his wife, of the one part, and C H, of the township of Swatara, in the county of Dauphin, in the State aforesaid, yeoman, of the other part: Witnesseth, that the said A M, and M his wife, for and in consideration of the sum of seven hundred dollars, to them in hand paid by the said C H, at and before the sealing and delivery hereof, the receipt whereof they do hereby acknowledge, and thereof acquit and forever discharge the said C H, his heirs, executors and administrators, and by these presents have granted, bargained, sold, aliened, enfeoffed, released and confirmed, and by these presents do grant, bargain, sell, alien, enfeoff, release and confirm, unto the said C H, and to his heirs and assigns, all that certain messuage, &c.

Together with all and singular other the houses, out-houses, buildings, barns, stables, ways, woods, waters, water-courses, rights, liberties, privileges, hereditaments and appurtenances whatsoever, thereunto belonging, or in any wise appertaining, and the reversions and remainders, rents, issues and profits thereof: And also, all the estate, right, title, interest, property, claim and demand whatsoever, of them, the said A M, and M his wife, in law or equity, or otherwise, howsoever, of, in, to, or out of the same.

To have and to hold the said messuage or tenement, and tract of one hundred acres of land, hereditaments and premises hereby granted or mentioned, or intended so to be, with the appurtenances, unto the said C H, his heirs and assigns, to the only proper use and behoof of the said C H, his heirs and assigns, forever.

In witness whereof, the said parties to these presents have hereunto interchangeably set their hands and seals, dated the day and year first above written. A M. [Seal.]

M. [Seal.]

Note.—It is usual in this State to recite with particularity, after describing the premises, the title by which the grantor holds it. Thus, in the case of an estate of intestate, conveyed by the heirs, who subsequently convey to the grantor, the title being originally derived from a patent, the following form is used:

"It being the same tract of land which the Commonwealth of Pennsylvania, by patent, bearing date the day of , A. D. (enrolled in the rolls office for the State of Pennsylvania, in Patent Book, No. 12, p. 53, &c.), for the consideration therein mentioned, did grant and confirm unto K E, in fee, who being thereof lawfully seized, died intestate, leaving issue E E, and N, intermarried with N S, to whom the same, by the laws of Pennsylvania, did descend and come. And the said E E, and N S, and N his wife, by their joint indenture, bearing date the day of , A. D. , for the consideration therein mentioned, did grant and confirm the same unto the said A M (party hereto), in fee, as in and by the said indenture (recorded, or intended to be recorded, &c.), relation being thereunto had, appears."

☞ Endorse on the conveyance a receipt for the consideration money, thus:

"Received, the day and year within, from the within named C H, the sum of dollars, being the full consideration money within mentioned. A M."

Form of deed of feoffment, with special covenants.

This indenture, made the day of , between A B of , of the one part, and C D of , of the other part: Witnesseth, that the said A B, for and in consideration of the sum of dollars, the receipt whereof is hereby acknowledged, hath granted, bargained, sold, aliened, enfeoffed, released and confirmed, and by these presents doth grant, bargain, sell, alien, enfeoff, release and confirm, unto the said C D, his heirs and assigns, forever, all that messuage or tenement, &c., and the reversion and reversions, remainder and remainders, rents, issues and profits thereof, and also, all the estate, right, title, interest, claim and demand whatsoever, of him, the said A B, of, in and to the said premises, and of, in and to every part and parcel thereof: To have and to hold the said messuage, tenement and premises above mentioned, with the appurtenances, unto the said C D, his heirs and assigns, forever. And the said A B, for himself, his heirs and assigns, doth covenant and grant to and with the said C D, his heirs and assigns, that he, the said A B, now is lawfully and rightfully seized, &c. And also, that he, the said A B, hath good right, full power, and lawful authority, in his own right, to grant, bargain, sell and convey, all and singular the said messuages and premises, with the appurtenances, unto the said C D, his heirs and assigns. And that he, the said C D, his heirs and assigns, shall and may, at all times forever hereafter, peaceably and quietly have, hold, occupy, possess and enjoy, all and singular the said message, lands, tenements, hereditaments and premises above mentioned, with the appurtenances, without the let, trouble, hindrance, molestation, interruption or denial of him, the said A B, his heirs or assigns, or of any other person or persons whatsoever, claiming or to claim, by, from, or under him, them, or any of them (except as hereinafter is excepted), and that freed and discharged, or otherwise well and sufficiently saved and kept harmless and indemnified, of and from all former and other bargains, sales, gifts, grants, leases, mortgages, jointures, dowers, uses, wills, entails, fines, post-fines, issues, amercements, seizures, bonds, annuities, statutes, recognizances, extents, judgments, executions, rents and arrears of rent, and of and from all former and other charges, estates, rights, titles, troubles and incumbrances, whatsoever, had, made, committed, done or suffered, or to be had, made, committed, done or suffered, by the said A B, or any person or persons whatsoever, claiming, or to claim, by, from, or under him, them, or any of them (except one indenture of lease granted by the said A B to E F of , of part of the said premises, for the term of years, under the yearly rent of dollars, which rent is intended to pass hereby). And further, that the said A B, and his heirs, and all and every other person and persons, having or claiming in the said premises above mentioned, or any part thereof, by, from, or under him (except as before excepted), shall and will, from time to time, and at all times hereafter, upon the reasonable request, and at the costs and charges of the said C D, his heirs and assigns, make, do and execute, or cause and procure to be made, done and executed, all and every such further and other lawful and reasonable act and acts, thing and things, devises, deeds, conveyances and assurances in the law whatsoever, for the further, better and more perfectly granting, conveying and assuring, of all and singular the said premises above mentioned, with the appurtenances, unto the said C D, his heirs and assigns, to the only proper use and benefit of the said C D, his heirs and assigns, forever, according to the true intent and meaning of these presents, as by the said C D, his heirs and assigns, or his or their counsel, shall be reasonably devised, advised and required. And lastly, the said A B hath made, ordained, constituted and appointed, and by these presents doth make, ordain, constitute and appoint E F of , and G H of , his true and lawful attorneys, jointly, and either of them severally, for him and in his name, into the said message, lands and premises, with the appurtenances, hereby granted and conveyed, or mentioned so to be, or into some part thereof, in the name of the whole, to enter, and full, quiet and peaceable possession and seisin thereof, for him, and in his name, to take and have, and such possession and seisin so thereof taken and had, the like full possession and seisin thereof, or of some part thereof, in the name of the whole, unto the said C D, or to his certain attorney, to give and deliver, to hold to him, the said C D, his heirs and assigns, forever, according to the true intent and meaning of these presents, hereby ratifying, confirming and allowing, and agreeing to ratify, confirm and allow, all and whatsoever his said attorneys, or either of them, shall do in the premises.

In witness whereof, the said parties to these presents have hereunto interchangeably set their hands and seals, dated the day and year first above written.

A B. [Seal.]
C D. [Seal.]

Form of a quit-claim deed.

Know all men by these presents, that I, A B, of , Esq., in consideration of the sum of , to me in hand paid by C D, of , the receipt whereof I do hereby acknowledge, have remised, released, and forever quit-claim, and by these presents do remise, release, and forever quit-claim unto the said C D, his heirs and assigns, a certain messuage, now in the seisin and possession of the said C D, situate, &c.

To have and to hold the aforesaid premises, with all the privileges and appurtenances to the said messuage, &c. belonging or appertaining, unto the said C D, his heirs and assigns, to his and their sole use forever, so that neither I, the said A B, nor my heirs, nor any person or persons claiming under me or them, shall, at any time hereafter, by any way or means, have, claim or demand any right or title to the aforesaid premises or appurtenances, or to any part or parcel thereof, forever.

In witness whereof, the said A B has hereunto set his hand and seal on this day of , in the year .

A B. [Seal.]

Form of mortgage to secure payment of money due on a bond.

This indenture, made the day of , A. D. , between A S of , in the county of , yeoman, of the one part, and J B of the city of , merchant, of the other part: Whereas the said A S, in and by a certain obligation or writing obligatory, under his hand and seal, bearing even date herewith, stands bound unto the said J B, in the sum of one thousand dollars, conditioned for the payment of five hundred dollars, on the day of next ensuing the date hereof, with lawful interest for the same, as in and by the said recited obligation and condition thereof, relation being thereunto had, more fully and at large appears: Now, this indenture witnesseth, that the said A S, as well for and in consideration of the aforesaid debt or sum of five hundred dollars, and for the better securing the payment thereof, with its interest, unto the said J B, his executors, administrators and assigns, in discharge of the said recited obligation, as of the further sum of one dollar, to him in hand paid by the said J B, at and before the sealing and delivery hereof, the receipt whereof is hereby acknowledged, hath granted, bargained, sold, released and confirmed, and by these presents doth grant, bargain, sell, release and confirm, unto the said J B, his heirs and assigns, all that messuage, &c., together with all and singular the buildings, improvements, ways, woods, waters, water-courses, rights, liberties, privileges, hereditaments and appurtenances whatsoever, thereunto belonging, or in any wise appertaining, and the reversions and remainders, rents, issues and profits thereof. To have and to hold the said messuage, &c., hereditaments, and premises hereby granted, or mentioned or intended so to be, with the appurtenances, unto the said J B, his heirs and assigns, to the only proper use and behoof of the said J B, his heirs and assigns, forever: Provided always, nevertheless, that if the said A S, his heirs, executors or administrators, shall and do well and truly pay, or cause to be paid, unto the said J B, his executors, administrators or assigns, the aforesaid debt or sum of five hundred dollars, on the day and time hereinbefore mentioned and appointed for payment thereof, with lawful interest for the same, according to the condition of the said recited obligation, without any fraud or further delay, and without any deduction, defalcation or abatement to be made of any thing, for or in respect of any taxes, charges or assessments whatsoever, then and from thenceforth, as well this present indenture, and the estate hereby granted, as the said recited obligation, shall cease, determine, and become absolutely null and void, to all intents and purposes, any thing hereinbefore contained to the contrary, in any wise, notwithstanding.

In witness whereof, the said parties to these presents have hereunto interchangeably set their hands and seals, dated the day and year first above written. A S. [Seal.]
J B. [Seal.]

Form of mortgage to secure endorsees in bank.

This indenture, made, &c. [here insert the parties]: Whereas the said C D and E F have endorsed for the said A B a certain promissory note for the sum of five hundred dollars, dated the day of last past, and payable months after date, which is now discounted at the bank of , in the city of , and which said note it is contemplated to renew from time to time; and the said A B being desirous to secure and save the said C D and E F against all responsibility as endorsers of the note aforesaid; therefore this indenture witnesseth, that the said A B, as well for and in consideration of securing the said endorsers from the payment of the note aforesaid, as the sum of one dollar to him in hand paid by the said C D and E F, at and before the sealing and delivery hereof, the receipt whereof is hereby acknowledged, hath granted, bargained, sold, released and confirmed, and by these presents doth grant, bargain, release and confirm unto the said C D and E F, their heirs and assigns, all that messuage, &c. [here describe the premises and recite the title], together with all and singular the buildings, improvements, ways, woods, waters, water courses, rights, liberties, privileges, hereditaments and appurtenances whatsoever thereunto belonging, or in any wise appertaining, and the reversions and remainders, rents, issues and profits thereof. To have and to hold the said messuage, &c., hereditaments and premises hereby granted or mentioned, or intended so to be, with the appurtenances, unto the said C D, his heirs and assigns, to the only proper use and behoof of the said C D, his heirs and assigns, forever: Provided always, nevertheless, that if the said A B, his heirs, executors or administrators, shall and do well and truly pay or cause to be paid unto the said bank the aforesaid promissory note for dollars, on the day and time hereinbefore mentioned and appointed for payment thereof, or by other lawful means, save, keep harmless and indemnified the said C D and E F, their heirs, executors and administrators, from the payment of the said note, and all costs, damages or charges as sureties aforesaid, then and from thenceforth, as well this present indenture and the estate hereby granted, as the said recited obligation shall cease, determine, and become absolutely null and void; any thing herein contained to the contrary notwithstanding.

In witness whereof, the said parties to these presents have hereunto interchangeably set their hands and seals, dated the day and year first above written.

——— ——— [Seal.]
——— ——— [Seal.]

Rhode Island.

Form of deed of bargain and sale.

Follow form under title " Alabama, p. 121, ante. There should be two attesting witnesses.

Form of mortgage deed.

Follow form under title "Pennsylvania."

Note.—The twelfth section of the act regulating conveyances of real estate provides as follows:

Any mortgagee of lands, tenements or other real estate, his heirs, executors, administrators or assigns, having received full satisfaction for the money due on such mortgage, shall, at the request of the mortgagor, his heirs, executors, administrators or assigns, and at his or their cost, acknowledge and cause satisfaction and payment to be entered on the margin or face of the record of such mortgage, and shall sign and seal the same; which shall forever afterwards discharge, defeat and release such mortgage, and perpetually bar all actions to be brought thereupon in any court. If any mortgagee, his heirs, executors, administrators or assigns, shall not, within ten days after a request made in that behalf, and a tender of all reasonable charges, repair to the clerk's office, and there make, sign and seal an acknowledgment as before directed, or otherwise make and execute a release and quit-claim of the estate so mortgaged, and acknowledge the same before some proper officer, he or they so refusing shall be liable to make good all damages that shall accrue for want of such discharge or release, to be recovered by an action of the case, in a court of record; and in case judgment shall pass against the party sued, he shall pay unto the plaintiff treble costs upon such suit: Provided, nevertheless, that nothing herein contained shall be construed to defeat, invalidate, annul or render ineffectual any other legal discharge, payment, satisfaction or release of any mortgage.

South Carolina.

Form of deed of conveyance.

The State of South Carolina:

Know all men by these presents, that I, A B, of , in the State aforesaid, in consideration of to me paid by C D of , in the State aforesaid, have granted, bargained, sold and released, and by these presents do grant, bargain, sell and release unto the said C D all that [here describe the premises], together with all and singular the rights, members, hereditaments and appurtenances to the said premises belonging, or in any wise incident or appertaining: to have and to hold all and singular the premises before mentioned, unto the said C D, his heirs and assigns, forever. And I do hereby bind myself, my heirs, executors and administrators, to warrant and forever defend all and singular the said premises unto the said C D, his heirs and assigns, against myself and my heirs, and against every person whomsoever, lawfully claiming or to claim the same, or any part thereof.

Witness my hand and seal this day of , in the year of our Lord , and in the year of the independence of the United States of America.

—— —— [Seal.]

Note.—This form the statute declares shall, to all intents and purposes, be valid and effectual to convey from one person to another, or others, the fee simple of any land or real estate, if the same shall be executed in the presence of, and be subscribed by two or more credible witnesses.

There is also a proviso that the act prescribing this form shall be so construed as not to oblige any person to insert the clause of warranty, or to restrain him from inserting any other clause or clauses in conveyances hereafter to be made, as may be deemed proper and advisable by the purchaser and seller, or to invalidate the forms heretofore in use within the State. So. Car. Stat. at Large, vol. v, pp. 255, 256.

TENNESSEE.

Mr. Thornton, who is a member of the bar in the city of Memphis, in this State, states in the last edition of his work on Conveyancing, that the courts of Tennessee have decided that if the conveyance be by deed, it does not matter in what manner or form it is drawn. See Jackson v. Dillon's lessee, 2 Tenn. 264-5; Thomas v. Blackmore, 5 Yerg. 124-26; Taul v. Campbell, 7 Ib. 338-9.

Form of deed of bargain and sale.

Follow form under title "Alabama," p. 121, ante. The wife, in Tennessee, is only entitled to dower in land of which the husband dies seized. It is not necessary that she should unite in deed to convey a mere dower right. In the use of a conveyance of her own property, she must unite in deed with her husband.

Form of a deed of trust.

Follow form under title "Alabama," p. 122, ante.

TEXAS.

Form of conveyance of fee simple estate.

The State of Texas:

Know all men by these presents, that I, A B, of , in the State aforesaid, in consideration of , to me paid by C D of , in the State aforesaid, have granted, bargained, sold and released, and by these presents do grant, bargain, sell and release, unto the said C D, all that [here describe the premises], together with all and singular the rights, members, hereditaments and appurtenances to the said premises belonging, or in any wise incident or appertaining: to have and to hold, all and singular the premises before mentioned, unto the said C D, his heirs and assigns, forever. And I do hereby bind myself, my heirs, executors and administrators, to warrant and forever defend, all and singular the said premises, unto the said C D, his heirs and assigns, against myself, and my heirs, and against every person whomsoever, lawfully claiming or to claim the same, or any part thereof.

Witness my hand and seal this day of , in the year of our Lord , and in the year of the independence of the United States of America. ——— ——— [Seal.]

Note.—This form, or the same in substance, the statute declares, shall, to all intents and purposes, be valid and effectual to convey from one person to another the fee simple to any land or real estate, if the same be executed in the presence of and be subscribed by two or more credible witnesses.

There is also a proviso, that no person shall be obliged to insert the clause of warranty, or be restrained from inserting any clause or clauses in conveyances, hereafter to be made, that may be deemed proper and advisable by the purchaser and seller, and other forms, not contravening the laws of the land, shall not be invalidated.

Vermont.

Form of deed conveying land.

Follow form on page 126, ante, under title "Connecticut."

XVI.

DOWER.

When a widow is entitled to hold during her life one-third part of her husband's real estate for her dower therein, and that third part yields a certain annual sum at the end of the year, it is often desirable to a party to ascertain the present value of the dower interest, and extinguish that interest by immediate payment of the value. 2 Rob. Prac. 380. The following table, prepared by Professor Wigglesworth, of Cambridge university, adopted by the supreme court of Massachusetts, 10 Mass. Rep. 322, is the one usually followed.

Ages.	Persons living.	Decrement of life.	Expectation of life.	Ages.	Persons living.	Decrement of life.	Expectation of life.
			yrs. dec.				yrs. dec.
At birth	4893	1264	28.15	50	1288	27	21.16
1	3629	274		51	1261	27	
2	3355	188		52	1234	27	
3	3167	132		53	1207	27	
4	3035	84		54	1180	27	
5	2951	58	40.87	55	1153	27	18.35
6	2893	55		56	1126	27	
7	2838	47		57	1099	27	
8	2791	40		58	1072	27	
9	2751	36		59	1045	27	
10	2715	28	39.23	60	1018	27	15.43
11	2687	27		61	991	27	
12	2660	27		62	964	27	
13	2633	27		63	937	27	
14	2606	27		64	910	27	
15	2579	42	36.16	65	883	37	12.43
16	2537	43		66	846	37	
17	2494	43		67	809	37	
18	2451	43		68	772	37	
19	2408	43		69	735	37	
20	2365	43	34.21	70	698	37	10.06
21	2322	42		71	661	37	
22	2280	42		72	624	37	
23	2238	42		73	587	38	
24	2196	42		74	549	38	
25	2154	40	32.32	75	511	37	7.83
26	2114	38		76	474	37	
27	2076	38		77	437	37	
28	2038	38		78	400	37	
29	2000	38		79	363	37	
30	1962	38	30.24	80	326	35	5.85
31	1924	38		81	291	34	
32	1886	38		82	257	34	
33	1848	38		83	223	34	
34	1810	38		84	189	34	
35	1772	35	28.22	85	155	21	4.57
36	1737	35		86	134	21	
37	1702	35		87	113	21	
38	1667	35		88	92	20	
39	1632	35		89	72	20	
40	1597	35	26.04	90	52	8	3.73
41	1562	35		91	44	7	
42	1527	35		92	37	7	
43	1492	35		93	30	7	
44	1457	34		94	23	7	
45	1423	27	23.92	95	16	6	1.62
46	1396	27		96	10	5	
47	1369	27		97	5	3	
48	1342	27		98	2	1	
49	1315	27		99	1	1	

Mr. Robinson, in vol. 2 of his Practice, edition of 1835, says:

"The present value of any yearly sum, payable at a future day, is so much money as, if put at interest, will, at the period when the yearly sum is payable, make with the interest added thereto the amount of such yearly sum. How much money, with the interest thereon to a specified time, will make at that time a given sum, may readily be ascertained by the rule of three. Thus if a sum of $240 is payable at the end of one year, and it is desired to know how much money with 6 per cent. interest thereon for one year will make $240, it may be ascertained as follows. $100 with the interest for one year will make $106; then, as $106 is to $100, so is $240 to the sum required.

```
106 : 100 : : 240
                100
              -----
        106)24000(226 44/106
            212
            ---
             280
             212
             ---
              680
              636
              ---
               44
```

The sum required is found to be $226 $\frac{44}{106}$. That the result is correct may be proved by calculating the interest on $226 $\frac{44}{106}$ for one year, and adding the year's interest to the principal. The $226 $\frac{44}{106}$ and the year's interest on it will make $240.

Mr. Hilary Baker, one of the commissioners of the circuit court of Henrico, has taken the case of a person 90 years old, whose expectation of life, according to Dr. Wigglesworth's table, is 3 years $\frac{73}{100}$, and has shown the value, in such a case, of a life estate the yearly income of which is $240. The following is furnished by him:

$226.41 $\frac{54}{100}$,	with	$13.58 $\frac{46}{100}$	interest	thereon for	1 year,	makes	$240.00
214.28 $\frac{58}{100}$,	with	25.71 $\frac{42}{100}$	"	"	2 years,	"	240.00
203.38 $\frac{98}{100}$,	with	36.61 $\frac{02}{100}$	"	"	3 years,	"	240.00
143.16 $\frac{08}{100}$,	with	32.03 $\frac{92}{100}$	"	"	$\frac{73}{100}$ year,	"	175.20
$787.25 $\frac{18}{100}$	plus	$107.94 $\frac{82}{100}$,	equal to				$895.20

Showing that a person whose income at the end of each of three years would be $240, and for $\frac{73}{100}$ of the fourth year would be $175.20, making together $895.20, would be entitled to receive a present sum of $787 25."

Judge *Allen*, in Wilson, &c. *v.* Davisson, 2 Rob. Va. Rep. 403, holds this language concerning Wigglesworth's table, and Mr. Baker's method of calculating the present value of annuities:

"In ascertaining the present worth of the annuity, the court adopted Wigglesworth's table of longevity, found in 2 Robinson's Practice, 381, and the method of calculating the present value of an annuity, which is there said to have been adopted by Mr. Baker, one of the commissioners of the circuit court of Henrico. That method is manifestly erroneous, as is strikingly exhibited in the present case. The one-third of the surplus is ascertained to be 150 dollars 34 cents, and the calculation gives the widow absolutely 122 dollars 2 cents, leaving to the reversioner, if there were one, but 28 dollars 32 cents. The error consists in calculating the discount at simple interest, instead of compound interest. The true rule, I think, is explained and illustrated very fully in a communication with which I have been favored by Judge *Smith*, who has had occasion to investigate the subject, and has furnished me with an exposition of his views, which will be handed to the reporter, to be published in a note to this case. There may possibly be some inaccuracies in the calculations, but the principle, I think, is the correct one."

Judge *Smith*, in the communication referred to by Judge *Allen*, says: "The results produced by taking Wigglesworth's table as a guide in respect to the duration of life, and calculating the discount by simple interest, have been so glaringly incorrect, that the table has been often thrown aside under an idea that the error must be in that, whereas the error is in the mode of calculation." Judge *Smith* does not question the correctness of the table as a guide in cases generally; but, taking the expectation of life as correct, he considers the true rule to be, to calculate the discount by compound interest. He refers to Pike's Arithmetic, 2d edition, enlarged, p. 268, where it is said, 'The purchasing annuities by simple interest is unjust and absurd, which may be easily made to appear by one instance only: the price of an annuity of £100, to continue 30 years, discounting at six per cent., will amount to nearly £2000, the interest of which, for one year only, exceeds the annuity; would it not, therefore, be highly absurd to give a sum which would yield me nearly £120 yearly, forever, for an annuity of £100, to continue only 30 years?' He refers also to the American edition of Nicholson's British Encyclopedia, title Annuities, where it is said, 'The present value of an annuity is that sum which, improved at *compound* interest, will be sufficient to pay the annuity;' and then proceeds as follows: "This is the correct rule, according to Pike, who, to facilitate calculations, has made out a table (p. 325), showing the present worth of an annuity of £1, for any number of years from 1 to 40, calculating by compound interest. I have found it very accurate, and will send you herewith an extract of so much of it as gives the present value, at 6 per cent., only changing the £1 into $1, as being more convenient. You will find it marked A. I may also remark, that I have seen in Jessee's Arithmetic, a table corresponding precisely with this, and the author gives it as the true rule.

"I have endeavored to test the correctness of these tables, and the principle upon which they are constructed; and I think I can give my views best by supposing a case, and sending you the calculations I have made, for your inspection. Let us suppose, then, that a widow, having her life estate in dower land, worth annually $60, agrees with the reversioner that they will sell out and out, and divide the money by the correct rule; that the land sells for $1000, and it is estimated and agreed that her expectation of life shall be put down at ten years: then, by a fair division of this money, the owner of the life estate ought to have what would be equivalent to $60 per annum for 10 years, and the reversioner ought to have what would be, in cash, a just equivalent for $1000, ten years hence. I have made a calculation of the value of the life estate, or rather the annuity for 10 years, discounting by simple interest; and it appears to be $458 93 $\frac{3}{10}$ cents. I send it that you may compare it with the others. It is marked B." [The principle of calculating by *compound* interest being that approved by the judges of the court of appeals, it is thought unnecessary to publish the table B.]

"I have also made a calculation, taking the discount of compound interest, which I contend is the true rule; and by this the life estate would be of the present value of $441 60. You will find this calculation, marked C.

"If, in dividing the $1000, the owner of the life estate gets $441 60, there will be left for the reversioner $558 40. Let this sum be improved at compound interest, for 10 years, to ascertain whether the reversioner will then have his proper sum of $1000. It comes out precisely. I send this calculation, marked D.

"Let me try this rule by another test. Suppose the owner of the life estate puts out her $441 60, taking bond for it, and stipulating that the borrower shall annually pay $60, to be credited on the bond: let us calculate when the bond would be discharged by such payments. It will be seen by the calculation I send, marked E, that the bond would be discharged precisely at the end of 10 years, and that the owner of the life estate will have received her $60 annually for the 10 years. Does it not follow that $441 60 is the true value of the life estate?

"But let us suppose for a moment that the expectation of life in the case I have been discussing were put down at 30 years, instead of 10 years; then it would be seen by calculation, if made according to the rule of simple interest, that of the $1000, the amount of the sale, there would be *nothing* to give to the owner of the reversion as his share. In fact, there would not be quite enough to make up the share of the owner of the life estate. The rule of simple interest must therefore, I humbly conceive, be abandoned."

[A.]

A TABLE *showing the present worth of an annuity of* $1 *for any number of years, from* 1 *to* 40, *at* 6 *per cent., calculating discount by compound interest.*

Years.	Present worth.	Years.	Present worth.
	$		$
1	0.94339	21	11.76407
2	1.83339	22	12.04158
3	2.67301	23	12.30338
4	3.46510	24	12.55035
5	4.21236	25	12.78335
6	4.91732	26	13.00316
7	5.58238	27	13.21053
8	6.20979	28	13.40616
9	6.80169	29	13.59072
10	7.36008	30	13.76483
11	7.88687	31	13.92908
12	8.38384	32	14.08398
13	8.85268	33	14.22917
14	9.29498	34	14.36613
15	9.71225	35	14.49533
16	10.10589	36	14.61722
17	10.47726	37	14.73211
18	10.82760	38	14.84048
19	11.15811	39	14.94270
20	11.46992	40	15.03913

[C.]

CALCULATION *to show the present value of an annuity of* $60, *for* 10 *years, by discounting at compound interest.*

1st year,	$56.604	with 1 year's int.	....	=	$60
2d "	53.40	" 2 years' compound int.	....	=	60
3d "	50.377	" 3 "	"	=	60
4th "	47.525	" 4 "	"	=	60
5th "	44.835	" 5 "	"	=	60
6th "	42.297	" 6 "	"	=	60
7th "	39.903	" 7 "	"	=	60
8th "	37.644	" 8 "	"	=	60
9th "	35.513	" 9 "	"	=	60
10th "	33.503	" 10 "	"	=	60
	$441.601, present value.				

By Table A, an annuity of $1 for 10 years is	$7.36008
	60
Multiplied by 60 (the annuity) is equal to............	$441.60480

Variance only $\frac{3}{10}$ of a cent.

[D.]

CALCULATION *of* $558.40, *reversioner's share, improved at compound interest for* 10 *years.*

Sum........................	$558.40
1st year, add 1 year's int..	33.504
	591.904
2d year, add year's int..	35.514
	627.418
3d year, add int..	37.645
	665.063
4th year, add int..	39.903
	704.966
5th year, add int..	42,297
	747.263
6th year, add int..	44.835
	792.098
7th year, add int..	47.525
	839.623
8th year, add int..	50.377
	890.000
9th year, add int..	53.400
	943.400
10th year, add int..	56.604
	$1000.004

[E.]

CALCULATION, *supposing* $441.60 *put to interest, bond taken, and* $60 *paid annually and credited.*

Amount on hand	$441.60
Add 1 year's int	26.496
	468.096
Deduct 1st year's credit	60
	408.096
Add 2d year's int	24.485
	432.581
Deduct 2d year's credit	60
	372.581
Add 3d year's int	22.354
	394.935
Deduct 3d year's credit	60
	334.935
Add 4th year's int	20.096
	355.031
Deduct 4th year's credit	60
	295.031
Add 5th year's int	17.701
	312.732
Deduct 5th year's credit	60
	252.732
Add 6th year's int	15.163
	267.895
Deduct 6th year's credit	60
	207.895
Add 7th year's int	12.473
	220.368
Deduct 7th year's credit	60
	160.368
Add 8th year's int	9.622
	169.990
Deduct 8th year's credit	60
	109.990
Add 9th year's int	6.599
	116.589
Deduct 9th year's credit	60
	56.589
Add 10th year's int	3.395
	59.984
Deduct 10th year's credit	60

Error in calculation, $1\frac{6}{10}$ cent only.

CALCULATION *of discount by compound interest may be stated in the rule of three, thus:*

1st year.	As 106 : 100 : : 60	: 56.604
2d year.	As 106 : 100 : : 56.604	: 53.40
3d year.	As 106 : 100 : : 53.40	: 50.377

XVII.

EXCHANGES.

Exchange of lands in fee.

This indenture, made and entered into this day of , in the year , between P H of , of the one part, and C J of , of the other part: Witnesseth, that for and in consideration of the messuage or tenement and premises hereinafter mentioned, to be granted and conveyed in exchange by the said C J, unto the said P H; and also, for and in consideration of the sum of dollars, lawful money of the United States, to the said P H in hand paid by the said C J, at or before the sealing and delivery of these presents, the receipt whereof he, the said P H, doth hereby acknowledge, he, the said P H, hath given, granted, bargained, sold, aliened, exchanged and released, and by these presents doth give, grant, bargain, sell, alien, exchange and release unto the said C J, all that lot, piece or parcel of land, situate, lying and being in county, and bounded as follows: beginning [here describe the land, and boundaries thereof], together with all and singular the appurtenances thereto belonging, or in any wise appertaining, with the reversion or reversions, remainder or remainders, rents, issues and profits thereof, and of every part and parcel thereof, and all the estate, right, title, interest, property, claim and demand whatsoever, of him, the said P H, of, in, to or out of the said lot, piece or parcel of land. To have and to hold the said lot, piece or parcel of land, with the appurtenances hereby granted, released and confirmed, or mentioned or intended so to be, unto the said C J, his heirs and assigns, forever, in exchange for the messuage or tenement, &c., hereinafter particularly mentioned and described, to be granted and conveyed in exchange by the said C J to the said P H. And this indenture witnesseth, that for and in consideration of the said lot, piece or parcel of land, with the appurtenances thereof, being so granted and conveyed unto the said C J, as aforesaid, and also, for and in consideration of the sum of dollars, lawful money of the United States, to the said C J in hand paid by the said P H, at or before the sealing and delivery of these presents, the receipt whereof he, the said C J, doth hereby acknowledge, he, the said C J, hath given, granted, bargained, sold, aliened, exchanged and released, and by these presents doth give, grant, bargain, sell, alien, exchange and release, unto the said P H, all that messuage or tenement, situate, lying and being in , and all houses, out-houses, barns, stables, buildings, yards, orchards and gardens, and the ground and soil thereof, ways, water-courses, and all the appurtenances thereof, with the reversion or reversions, remainder or remainders, rents, issues and profits thereof, and of every part and parcel thereof, and all the estate, right, title, interest, property, claim and demand whatsoever, of him, the said C J, of, in, to or out of the said messuage or tenement. To have and to hold the said messuage or tenement, with the appurtenances thereof, as aforesaid, hereby granted, released and confirmed, or mentioned, or intended so to be, unto the said P H, his heirs and assigns, forever, in exchange for the said lot, piece or parcel of land, and appurtenances hereinbefore granted and conveyed by the said P H to the said C J. And the said P H, for himself, his heirs, executors and administrators, doth covenant, promise and agree, to and with the said C J, his heirs and assigns, by these presents, in manner following (that is to say): that he, the said P H, is lawfully and rightfully seized of the said lot, piece or parcel of land, by him given, granted and conveyed in exchange to him, the said C J, his heirs and assigns, as above mentioned and recited, of and in a pure, perfect, absolute and indefeasible estate of inheritance, in fee simple, without any condition, contingent, proviso, power of limitation or revocation, or any other restraint, matter or thing whatsoever, to alter, change, charge, determine, lessen, incumber, defeat or make void the same. And the said P H, his heirs, &c., doth covenant and agree to and with the said C J, his heirs and assigns, that he, the said P H, his heirs, &c., the said lot, piece or parcel of land conveyed in exchange, unto the said C J, his heirs and assigns, shall and will warrant and forever defend by these presents, against him, the said P H, his heirs or assigns, and against all and every person or persons claiming by, through or under him, them, or any of them. And the said C J, for himself, his heirs, executors and administrators, doth covenant, promise and agree, to and with the said P H, his heirs and assigns, by these presents, in manner following (that is to say): that he, the said C J, is lawfully and rightfully seized of the said messuage or tenement by him given, granted and conveyed in exchange to him, the said P H, his heirs and assigns, as above mentioned and recited, of and in a pure, perfect, absolute and indefeasible estate of inheritance in fee simple, without any condition, contingent, proviso, power of limitation or revocation, or any other restraint, matter or thing whatsoever, to alter, change, charge, determine, lessen, incumber, defeat or make void the same. And the said C J, his heirs, &c., doth covenant and agree to and with the said P H, his heirs and assigns, that he, the said C J, his heirs, &c., the said messuage or tenement, &c., conveyed in exchange unto the said P H, his heirs and assigns, shall and will warrant and forever defend by these presents, against him, the said C J, his heirs or assigns, and against all and every person or persons claiming by, through or under him, them, or any of them.

In witness whereof, the parties to the above have hereunto set their hands and seals the day and year in the above indenture of exchange mentioned. ——— ——— [Seal.]

——— ——— [Seal.]

XVIII.

EXECUTORS, ADMINISTRATORS, AND OTHER FIDUCIARIES.

Account of executor or administrator.

In Burwell's ex'ors v. Anderson, adm'r, &c., 3 Leigh, 363, *Tucker*, president, said it would be better to adhere to a particular *formula*, that the mode of statement might become familiar to parties, to counsel, and to the court, who, he remarked, are often perplexed by complicated modes of statement, far more than they would be by executing the task of commissioner themselves. He accordingly prepared the following, which the commissioners of the courts of chancery in Virginia are required to observe:

☞ See Tables, pp. 186–7, and Notes, p. 188.

Form of executor's

DR. *The estate of* A B, *in ac-*

		Principal.	*Int'st.*
1820. Dec. 31.	To disbursements this year	5,000 00	
		$5,000 00	
1821. (1) Dec. 31.	To balance per contra	1,000 00	
	interest thereon	60 00	
	disbursements this year	1,940 00	
	balance due estate	2,000 00	
		$5,000 00	
1822. (3) Dec. 31.	To disbursements	2,000 00	
	balance due estate	5,000 00	120
		$7,000 00	$120
1823. (2) Dec. 31.	To disbursements	2,000 00	
	balance due estate	8,000 00	420
		$10,000 00	$420
1824. (2) Dec. 31.	To disbursements	3,000 00	
	balance due estate	6,000 00	900
		$9,000 00	$900
1825. (3) Dec. 31.	To disbursements	8,580 00	
	balance due estate (all interest)	800 00	
		$9,380 00	
1826. Dec. 31.	To disbursements	8,000 00	
	balance	2,000 00	800
		$10,000 00	$800
1827. (4) Dec. 31.	To disbursements	4,000 00	
		$4,000 00	
1828. (1) Dec. 31.	To balance per contra	1,080 00	
	interest thereon	64 80	
	balance due estate	10,000 00	
		$11,144 80	
1829. Dec. 31.	To disbursements	10,000 00	
	balance due estate (all interest)	....	600
		$10,000 00	$600
1830. Dec. 31.	To disbursements	500 00	
	balance (all interest)	100 00	
		$600 00	
1831. Dec. 31.	To disbursements	500 00	
	balance	3,500 00	100
		$4,000 00	$100

account.

count with C D, *his ex'or.* CR.

		Principal.	Int'st
1820. Dec. 31.	By receipts this year	4,000 00	
	balance due ex'or	1,000 00	
		$5,000 00	
1821. Dec. 31.	By receipts this year	5,000 00	
		$5,000 00	
1822. Dec. 31.	By balance per contra	2,000 00	
	interest thereon to date		120
	receipts	5,000 00	
		$7,000 00	$120
1823. Dec. 31.	By balance per contra	5,000 00	120
	interest on balance of principal		300
	receipts	5,000 00	
		$10,000 00	$420
1824. Dec. 31.	By balance per contra	8,000 00	420
	interest on balance of principal		480
	receipts	1,000 00	
		9,000 00	$900
1825. Dec. 31.	By balance per contra	6,000 00	
	interest on balance of principal	360 00	
	receipts	2,120 00	
	balance of interest brought into account of principal to meet the disbursements	900 00	
		$9,380 00	
1826. Dec. 31.	By balance per contra (interest)		800
	receipts	10,000 00	
		$10,000 00	$800
1827. Dec. 31.	By balance per contra	2,000 00	
	interest on above balance of principal	120 00	
	interest brought into account of principal to meet disbursements	800 00	
	balance due ex'or	1,080 00	
		$4,000 00	
1828. Dec. 31.	By receipts	11,144 80	
		$11,144 80	
1829. Dec. 31.	By balance per contra	10,000 00	
	interest thereon		600
		$10,000 00	600
1830.	By balance per contra (all interest) brought into column of principal to meet the disbursements.	600 00	
		$600 00	
1831. Dec. 31.	By balance (interest)		100
	receipts	4,000 00	
		$4,000 00	$100
	Balance due the estate with interest on the principal sum from December 31, 1831, till paid.	$3,500 00	$100

Notes (referred to on p. 186).

[1] In the years marked ([1]), the executor being in advance, is not only allowed interest, but that interest is aggregated with the principal; for when he is in advance to the estate, he is to be treated as a common creditor.

[2] In the years marked ([2]), a balance being due to the estate, the interest on that balance for the year is calculated, but kept in a separate column; and all the disbursements are exclusively applied to sink the principal.

[3] In the year marked ([3]), the disbursements exceeding the receipts of the current year, together with the balance of principal of former years, the interest on that balance is aggregated with the principal, in order to set off against the disbursements; and that aggregate being still insufficient to meet the disbursements, the interest of former years is brought into the aggregate, and set against the disbursements. A balance then appears due the estate of $800; but this being all interest, is, in the account of the succeeding year, carried back again into the interest column, on the credit side of the account.

[4] In the year marked ([4]), the disbursements discharge the whole of the principal and interest in arrear, and give a balance due to the executor. on which he is allowed interest in the next year.

Account of trustee.

The accounts of trustees, in ordinary cases, when the items are few, and the fund easily distributable, should be settled strictly on the principles of Debtor and Creditor. The following example will illustrate this mode of settlement:

R R, *Trustee—In account with the trust fund under deed from J B, dated —— day of ——*, Cr.

1866.	
January 1—To amount proceeds of sale under trust deed *	$5,000 00
1868.	
January 1—To interest thereon, two years, at 6 per centum per annum	600 00
	$5,600 00
Cr.	
1868.	
January 1—By amount paid J M, one of the creditors, secured by deed	2,600 00
	3,000 00
1868.	
October 1—To interest on $3,000, from January 1st, 1868, to date, 9 months	135 00
	3,135 00
Cr.	
1868.	
October 1—By cash paid A C, one of the creditors, secured by deed	25 00
	3,110 00
1869.	
January 1—To interest on $3,000 [not $3,110] from October 1st, 1868, to date, 3 months	46 65
	3,156 65
Cr.	
1869.	
January 1—By cash paid George G, amount of his debt, secured by said deed	3,156 65

* If trustee settles his account in time prescribed by law, he should be credited by his commissions.

In the example just given, J M, A C, and George G are paid their debts in full; and there is no balance in the hands of the trustee. No commission is allowed him because he has failed to settle his accounts in time. See Code Virginia, ch. 132, sec. 8. Of course, when the accounts are settled in the time directed by the statute, the commissions must be placed to his credit. Trustees, in an ordinary deed of trust made to secure the payment of debts, or for the indemnity of securities, are allowed 5 per cent. commission on the first three hundred dollars, and 2 per cent. on the residuum. Code Virginia, ch. 117, sec. 6. In other cases, the amount of commissions allowed is a matter of reasonable discretion. Usually five per cent. commissions are given; sometimes more, when the trust is of difficult execution, or there is much labor attending it.

It depends much upon the character of the trust, whether the mode of settlement above indicated should be adopted, or one of greater leniency to the trustee, or whether he should be held to even a stricter rule. In *Miller* v. *Beverly's*, 4 Hen. and Mun. 417, Chancellor Taylor said, "that a trustee was liable to pay interest upon the trust money in his hands, unless he can show that it was necessarily kept in hand for the purposes of the trust, and this he may do upon oath, subject to be controlled by other testimony and the circumstances of the case." In that case, the interest was charged from the time the money was received. The chancellor, however, relied somewhat on the fact, that Miller, the trustee, was a merchant, and the moment he received the money, had it, or might have had it, in active use.

The mode of computation adopted in *Raphael* v. *Boehm*, 11 Ves. 82, 13 Ves. 407, which was the case of an executor, (who was held to be *a trustee*), was extremely rigid. There were half yearly rests, and the interest was compounded with the principal. This goes farther than the supreme court of appeals of Virginia went in *Garrett, ex'or*, v. *Carr and ux.*, 1 Rob. Rep. 209, in which the executor was charged as *a guardian;* for, in the latter case, the rests were annual, not half yearly.

The following formula is prepared to meet a case in which the trustee has many transactions, and the fund is not easily distributable; a case in which the ordinary method adopted in the settlement of Debtor and Creditor accounts would be cumbrous, and the strict and rigid enforcement of the principles, applicable to Debtor and Creditor, would operate hardly upon the trustee.

Form of trustee's

DR. JOHN P, (*or, the trust fund under, &c.,*) *in ac-*

		Principal.	Interest.
1866. June 30—	To disbursements this year	100 00	
	To commission on receipts	60 00	
	To balance per contra	840 00	
		$1,000 00	
1867. June 30—	To disbursements this year	100 00	
	To commissions on receipts	1 00	
	To balance per contra	809 40	
		$910 40	
1868. June 30—	To disbursements this year	1,000 00	
	To commission on receipts	50	
		$1,000 50	
1868. June 30—	To balance	132 54	
1869. June 30—	To disbursements this year	300 00	
	To interest on balance brought into principal column, as an offset to receipts	7 95	
	To commission on receipts	75 00	
	To balance per contra	984 51	
		$1,500 00	
1870. June 30—	To disbursements this year	$— —	
	To commission on receipts	....	250 00
	To balance per contra	5,984 51	34 07
		$5,984 51	$284 07
1871. June 30—	To disbursements this year	$6,377 65	
	To amount of interest brought into principal column on credit side of account		34 07
		$6,377 65	$34 07

account.

count with ROBERT R, *trustee* (*or agent*). CR.

		Principal.	Interest.
1866. June 30—	By receipts this year	1,000 00	
		$1,000 00	
1866. June 30—	By balance to debit	$840 00	
1867. June 30—	By interest on do. one year	50 40	
June 30—	By receipts this year	20 00	
		$910 40	
1867. June 30—	By balance to debit	$809 40	
1868. June 30—	By interest on do. one year	48 56	
June 30—	By receipts this year	10 00	
June 30—	By balance	132 54	
		$1,000 50	
1869. June 30—	By receipts this year	$1,500 00	
		$1,500 00	
1869. June 30—	By balance to debit	984 51	
July 1—	By amount received from H. H.	5,000 00	
1870. June 30—	By interest on balance $984 51, one year		59 07
June 30—	By interest on money received from H. H., from the 1st day of October, 1869, (allowing the trustee *three* months to invest it), to date, (1)		225 00
		$5,984 51	$284 07
1870. June 30—	By balance to debit	$5,984 51	34 07
	By amount of interest brought into principal column, to meet disbursements	34 07	
1871. June 30—	By interest on $5,984 51, one year, brought into principal column	359 07	
		$6,377 65	$34 07

[1] A reasonable time for investment is the rule. What is a reasonable time will depend upon the circumstances of each case. In *Hooper, &c.* v. *Royster, &c.*, 1 Munf. 119, *six months* were allowed a guardian to invest.

Account of guardian.

The principles announced in *Garrett*, ex'or, v. *Carr* and ux, 1 Rob. Rep. 209, govern the settlement of guardians' accounts. The following formula is drawn in conformity with those principles:

Form for the settlement of an account

Dr. A B, *in account*

		Profits.	Principal.
1851.			
June 30—	To disbursements this year	104 50	
30—	To commission on profits	5 50	
30—	To commission on principal (1)	....	50 00
30—	To balance per contra	....	950 00
		$110 00	$1,000 00
1852.			
June 30—	To disbursements this year	50 00	
(2) 30—	To commission on profits (inclusive of interest)	7 85	
30—	To balance per contra	99 15	950 00
		$157 00	$950 00
1853.			
June 30—	To disbursements this year	100 00	
(2) 30—	To commission on profits (inclusive of interest)	28 14	
30—	To balance per contra	434 80	1,049 15
		$562 94	$1,049 15
1854.			
June 30—	To disbursements this year	475 00	
30—	To commission on profits	25 00	
30—	To balance per contra	....	1,483 95
		$500 00	$1,483 95
1855.			
June 30—	To disbursements this year	500 00	
(2) 30—	To commission on profits (inclusive of interest)	30 00	
30—	To balance per contra	70 00	1,483 95
		$600 00	$1,483 95
1856.			
June 30—	To disbursements this year	477 70	
(2) 30—	To commission on profits (inclusive of interest)	22 30	
30—	To balance per contra, (principal)	1,500 00	
		$2,000 00	

of a guardian or of a person acting as guardian.

with C D, *his guardian,* Cr.

		Profits.	Principal.
1851. June 30—	By receipts this year, (principal)........	....	1,000 00
June 30—	By receipts this year, (profits)........	110 00	
		$110 00	$1,000 00
1851. June 30—	By balance due per debit, in principal........	....	950 00
1852. June 30—	By interest on ditto to date........	57 00	
June 30—	By receipts this year, (profits)........	100 00	
		$157 00	$950 00
1852. June 30—	By balance due per debit, (profits and principal) (2)........	....	1,049 15
1853. June 30—	By interest on ditto to date........	62 94	
June 30—	By receipts this year, (profits)........	500 00	
		$562 94	$1,049 15
1853. June 30—	By balance due per debit, (profits and principal) (3)........	....	1,483 95
1854. June 30—	By receipts this year, (profits, exclusive of interest on balance of last year, which was loaned out by guardian, and no interest received) (4)........	500 00	
		$500 00	$1,483 95
1854. June 30—	By balance due per debit, (principal)........	....	1,483 95
1855. June 30—	By interest on ditto, from June 30, 1853, to date........	178 07	
June 30—	By receipts this year, (profits)........	421 93	
		$600 00	$1,483 95
1855. June 30—	By balance due per debit, (profits and principal), brought into account of profits to meet disbursements (5)........	1,553 95	
1856. June 30—	By interest on ditto to date........	93 23	
June 30—	By receipts this year, (profits)........	352 82	
		$2,000 00	

Dr. A B, *in account*

1857. June 30—	To disbursements this year	475 00	
(2) 30—	To commission on profits (inclusive of interest)	25 00	
June 30—	To balance per contra	....	1,500 00
		$500 00	$1,500 00

Act of 1856 *concerning guardians.*

The following important statute, first enacted in Sess. Acts '55-6, p. 36, and repeated in the Code of 1860, ch. 128, §§ 11, 12, p. 589, deserves special notice:

"Hereafter any person acting as guardian shall have the right to demand and recover of all obligors in bonds, payable to him as guardian and held by him for the benefit of his ward, not only the principal sum due with interest thereon after the rate now prescribed by law, but also, when the interest on the principal sum is not paid punctually at the end of each year, to demand and recover interest upon the interest so due and unpaid.

"Whenever a guardian shall collect any principal or interest belonging to his ward, he shall have thirty days to invest or loan the same, and shall not be charged with interest thereon until the expiration of said time, unless he shall have made the investment previous thereto; in which case, he shall be charged with interest from the time the investment or loan is made."

It surely was not the design of this statute to require guardians to pay interest on "profits" (though they exist in the shape of interest) where they are needed to meet current disbursements.

with C D, *his guardian*—(*Continued.*) Cr.

1856. June 30—	By balance per debit, (principal)	....	1,500 00
1857. June 30—	By interest on ditto to date	90 00	
	By receipts this year, (profits)	410 00	
		$500 00	$1,590 00
		Profits.	Principal.
1857. (6) June 30—	To balance per debit due ward, who has attained legal age,	....	1,500 00
	To interest on ditto to 30th June, 1858	....	90 00
	Cr.		1,590 00
	By cash then paid by guardian	....	590 00
	Dr.		1,000 00
	To interest on balance to 1st January, 1859	....	30 00
	Cr.		1,030 00
	By cash then paid by guardian	....	530 00
	Balance due ward 1st January, 1859,	....	$500 00

NOTES.

[1] The commission on the principal is charged to the *principal*, and the commission on the profits is charged to the *profits*. The commission for receiving or collecting any particular fund should be charged to the fund so received or collected, and to no other. In this case, however, if the commission for receiving the principal had been charged to the profits, the result would have been the same.

[2] The guardian is allowed commission on the interest upon the balance for the previous year, as well as upon other profits, although the balance was retained in his hands. If the balance had been invested or loaned out, the guardian would have been entitled to commission on the interest when received, and as the guardian is chargeable with compound interest, when the disbursements for any particular year are less than profits (inclusive of interest) credited for that year, there seems to be no good reason why he should not be allowed such commission, although the balance upon which the interest accrued remained in the guardian's hands. *Sed vide, C. V. ch.* 132, § 18, which authorizes such a commission, if the commissioner should think proper to allow it.

[3] The surplus of profits, carrying interest as well as the principal, is here aggregated with the principal, and the amount extended in the principal column. See *Garrett, exo'r*, v. *Carr*, 1 Rob. 196.

[4] When the money is loaned out or invested, the guardian is chargeable with only so much interest as he may have received. If he has received none, then none is credited. *Ibid.*

[5] Here, the aggregate amount of profits and principal is brought into the column of profits to meet the disbursements, which exceed the profits. *See C. V. ch.* 127, § 8, 9.

[6] The ward having attained legal age, the account between him and his guardian, for the rest of the period, is settled upon the ordinary principles that govern the settlement of accounts between debtor and creditor. 1 *Rob.* 196, 4 *Gratt.* 43.

XIX.

NOTARIES.

Notaries are authorized by the laws of Virginia to take depositions, affidavits, &c. They may also note and extend protests of negotiable notes, bills of exchange, and the like. They are also authorized to take depositions, under the act of congress of the United States.

The Code of Virginia imposes a tax on the seal of the notary, when annexed to any paper, except when affixed to a paper or document to be used in obtaining the benefit of a pension, revolutionary claim, money due on account of military services, or land bounty under an act of congress, or under a law of any State of the Union, or when a seal is annexed by a notary public to an affidavit or deposition. See Code, ch. 39, §§ 13, 15.

Notaries are required to make out an account of all taxes received by them on or after the first day of September in one year, and before the first day of September in the next year, and return it to the first auditor, on or before the fifteenth day of December following, to the correctness of which account the notaries are required to make oath, and the amount appearing due thereby they are required to pay into the treasury on or before the fifteenth December following, deducting therefrom a commission of five per centum for receiving and paying the same.

Form of protest of negotiable note.

Virginia—City of Richmond, to wit:

Know all men by these presents, that I, L N, a notary public in and for the city aforesaid, duly commissioned and qualified, at the request of the cashier of the Bank of Virginia, on the   day of   , in the year of our Lord 18   , presented the original note, of which the above is a copy, at the Bank of Virginia, where the same is payable, and demanded payment thereof (the period limited having expired), which was refused:

Wherefore, I, the said notary, do hereby protest the said note, as well against the maker as against the endorser, and all others whom it doth or may concern, for all loss, damages, principal, interest, costs, and charges sustained, or to be sustained, by reason of the non-payment and protest aforesaid. And I thereupon addressed written notices to the said endorser   , directed to   , that being his (or their) post-office, informing of the demand, non-payment, protest and dishonor of said note, and that the holders looked to for payment thereof.

In testimony of all which, I have hereunto subscribed my name and affixed my notarial seal, at the city of Richmond aforesaid, the day and year aforesaid. ——— ——— N. P.

Notarial charges, $

Notice to endorsers of non-payment of negotiable note.

RICHMOND, VA., August 26, 1851.

To :

Take notice, that R M R's note for $, dated the 23d day of June, 1851, and payable two months after date, to the order of H L, at the Bank of Virginia, and endorsed by you, being due and unpaid, the same was this day presented by me at said bank, and payment thereof then and there demanded, which was refused: whereupon, the said note was dishonored, and duly protested by me for non-payment, and the holders look to you for payment as endorser thereof, for principal, interest, damages, costs and charges.

Done at the request of the cashier of the Bank of Virginia.

L N, *Notary Public.*

Sometimes the endorser waives the necessity of demand, protest, and notice of non-payment. The following is the form:

Waiver of demand, protest, &c.

I agree to waive demand, protest, and notice of non-payment on a note drawn by H E, and endorsed by me, for the sum of $, dated the day of , and due on the 27-30th days of November, at the Bank of Virginia, and hereby hold myself as legally and as effectually bound for the same, as if the said note had been regularly protested, and the notice given.

Witness my hand this 30th day of November, 1851.

R J L.

Form of protest of bill of exchange.

Virginia—City of Richmond, to wit:

Know all men by these presents, that I, L N, a notary public in and for the city aforesaid, duly commissioned and qualified, at the request of the cashier of the Bank of Virginia, on the day of , in the year of our Lord 18 , presented the original bill, of which the above is a copy, and demanded payment thereof (the period limited having expired), which was refused:

Wherefore I, the said notary, do hereby protest the said bill, as well against the said drawer and endorser as against the said , and all others whom it doth or may concern, for all loss, damages, principal, interest, costs and charges, sustained, or to be sustained, by reason of the non-payment and protest aforesaid. And I thereupon on the same day addressed written notices to the drawer and endorser of the said bill, and directed the said notices to the said , at , and to the said , at , those being their respective post-offices, informing them of the demand, non-payment, protest and dishonor thereof, and that the holders looked to them for its payment, and deposited the said notices in the post-office in this city.

In testimony of all which, I have hereunto subscribed my name and affixed my notarial seal, at the city of Richmond aforesaid, the day and year aforesaid. L N, *N. P.*

Notarial charges, $.

Form of marine protest.

United States of America:

State of Virginia—County of Henrico;

By this public instrument of protest, be it known and made manifest to all whom these presents shall or may concern, that on the day of , in the year of our Lord one thousand eight hundred and forty , before me, W M F, notary public, in and for said county, duly commissioned and sworn, dwelling in the city of Richmond, personally came and appeared , master of the called the , belonging to the port of , of the burthen of tons, or thereabout, who, having duly noted a protest within twenty-four hours after his arrival at , now wishes to extend the same, and for that purpose has brought with him , mate, and , mariner, of said , who, being by me duly sworn according to law, do severally declare, and say of their own free will and accord, that they, the said master, mate and mariner sailed from the port of , on board of said , she being laden with , on the day of [here proceed to state the circumstances attending the loss of, or damage to, the vessel or its cargo].

And the said appearers did further severally declare, that the said , at the time of her departure from aforesaid, upon the said intended voyage, was tight, staunch and strong, and had her hatches well and sufficiently caulked and covered, and was well and sufficiently manned, provided and furnished with all things needful and necessary for the said voyage; and that during the said voyage the said appearers and ship's company used their utmost endeavors to preserve the said , and the goods of her loading, from damage.

And therefore the said did declare to protest, as by these presents he doth solemnly protest against all and every person or persons whom it shall or may concern; and doth declare that all damages, losses and detriments, that have happened to the said , and the goods of her loading, are and ought to be borne by the merchants and freighters interested, or whomsoever else it shall or may concern (by way of average, or otherwise), the same having occurred as is before mentioned, and not by or through the insufficiency of the said , or neglect of said first appearer, his officers, or any of his mariners.

All which matters and things were declared, alleged and affirmed, as is before set forth, in the presence of me, the said notary; and, therefore, I have hereunto subscribed my name, and affixed my notarial seal, being requested to testify and certify the premises.

Thus done and protested, at Richmond aforesaid, the day and year first above written. W M F, *N. P.*

Certificate to copy.

State of Virginia—County of Henrico, ss:

I, W M F, notary public in and for said county, duly commissioned and sworn, dwelling in the city of Richmond, do hereby certify the foregoing as a true and correct copy of the original protest of , master, of the record in my office.

Witness my hand and notarial seal this day of , in the year of our Lord one thousand eight hundred and fifty .

W M F, *N. P.*

Notice to take depositions.

Code of Virginia, ch. 176, § 28, enacts, that "In any pending case the deposition of a witness, whether a party to the suit or not, may, without any commission, be taken in this State by a justice or notary public, or by a commissioner, and, if certified under his hand, may be received without proof of the signature to such certificate."

By the 30th section of same chapter it is enacted, "that reasonable notice shall be given to the adverse party of the time and place of taking every deposition." In case the party be not a resident of Virginia, notice may be served on his counsel.

To C D and R S:

Take notice, that we shall, on the day of ,[1] at the office of S and S, in the city of Richmond, between the hours of 6 A. M. and 6 P. M. of that day, proceed to take the depositions of R G and others, to be read as evidence in our behalf in a certain action at law (or suit in equity) depending in the circuit court for the county of Henrico, wherein you are plaintiffs and we are defendants; and if, from any cause, the taking of the said depositions be not commenced on that day, or, if commenced, be not concluded on that day, the taking of the same will be adjourned and continued from day to day, or from time to time, at the same place and between the same hours until the same shall be completed.

Respectfully, yours, A B.
D L.

Caption of depositions, depositions, adjournment, attestation, &c.

The depositions of R G and others, taken before me, A H S, a notary public (or justice of the peace) for the city of Richmond, pursuant to notice hereto annexed, at the office of S & S, in the city of Richmond, on the day of , between the hours of 6 A M and 6 P M, to be read as evidence on behalf of A B and D L, in a certain action at law (or suit in equity) depending in the

[1] Where parties live within a convenient distance, five days' notice is usually given. In other cases, ten or fifteen days' notice will not be too much.

circuit court for the county of Henrico, wherein C D and R S are plaintiffs, and the said A B and D L are defendants.

Present: A M, attorney (or counsel) for plaintiffs.
J P, attorney (or counsel) for defendants.

R G, being duly sworn on the Holy Evangelists of Almighty God, deposeth and saith as follows:

1st question by J P, attorney (or counsel) for defendants. What is your age?

Answer. ———.

2d question by same. Do you know the parties to this suit?

Answer. ———.

[Continue the questions until conclusion of examination in chief as above, and in every instance, write the answers of witness, using his words.]

Cross-examined.

1st question by A M, attorney (or counsel) for plaintiffs. [Write questions and answers as before.]

Re-examined.

3d question by J P, attorney (or counsel) for defendants. Are you, &c. &c.

Answer. I am, &c. &c.

And further this deponent saith not. R G.

No other witness appearing, the further taking of these depositions is continued until to-morrow, at the same place and between the same hours. A H S, *N. P.*

Office of S & S, in the City of Richmond:
day of 18 .

Present: A M, attorney (or counsel) for plaintiffs.
J P, attorney (or counsel) for defendants.

K M, being duly sworn on the Holy Evangelists of Almighty God, deposeth and saith as follows:

1st question by attorney (or counsel) for defendants. [Write down questions and answers as in deposition of R G.]

And further this deponent saith not. K M.

State of Virginia—City of Richmond, to wit:

I, A H S, a notary public (or justice of the peace) for the city aforesaid, in the said State, do hereby certify, that the foregoing depositions were duly taken, sworn to and subscribed before me, at the times and place mentioned therein.

Given under my hand this day of 18 .[1]

A H S, *N. P.*

To compel the attendance of witnesses before notaries and others who may lawfully require their attendance, the 20th section of chapter 176 of Code of Virginia provides that a summons may be issued directing the witness to attend. If the witness fail to attend, the court of the county or corporation in which the attendance is desired, on a special report thereof by the person before whom there was the failure to attend, and on proof that there was paid to the witness (if it was required), a reasonable time before he was required to attend, the allowance for one day's attendance and his mileage and tolls, shall, after service to, or rule upon the witness to show cause against it (if no sufficient cause be shown against it), fine him not exceeding twenty dollars, to the use of the party for whom he was summoned, and may proceed by attachment to compel him to attend and give his evidence, at such time and place as the court may deem fit.

In case the witness attends, and yet refuses to be sworn or to give evidence or to produce any writing or document required, he may, by order of the person before whom he was summoned to attend, be committed to jail, there to remain until he shall, in custody of the jailor, give such evidence or produce such writing or document. See § 23, ch. 176, Code of Virginia.

The following are forms of the summons of the witness, and of the report of his non-attendance, should he fail or refuse to attend:

Form of summons requiring attendance of witness.

The Commonwealth of Virginia,

To the Sheriff of the City of Richmond, greeting:

We command you that you summon R G, L M and N O, to appear at the office of S and S, in the city of Richmond, on the day of , before A H S, a notary public for the said city, duly

[1] It has been the practice in Virginia, when depositions are taken by notaries, for the notaries to annex their seal. This is not required by the statute above cited. A certificate under the hand of the notary is sufficient.

commissioned and qualified (or a justice of the peace for said city), to testify and the truth to speak on behalf of A B and D L, in a matter of controversy pending in the circuit court for the county of Henrico, between C D and R S, plaintiffs, and the said A B and D L, defendants. And have then there this writ.

Given under my hand this day of , 18 .

A H S, *N. P.*

Report of non-attendance of witness.

To the Court for the City of Richmond:[1]

N O, who was duly summoned to appear before me, A H S, a notary public (or justice of the peace) for the city aforesaid, on the day of , at the office of S and S, in said city, to testify and the truth to say on behalf of A B and D L, in a matter of controversy pending in the circuit court for the county of Henrico, between C D and R S, plaintiffs, and the said A B and D L, defendants, has failed to attend at the time and place required, and I am requested to report the fact to this court, that proper means may be used to compel the attendance of the said witness.

Respectfully reported,

A H S, *N. P.*

[1] Statute requires report to be made to "a court of the county or corporation in which the attendance is desired." Is it intended to restrict it to the county or corporation court, or may it be made to the circuit court likewise?

XX.

NOTICES.

Notice to quit by a landlord to a tenant from year to year.

SIR:—I hereby give you notice, and require you to quit and deliver up to me, or my assigns, on the day of next, the possession of the messuage or dwelling-house (or rooms and apartments, or farm, lands and premises), with the appurtenances, which you now hold, or claim to hold, of me, situate in the (city, town or county) of .

Dated this day of , in the year of our Lord .

Yours, &c. ——— ———

To ——— ———

Notice by a tenant from year to year of his intention to quit.

SIR:—I hereby give you notice of my intention to quit, and that I shall, on the day of next, quit and deliver up the possession of the messuage, &c. (as above), which I now occupy, or which you may insist I hold of you, situate in the (city, town or county) of .

Dated this day of , in the year of our Lord .

Yours, &c. ——— ———

To ——— ———

Notice to tenant to quit by an agent for landlord.

SIR:—I do hereby, as the agent for and on behalf of your landlord, A B of , give you notice, and require you to quit and deliver up, on the day of next, the possession of the messuage, &c. (as above), which you now hold, or claim to hold, of the said A B, situate in the (city, town or county) of .

Dated this day of , in the year of our Lord .

Yours, &c. E F,

To ——— ——— *Agent for the said A B.*

Note.—Tenancy from year to year, without an express agreement to the contrary, terminates, by act of the assembly of Virginia, at the expiration of any current year: provided a notice to that effect shall have been given by either the landlord or tenant to the other, in writing. In cases of lands, lots or tenements being in city, borough, or incorporate town, at least *three* months before the end of the year, or where tenancy is in the country, *six* months before the end of the year; notice to be deemed duly given, on the part of the landlord, if proven to have been served upon any one interested in the lease as tenant, and upon the leased premises; and on the part of tenant, if served upon the owner of the rented premises, or his agent. Notice by one party sufficient. No notice required where there is a definite lease. See title "Affidavits," p. 2, ante.

Notice by one partner to another, of intention to dissolve the copartnership, pursuant to a power in articles for that purpose.

SIR:—I hereby require you to take notice, that it is my intention to retire from and determine the copartnership now subsisting between us, on the day of next, in pursuance of the power contained in the deed or articles, bearing date the day of , in the year , enabling me, as therein mentioned, to determine the said copartnership. And I hereby require that you will, on such dissolution of said copartnership, execute to me such bond of indemnity as in the said articles is mentioned, against the debts of the said copartnership, a draft of which bond will in due time be previously submitted to you for your approbation, I being ready to execute any such assignment or assurance as shall be requisite or proper, on my part, concerning the premises.

Dated, &c. ——— ———.

Notice from partner to partner, of intention to dissolve copartnership, where the partnership was for a limited time.

SIR:—I do hereby give you notice, that it is my intention to determine the copartnership subsisting between us in the trade or business of , on the day of next; and I do hereby require you, on or before that day, to render a just and true account, in writing, of all the moneys had and received by you for or on account of the said copartnership, and of all transactions relating thereto, I being on my part ready and willing to render and make such account or accounts, or any others that shall be requisite or proper concerning the premises; and I do hereby give notice in the mean time not to draw, accept or negotiate, or make or cause to be made or executed any bill of exchange or promissory note, or other security, for or on account of, or in the name of the said copartnership, or otherwise relating thereto, by means of which I might become liable to make any payment whatsoever.

Dated, &c. ——— ———

Notice of dissolution of partnership, and that one of the partners will continue the business.

Notice is hereby given, that the partnership heretofore carried on by and , under the name and style of , in , has this day been dissolved by mutual consent, and in future the business will be carried on by the said , on his separate account, who will pay and receive all debts due and owing to and from the said partnership in the regular course of business.

[Signed by parties.]

Notice of dissolution of partnership, and who to pay, requesting accounts to be sent in.

Notice is hereby given, that the partnership lately subsisting between and , heretofore carrying on trade under the firm of and , was, on the day of last, dissolved by mutual consent; all debts due and owing to the said partnership are to be received by the said , and all persons to whom the said partnership stands indebted are requested immediately to send in their respective accounts to said , in order that the same may be examined and paid.

[Signed by parties.]

Notice of dissolution of partnership as to one of the partners, and of new firm.

Notice is hereby given, that the partnership between and , transacting business under the name and style of , was dissolved on the day of last, so far as it relates to the said , and that all debts due to the said late partnership are to be paid, and those due from the same, discharged at their house in , where the business will in future be continued by the said and , and by , under the firm and style of .

Dated this day of .

[Signed by parties.]

Notice to tenants of a conveyance to a purchaser.

SIR:—I hereby give you notice, that by conveyance duly executed and dated, Mr. A. B of , your late landlord, and all other necessary parties, duly sold and conveyed all the estate and interest in the messuage, farm and lands, situate at, &c., and which you hold or claim to hold as tenant thereof, and that the right to such estate and premises is now vested in me, and that you must pay to me all rents accruing due since the day of , in the year , and observe and perform with me all covenants, and agreements, and terms upon which you hold or claim to hold the said premises.

Yours, &c. ——— ———

To ——— ———

XXI.

PARTNERSHIPS.

Form of limited partnership.

Certificate of limited partnership, with affidavit and acknowledgment.

This is to certify to all to whom these presents shall come, that we, whose names are hereto subscribed, to wit: A B of , C D of , E F of , &c., have entered into a limited partnership for the purpose of transacting and carrying on business in the [here describe the character of the projected business] within the State of Virginia, under and by virtue of the provisions of the 145th chapter of the Code of Virginia, upon the terms, conditions and liabilities hereinafter set forth, to wit:

1st. The said partnership is to be conducted under the firm of A B and C D.

2d. The general nature of the business intended to be transacted by the said partnership is [here describe the projected business].

3d. The place (or places) of said business is (or are) as follows [here specify the place or places]:

4th. The general partners are A B, residing in , C D, residing in ; and the special partners are E F, residing in, &c.

5th. Each of the special partners has contributed to the common stock of the said firm, the amount now herein set forth, to wit: E F has contributed the amount of dollars, &c.

6th. The said partnership is to commence immediately at and

after the making and signing of this certificate, and is to terminate on the day of , in the year .

Witness our hands and seals this day of .

A B. [Seal.]
C D. [Seal.]
E F. [Seal.]
G H. [Seal.]

County (or Corporation of), to wit:

I, , a justice of the peace (or notary public) for the county (or corporation) aforesaid, in the State of , do hereby certify, that the above named A B, one of the *general* partners of the firm of , referred to in the preceding certificate, personally appeared before me, in my county (or corporation) aforesaid, and made oath that the several sums of money specified therein to have been contributed by each of the *special* partners therein named, to the common stock, to wit: The sum of dollars by E F, &c., have been so contributed, and that said sums have been actually paid in cash.

Given under my hand and seal this day of , in the year . ——— ——— [Seal.]

County (or Corporation), to wit:

I, , a notary public (or justice of the peace) for the county aforesaid, in the State of Virginia, do hereby certify, that A B, C D, E F and G H, whose names are signed to the writing hereto annexed, bearing date on the day of , have acknowledged the same before me, in my county (or corporation) aforesaid.

Given under my hand this day of , in the year .

Articles of copartnership between two tradesmen.

Articles of agreement, had, made, concluded and agreed upon, this day of , in the year , between A B of , of the one part, and P M of , of the other part: Whereas, first, the said A B and P M have agreed, and by these presents do agree to become copartners together in the art or trade of , and all things thereto belonging, and also in buying, selling, vending and retailing all sorts of wares, goods and commodities belonging to the said trade of ; which said copartnership, it is agreed, shall continue from , for and during, and until the full end and term of years, thence next ensuing, and fully to be complete and ended. And to that end and purpose, he, the said A B, hath, on the day of the date of these presents, delivered in as stock the sum of , and the said P M, the sum of , to be used, laid out and employed in common between them, the said parties, and the said copartners, each for himself respectively, and for his own particular part, and for his respective executor and administrator, doth covenant, promise and agree with the other of them, his respective executor and administrator, by these presents, in manner and form following (that is to say): That they, the said copartners, shall not, nor will at any time hereafter, use, exercise or follow the trade of , aforesaid, or any other trade whatsoever, during the said term, to their private benefit or advantage; but shall and will, from time to time, and at all times during the said term (if they shall so long live), do their and each of their best and utmost endeavors, in and by all means possible, to the utmost of their skill and power, for their joint interest, profit, benefit and advantage; and truly employ, buy, sell and merchandise with the stock aforesaid, and the increase thereof, in the trade of aforesaid, without any sinister intention or fraudulent endeavors whatsoever; and also, that they, the said copartners, shall and will, from time to time, and at all times hereafter, during the said term, pay, bear and discharge equally between them the rent of the shop which they, the said partners, shall rent or hire for the joint exercising or managing the trade aforesaid. And that all such gain, profit and increase that shall come, grow or arise, for or by reason of the said trade or joint business as aforesaid, shall be, from time to time during the said term, equally and proportionably divided between them, the said copartners, share and share alike. And also, that all such losses as shall happen in the said joint trade, by bad debts, ill commodities, or otherwise, without fraud or covin, all wages, charges, expenses, purchases and payments whatsoever, relative to and in the said joint trade, shall be paid and borne equally and proportionably between them. And further, that neither of the said parties hereto shall take any apprentice into the said joint trade without their mutual consent; and that neither of the said parties shall or will sign or execute, or deliver any bond, judgment, or warrant of attorney to enter up judgment, nor give, sign, endorse, draw or accept any bill of exchange or promissory note whatsoever, whereby the said joint trade can be affected in any manner howsoever, or without the consent of the other of the said parties being first obtained, or the same being duly entered, in case of absence of the other of said parties, into the proper book or books of the transactions of the said copartnership; or use or employ the firm of the said copartnership in any transactions of notes or bills for accommodation, in any manner howsoever, or become bail in any court of law or judicature whatsoever, for any person or persons whomsoever. And further, it is agreed by and between the said copartners, that there shall be had and kept, from time to time, and at all times during the said term, and joint business and copartnership together as aforesaid, perfect, just and true books of accounts, wherein each of the said copartners shall duly enter and set down, as well all money by him received, paid, expended and laid out, in and about the management of the said trade, as also, all wares, goods, commodities and merchandise, by them, or either of them, bought and sold, by reason or means, or upon account of the said copartnership, and all other matters and things whatsoever to the said joint trade, and the management thereof, in any wise belonging or appertaining; which said books shall be used in common between the said copartners, so that either of them may have free access thereto, without any interruption by the other. And also, that they, the said copartners, upon the reasonable request of one of them, shall make, yield and render, each to the other, or to the executors or administrators of each other, a true, just and perfect account of all profits and increase by them, or either of them made, and of all losses by them, or either of them sustained, and also, of all payments, receipts, disbursements, and all other things whatsoever, by them made, received, disbursed, acted, done or suffered in the said copartnership and joint business as aforesaid, and the same account so made, shall and will clear, adjust, pay and deliver, each unto the other, at the time of making said account, their equal shares of the profits so made, as aforesaid. And at the end of the said term of   , or other sooner determination of these presents (be it by the death of one of the said copartners, or otherwise), they, the said copartners, each to the other, or in case of the death of either of them, the surviving party, to the executors or administrators of the party deceased, shall and will make a true, just and final account of all things as aforesaid, and divide the profits as aforesaid, and in all things well and truly adjust the same; and that, also, upon the making of such final accounts, all and every the stock and stocks, as well as the gains and increase thereof, which shall appear to be remaining, whether consisting of money, wares, debts, &c., shall be equally parted and divided between them, the said copartners, their executors or administrators, share and share alike.

In witness, &c.

A B. [Seal.]
P M. [Seal.]

Dissolution of partnership.

This indenture, made this day of , in the year , between A G of , of the one part, and S R of , of the other part: Whereas it was covenanted and agreed that the said A G and S R should become copartners and joint traders together in the said art and trade of , for the term of fourteen years from the day of , now next ensuing, upon a joint and equal capital to be made up between, upon and subject to the terms and conditions in the said indenture particularly mentioned, as in and by the said indenture may be seen by reference being had thereto: and whereas the said A G and S R have mutually consented and agreed to dissolve the said copartnership on the day of , next ensuing the date of these presents: and whereas all accounts relative to the receipts and disbursements on account of the said joint trade, and of all sums of money advanced and paid by the said parties, have been settled and adjusted up to the day of the date hereof: and whereas the said joint stock in trade hath been valued and appraised at the sum of dollars: and whereas it also appears that there are due and owing to the said copartnership, funds from sundry persons (the sum of dollars), and that the said copartnership stands indebted to sundry persons in the sum of dollars: Now, this indenture witnesseth, that the said A G and S R, in pursuance and performance of the said agreement, for themselves, their executors and administrators, have covenanted and agreed, and by these presents do covenant and agree to and with each other, their executors and administrators, that the said copartnership trade, and all dealings and transactions relative thereto, shall, from the said day of , next ensuing the date of these presents, cease and determine; and that the said indenture of copartnership, and every covenant, article, clause and agreement therein contained, as to the residue of the said term, shall from thenceforth cease and determine, and be absolutely void. And it is further covenanted and agreed, that the said S R shall collect, receive and get in all debts due and owing to the said partnership, and shall and will, from time to time, as such debts shall be received and got in, pay and apply the same towards the discharge of all demands on the said copartnership, and after such payment, shall and will, out of the surplus thereof, pay to the said A G, his executors or administrators, the share or interest of the said A G therein and thereto, as the same shall be made to appear by the accounts of the said copartnership. And for the better enabling the said S R to collect, receive and get in the debts due and owing to the said copartnership, the said A G doth hereby authorize and empower the said S R to ask, demand, sue for, levy, recover and receive the same, and to take all lawful ways and means to compel the payment thereof. And finally, the said parties hereto do mutually covenant and promise, the one unto the other of them, to sign and cause to be inserted in the , printed and published in , and in such other public newspapers as shall be deemed expedient, and as either of them shall require, due notice of the said dissolution of their said copartnership, and such other notification thereof, by letters or otherwise as may be found necessary.

In witness whereof, the said parties have hereunto set their hands and affixed their seals on the day and year first herein written as the date hereof.

A G. [Seal.]
S R. [Seal.]

XXII.

RECEIPTS.

Receipt for rent paid.

Received this day, the sum of dollars from B C, it being the first quarter's rent of the house situated in , due and ending this day, and by me rented to the said B C, as by an agreement bearing date day of , in the year .

Dated day of , in the year .

Receipt for interest on bond.

Received this day, from A B the sum of dollars, it being one-half year's interest on the sum of dollars, due to me from H R, on the day of , in the year , by his bond bearing date the day of , in the year .

Dated day of , in the year .

Receipt to an executor for a legacy.

Received, on the day of , in the year , from S T, the executor of the last will and testament of B T, deceased, the sum of dollars, it being the amount bequeathed to me as a legacy by the said B T, according to his last will and testament.

Dated the day of , in the year .

Receipt to an administrator for the payment of a debt of intestate.

Received this day, from C B, administrator of the goods and chattels, rights and effects of A H, deceased, the sum of dollars, in full of all demands against the estate of the said A H, for goods, &c., sold and delivered by me to the said A H, in his lifetime, and by him unpaid for.

Dated day of , in the year .

Receipt of an annuity.

Received this day of , in the year , from S H, the sum of dollars, it being the amount of an annuity, to be paid me by the said S H, out of the estate of B N, deceased, according to the provisions of his the said B N's last will and testament.

Dated day of , in the year .

——— ———

Receipt for award money.

Received this day of , in the year , the sum of dollars, it being the amount directed to be paid to me by C D, by an award made by and , arbitrators, indifferently chosen, and bearing date the day of , in the year , in full satisfaction of all claims and demands which I have against the said C D. ——— ———

XXIII.

RECORD OF WRITINGS IN THE SEVERAL STATES.

ACKNOWLEDGMENTS.

The forms of acknowledgment of deeds, &c., differ so widely, that it will be necessary to give forms for each State separately:

For Arkansas.

Acknowledgment of deed, for Arkansas.

State of Virginia—Henrico County, to wit:

Be it remembered, that on the day of , 18 , at the county aforesaid, before me [here give the name and style of the office], personally appeared Richard B, grantor in above deed, to me personally well known, and acknowledged that he voluntarily executed and delivered the foregoing deed, for the uses, purposes, and consideration therein expressed, and desired the same to be certified.

Given under my hand *and seal of office*,[1] on the day and date above named. A B. [Seal of office.]
[Describe his official character.]

Acknowledgment of deed by husband and wife, for Arkansas.

State of Virginia—Henrico County, to wit:

Be it remembered, that on the day of , 18 , [as last form to the word *certified*, inclusive, then add]: And on the same day, and at the same place, also came personally before me, Mary B, the wife of Richard B, and of full age, and to me personally well known, who being there by me examined in the absence of her said husband, and the contents of the foregoing deed being by me fully explained to her, she declared that she had of her free will executed the same, for the uses and purposes therein expressed, without compulsion or undue influence of her said husband, and desired the same to be certified.

Given under my hand *and seal of office*,[1] on the day and date above named. A B. [Seal of office.]
[Describe his official character.]

Before whom made. Before any court of the United States, or of any State or Territory having a seal, or the clerk of such court, or the mayor of any city or town having a seal of office, or the chief officer of any city or town having a seal of office. Also before any commissioner of deeds for Arkansas.

Witnesses. Two witnesses should subscribe the deed. And it seems that this form is not dispensed with by the acknowledgment of the parties before the officer.

For Alabama.

Acknowledgment of deed, for Alabama.

State of Virginia—County of Henrico:

I [here give the name and style of the officer], hereby certify that Richard B, whose name is signed to the foregoing convey-

[1] When the officer has one; if he have no such seal, then under his "official signature," and the words in *italics* will be omitted.

ance, and who is known to me, acknowledged before me, on this day, that being informed of the contents of the conveyance, he executed the same voluntarily, on the day the same bears date.

Given under my hand this day of , A. D. 18 .

A. B.

Acknowledgment of deed by husband and wife, for Alabama.

State of Virginia—County of Henrico:

I [here give the name and style of the officer], hereby certify that Richard B, and Jane B, his wife, whose names are signed to the foregoing conveyance, and who are known to me, acknowledged before me on this day, that being informed of the contents of the conveyance, they executed the same voluntarily, on the day the same bears date.

Given under my hand this day of , A. D. 18 .

A B.

Before whom made. These acknowledgments may be made before a judge or clerk of any federal court, a judge of any court of record in any State, a notary public, or a commissioner appointed by the Governor of Alabama. Mr. *Thornton*, in his work on Conveyancing, recommends that the certificate of the clerk of the court be added to the judge's certificate of acknowledgment had before him.

Witnesses. By Code of 1852, § 1266, " conveyances for the alienation of lands must be written or printed, on parchment or paper, and must be signed at their foot by the contracting party, or his agent having a written authority; or if he is not able to sign his name, then his name must be written for him, with the words 'his mark,' written against the same, or over it; the execution of such instrument must be attested by one, or where the party cannot write, by two witnesses who are able to write their names, as witnesses."

For California.

Acknowledgment of deed, for California.

State of Virginia—County of Henrico, ss:

On this day of , A. D. 18 , personally appeared before me [here describe the name and style of the officer], Richard

B, personally known to me to be the person described in, and who executed the foregoing instrument,[1] who acknowledged to me that he executed the same freely and voluntarily, and for the uses and purposes therein mentioned.

In testimony whereof, I have hereunto set my hand and affixed my seal of office (or the seal of said court), this day and date above written.

[Seal of court or of commissioner.] A B, Commissioner (or judge or clerk).

Acknowledgment of deed by husband and wife, for California.

State of Virginia—County of Henrico, ss:

On this day of , A. D. 18 , personally appeared before me [here describe the name and style of the officer], Richard B, and Mary his wife, personally known to me to be the persons described in, and who executed the foregoing instrument,[2] and the said Richard B then and there acknowledged to me that he executed the same freely and voluntarily, and for the uses and purposes therein mentioned; and the said Mary B, being made acquainted by me with the contents of said conveyance, did, on an examination apart from, and without the hearing of her husband, acknowledge to me that she executed the same freely and voluntarily, without fear or compulsion, or undue influence of her husband, and that she does not wish to retract the execution of the same.

In testimony whereof, I have hereunto set my hand and affixed my seal of office (or the seal of said court), this day and date above written.

[Seal of commissioner or of court.] A B, Commissioner (or judge or clerk).

Before whom made. Before some judge or clerk of any court of the United States, or of any State or territory having a seal, or

[1] Or "satisfactorily proved to me to be the person described in, and who executed the foregoing instrument, by the oath of John M, a competent and credible witness for the purpose, and the said Richard B."

[2] Or "satisfactorily proved to me to be the persons described in, and who executed the foregoing instrument, by the oath of John M, a competent and credible witness for the purpose."

before any commissioner of deeds appointed by the Governor of California.

FOR CONNECTICUT.

Acknowledgment of deeds, for Connecticut.

State of Virginia—County of , ss:

Personally appeared Richard B, signer and sealer of the foregoing instrument, and acknowledged the same to be his free act and deed, before me [here set forth the name and style of the officer], this day of , 18 . M R, Judge (or as the case may be).

Acknowledgment of deed by husband and wife, for Connecticut.

State of Virginia—County of , ss:

Personally appeared Richard B, and Mary B, his wife, signers and sealers of the foregoing instrument, and acknowledged the same to be their free act and deed, before me [here describe the name and style of the officer], this day of , 18 .

M R, Judge
(or as the case may be).

Before whom made. Before "a justice of the peace, a notary public, or before a judge of the supreme or district court of the United States, or of the supreme or superior court, or of the court of common pleas, or county court of any State, or before a commissioner or other officer having power to take acknowledgments of deeds."

Witnesses. Deeds should be attested by two witnesses.

FOR DELAWARE.

Acknowledgment of deed by husband, and privy examination of wife, for Delaware.

The State of Virginia—Henrico County, sct:

[*Seal of court.*] Be it remembered, that on the day of , in the year of our Lord one thousand eight hundred and , personally came before me the subscriber, N O, judge of the court of (being a court of record), Richard B, and Lucy B, his wife, parties to this *indenture* (or if by a deed poll, say *instrument*), known to me personally (or proved on the oath of) to be such, and severally acknowledged *said indenture to be their act and deed* (or *said instrument to be their act;* if under seal, add, *and deed*), respectively, and that the said , being at the same time privately examined by me, apart from her husband, acknowledged that she executed the said *indenture* (or *instrument*), without compulsion or threats, or fear of her husband's displeasure.

In testimony whereof, I have hereunto set my hand and affixed the seal of my said court, on the day and year last aforementioned. N O, Judge.

When taken by a judge, the seal of the court may be affixed to a certificate of attestation by the clerk, or keeper of the seal. In that case, in his certificate the judge will omit the seal, and the clerk or keeper of the seal will certify under seal that he is a judge, &c. When the clerk certifies, the following is the form of his certificate:

Clerk's certificate to attestation of judge.

State of Virginia—Henrico County, to wit:

[*Seal of court.*] I, Robert E, clerk of the court of , in the said State (which is a court of record), do hereby certify that N O, before whom the foregoing acknowledgment was made, is judge of the aforesaid court, duly commissioned and qualified, and that the foregoing signature, purporting to be his, is genuine.

In testimony whereof, I have hereunto set my hand, and affixed the seal of said court, the day of , in the year of our Lord . ROBERT E, Clerk.

A certificate of a similar character may be made by any keeper of the seal of court.

Before whom taken. Before the judge of any district or circuit court of the United States, or the chancellor or any judge of a court of record of any State, territory or country, or the mayor or chief officer of any city or borough (certifying under their hands and the seal of the court, city or borough), or before a court, the clerk, &c. certifying under its seal; or before a commissioner of deeds for Delaware certifying under his hand and seal.

For Florida.

Acknowledgment of deed, for Florida, when taken by a judge.

State of Virginia—County of , to wit:

This day of , A. D. 18 , Richard B, party to a certain deed, bearing date the day of , A. D. 18 , and hereto annexed, personally appeared before me, M M, judge of the circuit court of the said county of , and within the jurisdiction of said court (there being no commissioner of deeds in the said county authorized to take acknowledgments to deeds for recordation in the State of Florida), and the said Richard B being personally known to me to be the individual described in, and who executed said deed, acknowledged that he did sign, seal and deliver the foregoing deed, as and for his own act and deed, and for the purposes expressed therein.

In witness whereof, I have hereunto set my hand this day and date above written. M M, Judge.

Clerk's Office of the Circuit Court of the
County of , in the State of Virginia:

I, James R, clerk of the circuit court of the county of , in the State of Virginia, do hereby certify, that M M, whose name is affixed to the foregoing certificate, is now, and was at the time the said certificate bears date, an acting judge of my said court, duly commissioned and qualified, and that to all his official acts as such, full faith and credit are due: and I further certify, that the foregoing signature, purporting to be the signature of said M M, judge as aforesaid, is genuine.

[*Seal of court.*] In testimony whereof, I have hereunto signed my name, and affixed the seal of the said court, this day of , A. D. 18 .

JAMES R, Clerk.

Relinquishment of dower, &c. by married woman, for Florida.

The acknowledgment of a married woman ought to be made thus: She should "acknowledge, on a separate or private examination by the officers taking her acknowledgment, apart from her husband, that she executed such deed, conveyance, or instrument under seal, freely, and without any fear or compulsion of her husband." A wife may part with her dower, by making herself a party to the conveyance, for the purpose of relinquishing the same, "or she may, by a separate relinquishment under her hand and seal, executed in the presence of two witnesses, renounce her right of dower." Such separate relinquishment must be accompanied by an acknowledgment under the hand and seal of the wife (taken and made separately and apart from her husband, before some judicial officer of the State, when it shall have been made therein), that the said relinquishment and renunciation of dower is made freely and voluntarily, and without any compulsion, constraint, apprehension, or fear of, or from, the husband of the party making said relinquishment."

Certificate of execution of deed by married woman, for Florida.

State of Virginia—County of :

Before me, the subscriber [describe the official capacity, as in certificate on page 220], personally came A B, the wife of C B, whose name is subscribed to the foregoing deed, and upon a separate and private examination, apart from her husband, acknowledged that she executed such deed freely, and without any fear or compulsion of her said husband.

In testimony whereof, &c. (conclude as in certificate on page 220).

Relinquishment of dower by married woman, for Florida, she not having united in the deed of husband.

State of Virginia—County of , sct:

Know all men by these presents, that I, Mary B, the wife of Richard B, the grantor in the annexed deed, for and in consideration of the premises therein specified (and in consideration of the sum of dollars, to me in hand paid, the receipt whereof is hereby acknowledged), have renounced, relinquished and released, and by these presents do renounce, relinquish and release, to E F, the grantee in said deed, all my dower and right of dower, in and to the property therein conveyed: To have and to hold the same unto the said E F, his heirs and assigns, forever.

In witness whereof, I have hereunto set my hand and seal this day of , A. D. 18 .

Signed and sealed in presence of G L. R K. MARY B. [Seal.]

State of Virginia—County of :

I do hereby acknowledge, that the foregoing relinquishment and renunciation of dower is made freely and voluntarily, and without any compulsion, constraint, apprehension or fear, from my husband, Richard B.

In witness whereof, I hereunto set my hand and seal this day of , A. D. 18 . MARY B. [Seal.]

State of Virginia—County of :

I, M M, judge of the circuit court of the said county of , and within the jurisdiction of said court (there being no commissioner of deeds in the said county authorized to take acknowledgments to deeds, for recordation in the State of Florida), do hereby certify, that Mary B, wife of Richard B (the said Mary B being personally known to me to be the individual described in, and who executed the foregoing relinquishment of dower), and the said Mary B being examined by me separately and apart from her husband, did acknowledge that the above relinquishment and renunciation of dower was made by her freely and voluntarily, and without any compulsion, constraint, apprehension, or fear of or from her husband, and did in my presence sign and seal the foregoing acknowledgment, in evidence of the same.

In testimony whereof, &c. (conclude as in certificate on page 220, and annex certificate of clerk, as there found).

Sometimes the relinquishment is made before the clerk of a court. In that event, the following certificates ought to be used:

Certificate of relinquishment of dower, for Florida, when made before a clerk of a court.

State of Virginia—County of :

Be it remembered, that on the day of , A. D. , at the county aforesaid, before me the subscriber, clerk of [here describe the court], which said court is a court of record, and in the presence of , judge (or justice) of said court, came Mary B, the wife of Richard B, grantor in the foregoing deed of conveyance, the said Mary B being personally known to me to be the individual described in, and who executed the foregoing relinquish-

ment of dower, and the said Mary B being examined by me separately and apart from her husband, did acknowledge, &c. (as in last form).
J R, Clerk.

State of Virginia—County of :

I, , judge (or justice) of the court of the said county, do hereby certify, that the foregoing acknowledgment was made in my presence, and that J R, who subscribed the foregoing certificate, was, at the time of signing the same, the clerk of said court.

Given under my hand this day of , A. D. .

——— ———, Judge (or justice).

Before whom acknowledgment or relinquishment of dower made. Before a commissioner of deeds for Florida, and in cities and counties where no commissioner has been appointed, before the chief justice, judge, presiding justice, or president of any court of record of the United States, or of any State or territory thereof, having a seal, and a clerk or prothonotary. The acknowledgment, &c. to be made *within* the respective jurisdictions of such judges, &c.

For Illinois.

Form of acknowledgment of husband and wife, for Illinois.

State of Virginia—Henrico County, ss:

This day personally appeared before the undersigned, a notary public for the county of Henrico, in the State of Virginia, A B, and Jane B his wife, who are personally known to me to be the persons whose names are subscribed to the foregoing deed (or other instrument of writing, as the case may be), as having executed the same, and acknowledged that they had executed the same for the uses and purposes therein expressed; and the said Jane B, wife of the said A B, being of lawful age, and having been by me, separately and apart from her husband, examined, and the full contents of said deed (or other instrument of writing) made known and explained to her, acknowledged that she had executed the same, and relinquished her dower to the lands and tenements therein mentioned, voluntarily, freely, and without compulsion of her said husband.

Witness my hand and seal, at the county aforesaid, this day of , A. D. .

E F, Notary Public. [Seal.]

Before whom acknowledgment, &c. made. Without the limits of Illinois, and within the United States, before a judge of the supreme or district court of the United States, a commissioner of deeds for Illinois, a judge or justice of the supreme, superior or circuit court of any of the United States or their territories, or the district of Columbia, a clerk of a court of record, a mayor of a city, a notary public, or a justice of the peace.

For Indiana.

Form of acknowledgment of husband and wife, for Indiana, when wife is over 21 years of age.

State of Virginia—County of Henrico, ss:

Before me, J M, a notary public for the county of Henrico, in the State of Virginia, this day of , 18 , A B, and Jane B, his wife, acknowledged the execution of the annexed deed (or mortgage, or as the case may be).

J M, Notary Public. [Seal.]

Form of acknowledgment of husband and wife to deed for husband's land, for Indiana, when wife is between the ages of 18 and 21 years, with declaration of mother or of father, as required by Indiana statute.

State of Virginia—County of Henrico, ss:

Before me, J M, a notary public for the county of Henrico, in the State of Virginia, this day of , 18 , A B, and Jane B, his wife, the said Jane being over the age of eighteen years and under twenty-one years of age, acknowledged the execution of the annexed deed, and R O, the father (or the mother) of the said Jane B, this day declared before me the said notary, that he (or she) believes that the said annexed deed is for the benefit of the said Jane B, and that it would be prejudicial to the said Jane, and her husband, the said A B, if they were prevented from thus disposing of the lands thus conveyed.

J M, Notary Public. [Seal.]

Annex endorsement of father or mother, as follows:

State of Virginia—County of Henrico, ss:

I, R O, the father (or mother) of the within named Jane B, do declare before J M, the notary public who took the acknowledgment of the said Jane B to the annexed deed, that I believe such conveyance is for the benefit of the said Jane B (who is over the age of eighteen years and under the age of twenty-one years), and that it would be prejudicial to her, and her husband, the within named A B, if they were prevented from disposing of the lands thus conveyed. R O.

Signed in our presence: A R. M P.

Sworn to before me, this day of , 18 .

R M, Notary Public.

Before whom acknowledgments, &c. made. Before any judge, clerk of a court of record, justice of the peace, recorder, notary public, or mayor of a city in any State of the Union, or before a commissioner of deeds for Indiana.

For Iowa.

Form of acknowledgment of husband and wife, for Iowa.

State of Virginia—County of Henrico, sct:

Be it remembered, that on this day of , personally appeared before me, R M, a notary public for the county and State aforesaid, duly commissioned and qualified, A B, and Jane B, his wife, to me personally known (or proved by the oath of C D, a credible witness) to be the identical persons whose names are affixed to the within conveyance, and acknowledged that the within conveyance is their voluntary act and deed.

In testimony whereof, I have hereto set my hand and affixed my notarial seal, on the day and date above written.

[Seal of notary.] R M, Notary Public.

Before whom acknowledgment, &c. made. Without the State of Iowa, before some court of record, or clerk or officer holding the seal thereof, or before some commissioner of deeds for Iowa, or before some notary public.

FOR KENTUCKY.

Form of acknowledgment by husband and wife, for Kentucky.

Commonwealth of Virginia—County of Henrico, sct:

I, W F, clerk of the county court of Henrico county, in the State of Virginia, do certify, that this instrument of writing from A B, and Jane B, his wife, was this day produced to me by the parties, and the said instrument of writing was acknowledged by the said A B to be his act and deed, and the contents and effect of the instrument being explained to the said Jane B by me, separately and apart from her husband, she thereupon declared that she did freely and voluntarily execute and deliver the same, to be her act and deed, and consented that the same might be recorded.

Given under my hand and seal of office, at the clerk's office of the said court, on this day of , 18 .

[Seal of office.] W F, Clerk.

Form of acknowledgment by husband alone.

Commonwealth of Virginia—County of Henrico, sct:

Be it remembered, that on this day of , A. D. 18 , before me, W F, the clerk of the county court of Henrico county, in the State of Virginia, at my office, in the said county and State, personally came A B, to me known to be the person described in, and who executed the foregoing conveyance, and acknowledged that he executed the same.

Witness my hand and seal of office, at the office of the said court, on this day of , 18 .

[Seal of office.] W F, Clerk.

Before whom acknowledgment made. Deeds may be executed, *out of Kentucky*, before a clerk of a court, certifying under his seal of office, or under seal of office before a mayor of a city or the secretary of state, or commissioner of deeds for Kentucky, or before a judge, *under the seal of his court.*

FOR LOUISIANA.

In this State, the civil law prevails. The mode of conveyance is by an "Authentic act" passed before the proper officer. Beyond the limits of Louisiana, the act should be passed before one of the commissioners for Louisiana, appointed in the several States. See pp. 141, 142, 143, ante.

For Maine.

Form of acknowledgment, for Maine.

State of Virginia—County of Henrico, sct:

December 19th, 1865. Personally appeared A B, and acknowledged the foregoing instrument, by him signed and sealed, to be his free act and deed, before me.

[Seal of office.] R D W, Notary Public.

Form of acknowledgment by husband and wife, when property in the wife's right[1] *is conveyed.*

State of Virginia—County of Henrico, sct:

December 19th, 1865. Personally appeared A B, and Jane B his wife, and acknowledged the foregoing instrument, by them signed and sealed, to be their free act and deed, before me.

[Seal.] R D W, Notary Public.

Before whom acknowledgment made. Before a justice of the peace of any State, justice of a court of record, a notary public, or a commissioner of deeds for Maine.

For Maryland.

Form of acknowledgment by husband and wife, for Maryland.

State of Virginia—County of , ss:

Be it remembered, that on this day of January, in the year 18 , before me the undersigned, G L, a commissioner, resident in the county aforesaid, duly commissioned and qualified by the

[1] To convey a wife's right of dower, no acknowledgment is necessary. Instead of that, the attesting clause of the deed runs as follows, and this answers for the acknowledgment:

"In witness whereof, I, the said A B (the husband), and I, the said Jane, wife of the said A B, in consideration of one dollar to me paid by the said R N, in token of a full relinquishment of all my right to dower in the premises, have hereunto set our hands and seals this day of , in the year of our Lord one thousand eight hundred and ."

Executive authority, and under the laws of the State of Maryland, to take the acknowledgment of deeds, &c., to be used or recorded therein, personally appeared A B, and Jane B his wife, they being known to me (or they being satisfactorily proven by oral testimony, under oath, received by me) to be the persons who are named and described as and professing to be the parties to the foregoing deed (or indenture), and do severally acknowledge the said instrument of writing (or indenture) to be their respective act and deed; the said Jane B having signed and sealed said instrument of writing (or indenture) before me, out of the presence and hearing of her said husband; and the said Jane B being by me examined, out of the presence and hearing of her said husband, "whether she doth execute and acknowledge the same, freely and voluntarily, and without being induced to do so by fear, or threats of or ill usage by her husband, or by fear of his displeasure," declareth and saith, that she doth.

In witness whereof, I have hereunto set my hand and affixed my

[Seal.] official seal, the day and year aforesaid.

G L, Commissioner.

Before whom acknowledgments made. Before a commissioner of deeds for Maryland, or judge of the United States court, or judge of a court of record.

For Massachusetts.

Form of acknowledgment of husband and wife,[1] *for Massachusetts.*

State of Virginia—County of Henrico, ss:

December 19th, 1865. Then personally appeared the above mentioned A B, and Jane B his wife, and acknowledged the foregoing instrument to be their free act and deed, before me.

R D W, Notary Public.

[1] It is not necessary for the wife to acknowledge the deed to part *with her right of dower*. When the husband conveys his estate, the usual form of the clause in the deed releasing dower on the part of the wife, is as follows: "In witness whereof, I the said A B (the husband), and I the said Jane B, my wife, in token of her relinquishment of dower in the premises, have hereunto set our hands and seals this day of ," &c. This is instead of the acknowledgment of the deed by the wife.

Before whom acknowledgment made. Before any justice of the peace, magistrate or notary public within the United States, or before any commissioner of deeds for Massachusetts.

FOR MICHIGAN.

Form of acknowledgment by husband and wife, for Michigan.

Deeds for Michigan, when executed in any other State, ought to be acknowledged according to the laws of the State in which the acknowledgment, &c. are taken, and there should be a certificate under seal, by a clerk of a court of record, that the person taking the acknowledgment is an officer, and that the deed is properly executed. When a commissioner of deeds for Michigan certifies the acknowledgment, &c. under his seal, the seal of the clerk is unnecessary.

In deeds executed in Virginia, for lands lying in Michigan, follow the forms of acknowledgment, &c. for Virginia, and then add:

Clerk's Office of the Court of the ,
State of Virginia, sct:

I, W F T, clerk of the said court, being a court of record, do hereby certify, that J M, who hath given the preceding certificates of acknowledgment by A B, and of relinquishment by Jane B, annexed to the deed from said A B, and Jane his wife, to , dated the day of , was, at the time of giving said certificates, and taking such acknowledgment and relinquishment, a notary public (or other officer, as the case may be,) in and for the said , and authorized under the laws of Virginia to take acknowledgments and relinquishments as aforesaid, and that the said deed is properly executed, in conformity with the laws of Virginia.

Witness my hand and seal of the said court, on this day
[Seal of court.] of , 18 . W F T, Clerk.

When a commissioner of deeds takes an acknowledgment, &c., his certificate is as follows:

Form of acknowledgment by husband and wife, taken by a commissioner of deeds for Michigan.

State of Virginia—County of , ss:

On this day of , one thousand eight hundred and sixty , personally came the abovenamed A B, and Jane B his wife, known to me to be the persons who executed the foregoing instrument, and acknowledged the same to be their free act and deed. And the said Jane B, wife of the said A B, being by me privately examined, separate and apart from her husband, acknowledged that she executed the same freely, and without any fear or compulsion from any one.

Witness my hand and seal of office.

[Seal of office.] R D, Comm'r of deeds
For Michigan.

For Minesota.

Form of acknowledgment, &c. by husband and wife, for Minesota.

State of Virginia—County of , ss:

Be it known, that on the day of , A. D. 18 , before the undersigned, personally came A B, and Jane B his wife, the grantors to the foregoing and within deed from them as such grantors to M N, to me known to be the identical persons described, and who executed the said deed, and they acknowledged that they executed the said deed freely and voluntarily, for the uses and purposes therein expressed. And the said Jane B, wife of the said A B, in a private examination by me made, apart from her said husband, acknowledged that she executed the said deed freely, and without any fear or compulsion from her said husband.

In testimony whereof, I hereunto subscribe my name on the day and year aforesaid. R M, Comm'r of deeds
For Minesota.

Before whom acknowledgment, &c. made. When the grantor lives out of Minesota, the deed may be executed according to the laws of the State, &c. where the deed is executed, and the execution acknowledged before any judge of a court of record, notary public, justice of the peace, or other officer authorized by the laws of such State, &c. to take the acknowledgment of deeds therein, or before a commissioner of deeds for Minesota. When taken by any other officer than a commissioner of deeds, the deed should have attached thereto a certificate of a clerk of a court of record of the county or district within which such acknowledgment is taken, under the seal of his office, that the person whose name is signed to the certificate of acknowledgment, was, at the date thereof, such officer as he is represented to be, that he believes the signature of such person subscribed thereto to be genuine, and that the deed is executed and acknowledged according to the laws of such State, &c.

For Mississippi.

Acknowledgment by husband and wife, for Mississippi.

State (or Territory) of :
County (or City) of , ss:

Personally appeared before me, chief justice of the supreme court of the United States,[1] in the State (or territory) and county (or city) aforesaid, A B, and C B his wife, the grantors in the within indenture (or instrument) named, and severally acknowledged the same to be their voluntary act and deed, for the uses and purposes therein mentioned. And the said C B did, moreover, on a private examination, made of her by me, apart from her husband, acknowledge that she signed, sealed and delivered the same, as her voluntary act and deed, freely, without any fear, threats or compulsion of her said husband.

As witness my hand and seal this day of , 18 .

——— ——— [Seal.]

Before whom made. Before any one of the officers named in above form; and when made before any of them, it seems to the writer that the certificate of a clerk, under his seal of office, is not required. Also before one of the commissioners of deeds for Mississippi. Also before either of the following officers, viz: by the judge of any inferior or county court of record, or any justice of the peace of the State or territory and county where the person executing the conveyance resides. When a judge of an inferior or county court of record takes the acknowledgment, the certificate of the clerk or register of the superior or circuit court of such county, with a seal of his court thereto affixed, should be appended; when the acknowledgment is made before a justice of the peace, either the clerk or register of a superior or circuit court, or the clerk of such inferior or county court of record of such county, should append his certificate, with the seal of his office affixed.

[1] Or one of the associate justices of the supreme court of the United States; or district judge for the court of the United States; or judge of the supreme (or superior) court of ; or justice of the court of .

Form of certificate of clerk, &c.

State (or Territory) of :
County (or City) of , ss:

I, J E, clerk of the court of for the county (or city) and State (or territory) aforesaid, do hereby certify, that J T, whose name is subscribed to the foregoing certificate of acknowledgment, is and was at the time he subscribed the said certificate, a judge of the court of (or a justice of the peace, as the case may be), of the State and county aforesaid, duly commissioned, qualified and acting; that the same is his genuine signature, and full faith and credit are due to his official acts as such.

In testimony whereof, I have hereunto set my hand and affixed
[Official seal.] my seal of office, this day of , 18 .

J E, Clerk.

FOR MISSOURI.

Acknowledgment by husband and wife, for Missouri.

State of : County (or City), ss:

Be it remembered, that on the day of , in the year 18 , personally came before me, clerk of the court of , A B, the wife of James B, named in the within deed as parties thereto, and was by me examined, privily and apart from her said husband, and upon that examination, was made acquainted with the contents of said deed, and thereupon acknowledged the same to be her act and deed, and that she executed the same; and the said A B then and there declared to me that she relinquished her dower (or released and conveyed all her right and interest) in the real estate therein mentioned, freely, and without any compulsion or undue influence of her husband; the said A B being also personally known to me to be the person whose name is subscribed to the within deed (or instrument), as a party thereto (or if not known to the officer, say: proved by E F and G H, two credible witnesses, to be the person whose name is subscribed to said deed as a party thereto).

Taken and certified under the seal of said court, by me, this day
[Seal of court.] and year aforesaid.

J E, Clerk.

Before whom made. Before any court of the United States, or of any State or territory having a seal, or the clerk of any such court. Also before commissioners of deeds for Missouri.

FOR NEW HAMPSHIRE.

Acknowledgment by husband and wife, for New Hampshire.

State (or Territory) of :

County (or Town) of , ss:

On the day of , A. D. 18 , the above (or within) named Alexander B, and Caroline B his wife, personally appeared and acknowledged the above (or within) written instrument, by them subscribed, to be their voluntary act and deed, before me, a justice of the peace (or notary public) for the State (or territory) and county (or town) aforesaid.

JAMES E, *J. P.* (or *N. P.*)

Before whom made. Before a justice of the peace, notary public, or commissioner.

Witnesses. There should be two or more attesting witnesses to the deed, in addition to the certificate of acknowledgment by the officer.

FOR NEW JERSEY.

Form of acknowledgment by husband and wife, for New Jersey.

State of : County (or City), to wit:

On this day of , Anno Domini 18 , personally appeared before me, Oliver P, one of the judges of the court of , in the State and county (or city) aforesaid, Alexander B, and Caroline B his wife, and (I being satisfied that they are the grantors mentioned in the within conveyance, and having also first made known the contents thereof to each of them,) they did severally acknowledge that they signed, sealed and delivered the same, as their voluntary act and deed. And the said Caroline B, on a private examination apart from her husband, before me, acknowledged that she signed, sealed and delivered the same as her voluntary act and deed, freely, without any fear, threats, or compulsion of the husband.

Witness my hand. OLIVER P, Judge, &c.

☞ The certificate of clerk to be appended when acknowledgment is taken by a judge of a court of common pleas. See below.

Before whom made. Before the chief justice of the United States supreme court, or an associate justice of the supreme court of the United States, or district judge of the same, or any judge or justice of the supreme or superior court of any State in the Union, or territory thereof, or in the District of Columbia, or judge of any court of common pleas, or mayor or other chief magistrate of any city in any State in the Union, or territory thereof; or by a commissioner of deeds for New Jersey.

If a judge of a court of common pleas take the acknowledgment, then a certificate under the great seal of the State, or under the seal of the county court in which it is taken, that he is such judge, must be approved. The certificate may be as follows:

State of : County of , sct:

I, William F, clerk of the county court of said county and State, do hereby certify, that Oliver P, before whom the foregoing acknowledgment was made, is a judge of the court of common pleas of , as stated in his above certificate, and that to all his official acts as such, full faith and credit are due and ought to be given.

In testimony whereof, I have hereunto set my hand and affixed the seal of my said court, this day of , 18 .

[Seal of court.]

WM. F, Clerk.

For New York.

Form of acknowledgment by husband and wife, for New York.

State of : County (or City) of , to wit:

On this day of , one thousand eight hundred and sixty , before me, personally came William S, and Sarah his wife, to me known to be the individuals described in and who executed the foregoing conveyance, and acknowledged that they executed the same; and the said Sarah, on a private examination, separate and apart from her husband, acknowledged that she executed the same freely, and without any fear or compulsion of her said husband.

SAMUEL R, Judge of, &c.

Before whom taken. Before the chief justice, or one of the associate justices of the supreme court of the United States; district judges of the United States; the judges or justices of the supreme, superior or circuit court of any State or territory within the United States, and the chief judge or any associate judge of the circuit court of the United States in the District of Columbia. The acknowledgment must be taken within some place or territory to which the jurisdiction of the court to which he belongs shall extend. Before a commissioner of deeds for New York, or before any officer of the State or territory of the United States in which it is taken, authorized by the laws of such State or territory to take the proof and acknowledgment of deeds; but in this last mentioned case, there must be a certificate under the name and official seal of the clerk or register of the county in which such officer resides, specifying that such officer was at the time of taking such proof or acknowledgment, duly authorized to take the same, and that such clerk or register is well acquainted with the handwriting of such officer, and verily believes that the signature to said certificate of proof and acknowledgment is genuine.

FOR NORTH CAROLINA.

Form of acknowledgment of husband and wife, for North Carolina.

State of , day of , 18 :

Before me, James Jones, judge of the superior court of law (or other court, as the case may be,) for , in the State aforesaid, personally came Benjamin B and Caroline B, the bargainors in the foregoing deed (or power of attorney), and acknowledged the execution thereof, she the said Caroline B being first examined by me privily and apart from her husband, the said Benjamin B, touching the execution thereof, and it appearing that she hath executed the same freely and of her own accord, without fear or compulsion of the said Benjamin B her husband, and that she doth voluntarily assent thereto. Let it be recorded.

JAMES JONES, Judge, &c.

Before whom made. Before a commissioner of deeds for North Carolina; before some one of the judges of the court of supreme jurisdiction, or before some one of the judges of the superior courts of law, or circuit courts of law of superior jurisdiction within any State, territory or district. Or before two or more commissioners duly authorized to take the acknowledgment of the wife under a commission issued from some court of record in the State, territory or district in which the acknowledgment is taken. When taken before a judge, or the two commissioners before named, the certificate of the State or territory, or in the District of Columbia, the certificate of the Secretary of State of the United States, duly authenticated, must be annexed to the deed, that the judge before whom the acknowledgment was taken, was at the time of taking thereof one of the judges of the courts before mentioned, or that the court which issued such commissions was a court of record, and the person signing said commission is clerk of said court.

For Ohio.

Form of acknowledgment by husband and wife, for Ohio.[1]

State of : County of , sc:

Personally appeared before me, the undersigned, on this day of , 18 , James Jones, and Julia his wife, who acknowledged that they did sign and seal the foregoing instrument, and that the same is their free act and deed. And I do further certify, that I did examine the said Julia Jones separate and apart from her said husband, and did then and there make known to her the contents of the foregoing instrument, and upon that examination she declared that she did voluntarily sign, seal and acknowledge the same, and that she is still satisfied therewith.

ROBERT R, Notary Public.

Before whom made. Before a judge of the supreme court, or of common pleas, a justice of the peace, notary public, mayor or other presiding officer of any incorporated town or city, or before any officer of the State in which the acknowledgment is taken, authorized to take acknowledgments. In the latter case, annex to the officer's certificate of acknowledgment the certificate of the clerk of the court of the county in which it is taken, under his seal of office, certifying that the officer taking the acknowledgment is authorized to take acknowledgments of deeds in his State, and that his signature is genuine.

[1] This form may be adopted; or a form similar to that used in the State or territory in which the acknowledgment is taken. The acknowledgment must be certified on the same sheet of paper on which the deed is printed or written.

FOR PENNSYLVANIA.

Form of acknowledgment of husband and wife, for Pennsylvania.

State of : County of , sc:

Be it remembered, that on this day of , 18 , before me, James Jones, a judge (or justice) of the court of common pleas (or other court), of the State and county aforesaid, personally appeared Benjamin B, and Caroline his wife, and acknowledged the above written conveyance as and for their act and deed, and desired that the same might be recorded as such, according to law; she the said Catharine being of full age, and being by me examined separate and apart from her said husband, and the full contents of said deed being by me first made known to her, did, on such examination, declare and say, that she did voluntarily and of her own free will and accord, sign, seal, and without any coercion or compulsion of her said husband, as of her own free act and deed, deliver the said conveyance.

In testimony whereof, I have hereunto set my hand and caused the seal of my said court to be affixed, this day and year aforesaid.

JAMES JONES, Judge. [Seal of court.]

Before whom taken. Before one or more of the judges or justices of the supreme court of the United States, or before a judge of the district court of the United States, or before any one of the judges or justices of the supreme or superior court, or courts of common pleas of any State or territory in the United States, or before any one of the judges or justices of a court of probat, or court of record of any State or territory in the United States, or before a commissioner of deeds for Pennsylvania.

FOR RHODE ISLAND.

Form of acknowledgment by husband and wife, for Rhode Island.

State of : day of , 18 .
City of , to wit:

Then personally appeared the within named Benjamin B (grantor), and acknowledged the within instrument to be his voluntary act and deed, hand and seal; and at the same time personally appeared the within named Caroline B, wife of the said Benjamin

B, and being examined by me privily and apart from her said husband, and the said instrument being then shown to her by me, she the said Caroline B then and there acknowledged the same to be her free and voluntary act and deed, hand and seal, and that she did not wish to retract the same. Before me.

WILLIAM W. (Style of officer.)

Before whom taken. Before a commissioner of deeds for Rhode Island. Before any judge, justice of the peace, mayor of a city, or notary public.

For South Carolina.

Form of acknowledgment for South Carolina.

State of , County:

Personally appeared before me, James Jones, commissioner, &c., on this day of , Anno Domini 18 , Benjamin B, the grantor in the within instrument of conveyance named, and acknowledged that he did sign and seal and deliver the same, for the uses and purposes therein mentioned.

BENJAMIN B, Grantor.

Acknowledged and sealed before me, the day and year aforesaid.

JAMES JONES, [Seal.]
Commissioner of deeds for South Carolina.

Form of relinquishment by married woman, for South Carolina.

State of , County, to wit:

I, James Jones, commissioner, &c., do certify unto all whom it may concern, that Caroline B, the wife of the within named Benjamin B, did this day appear before me, and upon being privately and separately examined by me, did declare, that she does freely, voluntarily, and without any compulsion, dread or fear of any person or persons whomsoever, renounce, release, and forever relinquish unto the within named [here insert name of grantee or releasee], his heirs and assigns, all her interest and estate, and also all her right and claim of dower of, in or to all and singular the premises within mentioned and released.

CAROLINE B.

Given under my hand and seal this day of , Anno Domini 18 .

JAMES JONES. [Seal.]
Commissioner of deeds for South Carolina.

Before whom taken. Before a commissioner of deeds for South Carolina.

FOR TENNESSEE.

Form of acknowledgment of husband and wife, for Tennessee.

State of ; County (or City) of , ss:

Personally appeared before me the undersigned, a notary public for the county (or city) aforesaid, in the State aforesaid, Benjamin B, the grantor in the foregoing instrument, with whom I am personally acquainted, who acknowledged that he executed the said instrument for the purposes therein set forth and declared. And Caroline B, the wife of said Benjamin B, having also personally appeared before me, privately and apart from her said husband, acknowledged the execution of said deed to have been done by her freely, voluntarily and understandingly, without compulsion or restraint from her said husband, and for the purposes therein expressed.

Witness my hand and seal of office this day of , 18 .

JAMES JONES, Notary Public. [Seal of office.]

Before whom taken. In some court of record in some one of the United States, and certified to by the clerk under his seal of office, and attested by the presiding judge or justice of the court; before a notary public, under his seal of office; before a judge of a supreme or superior court, who shall certify the same under his hand; and the clerk must sustain his (the judge's) official character by his seal of office; before commissioners of deeds for Tennessee.

FOR TEXAS.

Form of acknowledgment, for Texas.

State of : County of , to wit:

I, James Jones, judge of the court of , in the State and county aforesaid, which is a court of record, do hereby certify, that Charles C, a party to a certain deed, bearing date on the day of , 18 , and hereto annexed, personally appeared before me, in my county aforesaid, and acknowledged the same to be his act and deed, and desired me to certify the same to the clerk of the county court of , in the State of Texas, in order that said deed may be recorded.

Given under my hand and seal this day of , 18 .

JAMES JONES, Judge. [Seal.]

☞ Add certificate of clerk. See below.

Form of acknowledgment by wife, for Texas.

State of : County of , ss:

Before me, James Jones, judge of the court of , in the State and county aforesaid, which is a court of record, personally appeared Caroline C, wife of Charles C, parties to a certain deed or writing, bearing date on the day of , and hereto annexed, and having been examined by me privily and apart from her husband, and having the same fully explained to her, she the said Caroline C acknowledged the same to be her act and deed, and declared that she had willingly signed, sealed and delivered the same, and that she wished not to retract it, to certify which, I hereto sign my name and affix my seal, this day of , A. D. 18 .

JAMES JONES, Judge. [Seal.]

☞ Add certificate of clerk. See below.

Certificate of clerk to judge's official character.

State of : County of , ss:

I, William R, clerk of the court of , in the county and State aforesaid, do certify, that James Jones, whose name is subscribed to the foregoing certificate, is, and was at the time he subscribed the same, judge of the said court, duly commissioned, qualified and acting, and that full faith and credit are due to his official acts as such.

In witness whereof, I have hereunto signed my name and affixed the seal of the said court, this day of , A. D. 18 .

[Seal of court.]

WILLIAM R, Clerk.

Before whom taken. Before a commissioner of deeds for Texas; before any judge of a court of record having a seal, in any of the States or territories of the United States.

FOR VERMONT.

Form of acknowledgment of husband and wife, for Vermont.

State of : County (or City) of , to wit:

At , in the State aforesaid, on the day of , 18 , personally appeared before me the undersigned, Benjamin B, signer and sealer of the within deed, and acknowledged that he had signed, sealed and delivered the same for the purposes therein mentioned; and at the same time also personally appeared Caroline B, the wife of the said Benjamin B, likewise a party to the within deed, who being by me examined privily and separate from her husband, acknowledged that she did, voluntarily and freely, without any fear or compulsion of her said husband, sign, seal and deliver the same for the purposes therein mentioned. Before me,

JAMES JONES, [Style of officer.]

Before whom taken. Before a commissioner of deeds for Vermont; before a justice of the peace, magistrate, or notary public within the United States.

FOR VIRGINIA.

Form of acknowledgment, for Virginia.

State of : County (or Corporation) of , to wit:

I, James Jones, a notary public for the county (or corporation) aforesaid, in the State of , do certify, that Robert H, whose name is signed to the writing above (or hereto annexed), bearing date on the day of , hath acknowledged the same before me, in my county (or corporation) aforesaid.

Given under my hand this day of , 186 .

JAMES JONES, N. P.

Form of relinquishment by married woman, for Virginia.

State of : County (or Corporation) of , to wit:

We, James Jones and Samuel Smith, notaries public for the county (or corporation) aforesaid, in the State of Virginia, do certify, that Caroline H, the wife of Robert H, whose names are signed to the writing above (or hereto annexed), bearing date on the day of , 18 , personally appeared before us in the county (or corporation) aforesaid, and being examined by us privily and apart from her said husband, and having the writing aforesaid fully explained to her, she the said Caroline H acknowledged the said writing to be her act, and declared that she had willingly executed the same, and does not wish to retract it.

Given under our hands this day of , 186 .

JAMES JONES, N. P.
SAMUEL SMITH, N. P.

Before whom taken. An acknowledgment by other than a married woman may be taken, *in the State of Virginia*, before the clerk of the court of any county or corporation, or before the court itself, or before a justice of the peace or notary public; *beyond the State of Virginia, and in the United States*, before the clerk of any court, or before a justice of the peace or notary public within the United States, or before a commissioner of deeds for Virginia; *beyond the United States*, before any minister plenipotentiary, charge d'affaires, consul general, consul, vice-consul or commercial agent appointed by the government of the United States to any foreign country (under his official seal), or of the proper officer of any court of such country, or the mayor or other chief magistrate of any city, town or corporation therein, under official seal.

Married woman. An acknowledgment or relinquishment of a married woman may be taken, *in the State of Virginia*, before the clerk of the court of any county or corporation authorized to admit the writing to record, or before the court itself, or before two justices of the peace (present at the same time), or before two notaries public (present at the same time); *beyond the State of Virginia, and in the United States*, before two justices of the peace (who shall be present together), or before two notaries public (who shall be present together), or before a commissioner of deeds for Virginia; *beyond the United States*, before any minister plenipotentiary, charge d'affaires, consul general, consul, vice-consul or commercial agent appointed by the government of the United States to any foreign country, or before any court of such country, or the mayor or other chief magistrate of any city, town or corporation therein, under the official seal of the officer taking the acknowledgment or relinquishment.

For Wisconsin.

Form of acknowledgment, for Wisconsin.

State of : County (or Corporation) of , to wit:

I, James Jones, a notary public for the county (or corporation) aforesaid, in the State of , do certify, that Robert H, whose name is signed to the writing above (or hereto annexed), bearing date on the day of , hath acknowledged the same before me, in my county (or corporation) aforesaid.

Given under my hand this day of , 186 .

JAMES JONES, N. P.

Form of relinquishment by married woman, for Wisconsin.

State of : County (or Corporation) of , to wit:

We, James Jones and Samuel Smith, notaries public for the county (or corporation) aforesaid, in the State of Wisconsin, do certify, that Caroline H, the wife of Robert H, whose names are signed to the writing above (or hereto annexed), bearing date on the day of , 18 , personally appeared before us in the county (or corporation) aforesaid, and being examined by us privily and apart from her said husband, and having the writing aforesaid fully explained to her, she the said Caroline H acknowledged the said writing to be her act, and declared that she had willingly executed the same, and does not wish to retract it.

Given under our hands this day of , 186 .

JAMES JONES, N. P.
SAMUEL SMITH, N. P.

☞ Add certificate of clerk, as on p. 244.

It will be noticed that the forms just given are the same as those given under the title *Virginia*. They have been drawn thus, in order, in Virginia, to comply with the Wisconsin statute, which declares that "all deeds and conveyances of lands, tenements and hereditaments, situate, lying and being within this territory [State], which shall hereafter be made and executed in any other territory, State or country, whereby such lands, &c. shall be conveyed, in whole or in part, or otherwise affected or encumbered in law, shall be acknowledged or proved and certified according to and in conformity with the laws and usages of the territory, State or country in which deeds or conveyances were acknowledged and proved." It is safer, when the acknowledgment is not taken by a commissioner of deeds, to append the following:

Certificate of clerk of county court.

State of : County of , sct:

I, William F, clerk of the county court of , do certify, that James Jones (or in case of relinquishment of dower, or acknowledgment by married woman, say, James Jones and Samuel Smith), who hath (or have) taken and certified the preceding acknowledgment, was (or were), at the time of taking and certifying the same, a notary public (or notaries public) for the county aforesaid, in the said State, and duly authorized by the laws of the said State to take and certify acknowledgments (or relinquishments of dower and other estate, on the part of married women) to deeds conveying lands; and that his (or their) said certificate is in due form.

In witness whereof, I have hereto set my hand and affixed the seal of said court, this day of , A. D. 18 .

[Seal of court.]

WILLIAM F, Clerk.

Before whom taken. Before a commissioner of deeds for Wisconsin; before officers authorized to take acknowledgments to deeds, for record in the State or territory in which the acknowledgment is taken.

☞ Since the forms of deeds in the several States were printed, the following form of deed, with general warranty, for Wisconsin, has been furnished the writer:

Form of deed, with general warranty, for Wisconsin.

This indenture, made the day of , in the year of our Lord , between of the first part, and of the second part: Witnesseth, that the said party of the first part, for and in consideration of the sum of , in hand paid by the said party of the second part, the receipt whereof is hereby confessed and acknowledged, has given, granted, bargained, sold, remised, released, aliened, conveyed and confirmed, and by these presents doth give, grant, bargain, sell, remise, release, alien, convey and confirm unto the said party of the second part, and to his heirs and assigns, forever, all of the following described real estate, &c. &c., together with all and singular the hereditaments and appurtenances thereunto belonging, or in any wise appertaining; and all the estate, right, title, interest, claim or demand whatsoever, of the said party of the first part, either in law or equity, either in possession or expectancy, of, in, or to the above bargained premises, and their hereditaments and appurtenances.

To have and to hold the said premises, as above described, with the hereditaments and appurtenances, unto the said party of the second part, and to his heirs and assigns, forever.

And the said parties of the first part, for themselves, their heirs, executors and administrators, do covenant, grant, bargain and agree, to and with the said party of the second part, his heirs and assigns, that at the time of the ensealing and delivery of these presents, they are well seized of the premises above described, as of a good, sure, perfect, absolute and indefeasible estate of inheritance in the law in fee simple, and that the same are free and clear from all incumbrance whatever, and that the above bargained premises in the quiet and peaceable possession of the said party of the second part, his heirs and assigns, against all and every person or persons lawfully claiming the whole or any part thereof, they will forever warrant and defend.

In witness whereof, &c., have set their hands and seals the day and year first above written.

Signed, sealed and delivered in presence of John Smith, Thomas Jones.	——— ——— [Seal.] ——— ——— [Seal.]

XXIV.

RELEASES OR DISCHARGES.

A general release or discharge from one to one.

Know all men by these presents, that I, A B of , for and in consideration of the sum of dollars, lawful money of the United States, to me in hand well and truly paid by B C of , have remised, released and forever discharged, and by these presents do, for me, my heirs, executors and administrators, remise, release and forever discharge the said B C, his heirs, executors and administrators, of and from all and all manner of action and actions, cause or causes of actions, suits, debts, dues, sum and sums of money, accounts, reckonings, bonds, bills, specialties, covenants, contracts, controversies, agreements, promises, variances, damages, judgments, extents, executions, claims and demands whatsoever, in law and equity, which, against the said B C, I ever had, now have, or which I, my heirs, executors or administrators, hereafter can, shall or may have, for, upon, or by reason of any matter, cause or thing whatsoever, from the beginning of the world to the day of the date of these presents.

In witness, &c. (as before, on page 48).

——— ——— [Seal.]

Release to a guardian.

Know all men by these presents, that A B of (son and heir of , deceased), hath remised, released and forever quit-claimed, and by these presents doth remise, release and forever quit-claim unto C D of , his guardian, all and all manner of action and actions, suits, reckonings, accounts, debts, dues and demands whatsoever, which he the said A B ever had, now hath, or which he, his executors or administrators, at any time hereafter can or may have, claim or demand against the said C D, his executors or administrators, for, touching and concerning the management and disposition of any of the lands, tenements and hereditaments of the said A B, situated in , or any part thereof, or for or by reason of any moneys, rents or profits by him received out of the same, or any payments made thereout during the minority of the said A B, or by reason of any matter, cause or thing, whatsoever, relating thereto, from the beginning of the world to the day of the date hereof.

In witness, &c. (as before, on page 24).

—— —— [Seal.]

Release from creditors to a debtor, under a composition.

To all men to whom these presents shall come, we who have hereunto set our hands and seals, creditors of A B of , send greeting: Whereas the said A B is indebted to us, his said creditors, in several sums of money, which he is not able fully to satisfy and discharge, we therefore have agreed, and do hereby agree, to accept of the sum or value of dollars, good and lawful money of the United States, in full payment and satisfaction of all the debts owing to us, respectively, at the date hereof, by and from the said A B, which is paid and delivered by or for the said A B, to C and E, or one of them, creditors also, for the use of, and to the intent that the same may be shared and divided amongst us, his creditors, in proportion and according to the debts to us severally due and owing: Now, therefore, know ye, that for the consideration aforesaid, we, the said creditors, who have hereunto set our hands and seals, each for himself, his heirs, executors and administrators, do by these presents remise, release and forever discharge the said A B, his heirs, executors and administrators, of and from our said several debts, and all and all manner of action and actions, suits, reckonings, accounts, debts, dues and demands, in law or equity, which, against the said A B, each and every of us, the said creditors, now hath, or which each and every of our heirs, executors or administrators, respectively, hereafter, may have claim or demand for, upon or by reason of the said several and respective debts to us severally due and owing, or for, or by reason of any other matter, cause or thing whatsoever, from the beginning of the world to the day of the date of these presents.

Witness, &c. (as before, on page 208).

—— —— [Seal.]

Release or confirmation (by endorsement) of a deed by an infant, on his coming of age, who had been made a party thereto during his minority.

Whereas the within named E C did, on or about the day of last past, attain the age of twenty-one years: and whereas the within named C F hath this day paid to the within named J C and E C (or one of them) the sum of dollars, good and lawful money of the United States, within mentioned to have been retained by the said C F, out of the within mentioned sum of dollars, of lawful money as aforesaid, the consideration of the within written indenture of conveyance, and also the sum of dollars, for interest of the said sum of dollars (so retained by the said C F, as aforesaid), after the rate of dollars for each hundred dollars, by the year, from the day of the date of the within written indenture, which they the said J C and E C do hereby respectively acknowledge: And whereas the said E C, in pursuance of the covenants in the within written indenture entered into by the said J C, on the part of the said E C, to be performed, and also in consideration of the said sum of dollars, good and lawful money of the United States, with the interest thereon as aforesaid, so paid to the said J C and E C (or one of them) as aforesaid, hath duly sealed and delivered the said within written indenture, and hath also subscribed his name to the receipt for the consideration money hereon endorsed, and hath agreed to ratify and confirm the same indenture, in manner hereinafter mentioned. And the said C F, in consideration of the said E C having executed the said indenture, and of his ratifying and confirming the same, hath agreed to release the said J C of and from the covenants so entered into by him as aforesaid, in manner hereinafter expressed: Now, therefore, these presents witness, that in consideration of the said agreement on the part of the said J C, he the said E C hath ratified and confirmed, and by these presents doth ratify and confirm the said within written indenture, so executed by him the said E C as aforesaid, and every article, clause and thing therein contained. And the said C F, in consideration of the said agreement on his part to be performed, hath released and forever discharged, and by these presents doth release and forever discharge the said J C, his executors and administrators, of and from the within mentioned covenants, so entered into by him the said J C as aforesaid, and of and from all action and actions, suit and suits, cause and causes of action, and suit, claim and demands whatsoever, in respect thereof, or for compelling the performance thereof, or otherwise, howsoever.

In witness whereof, &c. (as before, on page 22).

——— ——— [Seal.]

XXV.

SEPARATIONS.

Deed of separation between a man and his wife, where the husband allows the wife an annuity.

This indenture, made the day of , in the year , between A B of , of the one part, and D E of , and C, wife of the said A B, of the other part: Whereas some unhappy differences have lately arisen between the said A B, and C his wife, and they have mutually agreed to live separate and apart from each other, and previous to such separation, he, the said A B hath consented thereto, and also proposed and agreed that he, out of his own proper moneys, would allow and pay the said C, his wife, during the term of her natural life, for her better support and maintenance, the annuity or yearly sum of dollars, clear of all taxes, charges and deductions whatsoever, payable to her in such manner as hereinafter mentioned (subject, nevertheless, to the proviso hereinafter contained, respecting the payment of the said annuity). And also, that in case the said C his wife should die before the said A B, that then the said A B should pay her executors or administrators the sum of dollars towards defraying her funeral charges: Now, this indenture witnesseth, that the said A B, in pursuance of his aforesaid proposal and agreement, doth hereby, for himself, his executors and administrators, and for every of them, covenant, promise and agree, to and with the said D E, his executors, administrators and assigns, in manner and form following (that is to say): that it shall and may be lawful to and for the said C, his wife, and that he the said A B shall and will permit and suffer her the said C, from time to time, and at all times from henceforth, during her natural life, to live separate and apart from him, and to reside and be in such place and places, and family and families, and with such relations, friends and other persons, and to follow and carry on such trade and business as she the said C, from time to time, at her will and pleasure (notwithstanding her present coverture, and as if she was a *feme sole*, and unmarried), shall think fit. And that the said A B shall not nor will, at any time or times hereafter, sue, molest or trouble her for so living separate and apart from him, or any other person or persons whatsoever, for receiving, harboring or entertaining her, nor shall nor will, without the consent of the said C, visit her, or knowingly come into any house or place where she shall or may dwell or reside, or be; or send or cause to be sent any letter or message to her, nor shall or will, at any time hereafter, claim or demand any of the moneys, rings, jewels, plate, clothes, linen, woollen, household goods or stock in trade, which the said C now hath in her custody, power or possession, or which she shall or may hereafter buy and purchase, or which shall be devised or given to her, or she shall otherwise acquire, and that she shall and may enjoy and absolutely dispose of the same, as if she were a *feme sole*, and unmarried. And further, that the said A B, his executors or administrators, or some one of them, shall and will well and truly pay, or cause to be paid unto the said C his wife, or her assigns, during the term of her natural life, for and towards her better support and maintenance, one annuity or yearly sum of dollars, good and lawful money of the United States, free and clear of all charges, taxes and deductions whatsoever, the said annuity or yearly sum of dollars, to be paid and payable to her the said C, and her assigns, during her natural life, at or upon the quarterly days of payment (that is to say): on the day of , the day of , the day of , and the day of , or within ten days next after each of the said quarterly days of payment, in four equal shares or proportions, the first quarterly payment to begin and be made on the day of : which said sum of dollars, paid annually unto the said C, in manner aforesaid, she the said C doth hereby agree to accept and take in full satisfaction for her support and maintenance, and all alimony whatsoever, during her coverture: Provided, always, and it is hereby expressly agreed and declared by and between all the parties hereunto, and the true intent and meaning of them, and of these presents, is and are, that in case he the said A B, his executors or administrators, shall at any time hereafter be obliged to, and shall actually pay any debt or debts which she the said C, his wife, shall, at any time hereafter, during her present coverture, contract with any person or persons whatsoever, that then and in such case it shall and may be lawful to and for the said A B, his executors and administrators, to deduct, retain and reimburse to him and themselves, out of the said annuity or yearly sum of dollars, so hereby made payable to her the said C, as aforesaid, all and every such sum and sums of money as he and they shall be obliged to and shall so actually pay, for or on account of any such debt or debts, to be by her the said C, at any time hereafter, so contracted as aforesaid, together with all costs, charges and damages which he or they shall or may pay or sustain on account thereof, anything herein contained to the contrary notwithstanding.

In witness, &c. (as before, on page 16).

——— ——— [Seal.]
——— ——— [Seal.]

Deed of separation, where the husband gives to the wife all the estate he was entitled to by the marriage.

Articles of agreement, had, made and entered into, this day of , in the year , between D A of , of the one part, and C C (for and on behalf of F A, the wife of the said D A), of the other part: Whereas the said D A, by virtue of his marriage with the said F, and of several deeds and settlements made by her, and others for and on her behalf, is seized of or entitled to divers messuages, lands, tenements and hereditaments, of a very considerable value, and is likewise possessed of some jewels, plate, furniture and other goods and chattels, which before their intermarriage belonged to and were the estate and property of the said F: And whereas the said D A and F have by mutual consent agreed to live separate and apart, and to the intent that the said F may maintain and support herself in a manner suitable to her rank and quality, he the said D A hath agreed to convey, surrender and yield up all the estates and effects, both real and personal, which he is now, or at any time or times hereafter shall be, seized or possessed of, or in any wise entitled to, in right of the said F, or by or from or under her; to be held and enjoyed by her from henceforth, to her sole and separate use, and to be at all times fully and absolutely at her disposal, as if she were *sole* and unmarried, without being subject to his debts, incumbrances or control, or to any claim or demand by, from or under the said D A, on any account whatsoever: Now, for the more effectually carrying the said agreement into execution, he the said D A, doth hereby, for himself, his heirs, executors and administrators, covenant, promise and agree, to and with the said C C, his heirs, executors and administrators, in manner following (that is to say): that he the said D A, and his heirs, shall and will, from time to time, and at all times hereafter, at and upon the request, costs and charges in law of the said C C, his heirs, executors or administrators, well and sufficiently grant, convey and assure unto the said C C, his heirs, executors, administrators and assigns, and permit him and them to take and receive the rents, issues and profits of all the said messuages, lands, tenements and hereditaments, and all the right, title and interest which he the said D A hath, in possession, reversion or expectancy, of, in and to the same, and all rents and arrears of rent, and other profits and advantages whatsoever, which are now due and owing, or accruing to the said D A, or which may, at all or any times hereafter arise or become due to him out of or for the same, or any part thereof, from any person or persons whatsoever. And also that he, the said D A, his executors or administrators, shall and will bargain, sell, assign, transfer and deliver to the said C C, his executors, administrators and assigns, all jewels, plate, household goods, furniture, and all other goods and chattels whatsoever, now remaining in the possession of the said D A, or any other person or persons in trust for him, or for his benefit, which he became seized or possessed of, or entitled to, by his intermarriage with the said F, or otherwise, by, from or under her, or which were at any time her property or estate, and all the estate, right, title, interest, property, claim and demand of him the said D A in and to the same, or any part thereof, free and clear from the debts, incumbrances and engagements of the said D A. And further, that it shall and may be lawful to and for the said F, her heirs, executors, administrators and assigns, from time to time, and at all times hereafter, to have, hold and enjoy, to and for their own sole and separate use, all and singular the said messuages, lands, tenements and hereditaments, and all rents and arrears of rent, and other profits and advantages now due or accruing to him the said D A, or which shall hereafter grow due or accrue, for or in respect of the same, from any person or persons whomsoever; and also all and every the said jewels, plate, furniture, goods and chattels. And moreover, that it shall and may be lawful to and for the said F, notwithstanding her coverture, and she is hereby authorized and empowered, from time to time, and at all times, freely and absolutely, to dispose of all or any of the premises, at her will and pleasure, either in her lifetime, or by any writing purporting to be her last will and testament, without the control, or any let, molestation or denial from or by him, the said D A, or any other person or persons claiming, or to claim, by, from, or under him, and as fully and amply as if she were *sole* and *unmarried*. And that he, the said D A, his executors and administrators, shall and will permit and suffer the probate of such will, by the executor or executors thereof. And in consideration of the premises, the said C C, for and on behalf of the said F, doth covenant and promise, to and with the said D A, his heirs, executors, administrators and assigns, that she, the said F, shall and will, at any time when thereunto requested by the said D A and his heirs, assign, release, surrender and give up all right and title which she, the said F, hath, or may have to any jointure, dower, or thirds, in to or out of the estate, real or personal, of the said D A, or any part thereof. And likewise, that she, the said F, her heirs, executors and administrators, shall and will indemnify and save harmless the said D A, his heirs, executors and administrators, from all debts, charges and incumbrances, contracted, or to be contracted by her, the said F, at any time, or upon any account whatsoever. And lastly, the said several parties hereunto do mutually promise and agree, to and with each other, to sign, seal and execute all such other deeds and conveyances, for the better confirming and executing the several articles aforesaid, according to the true intent and meaning thereof, as by their, or any of their counsel shall be advised or devised and required, and at such time or times as either of the said parties shall tender and require the same to be signed and executed.

In witness, &c. (as before on page 16).

——— ——— [Seal.]

XXVI.

SETTLEMENT.

Marriage settlement of a wife's fortune to her use, as a separate and distinct estate.

An indenture tripartite, made and entered into this day of , in the year , between A B, of , of the first part, C D, of , of the second part, and H K, of , of the third part. Whereas the said C D is seized and possessed of certain lands, tenements and hereditaments, situate, lying and being in ; and whereas a marriage is agreed upon, and intended to be shortly had and solemnized by and between the said A B and C D; and whereas, it was agreed upon, by and between the said A B and C D, that the said C D should, notwithstanding her intended marriage, have, hold, enjoy and possess all her said property above described, with all and every the rights, titles, interests, and profits of, to, in and out of the same; free and separate from all the claims or demands of the said A B, arising from the consummation of the above marriage. And whereas, the said C D hath relinquished, discharged and forever quit-claim to all and every part of the property, real and personal, of him, the said A B, to which she, the said C D, might, on the perfecting of the above marriage, be entitled to, by virtue of dower, or in any other way however. Now, this indenture witnesseth, that in consideration of the said intended marriage, and in pursuance and perfecting of the said hereinbefore mentioned agreements, and in consideration of the sum of dollars, good and lawful money of the United States, to the said C D in hand paid by the said H K, at or before the sealing and delivery of these presents, the receipt whereof is hereby acknowledged, she, the said C D, with the consent and approbation of the said A B, testified by his being a party to, and sealing and delivering these presents, hath bargained, sold, assigned, transferred and set over, and by these presents doth bargain, sell, assign, transfer, and set over unto the said H K, his executors, administrators and assigns, all [here describe the property] to have and to hold the said property hereby conveyed unto the said H K, his executors, administrators and assigns. But nevertheless, upon the trusts, and for the intents and purposes hereinafter expressed and declared of and concerning the same. That he, the said H K, his executors, administrators or assigns, shall hold and manage the said property, and all and every part and parcel thereof, to and for the sole and separate use, benefit and disposal of the said C D, her said marriage notwithstanding. And that the same, in no manner whatsoever, shall be subject to the direction, control or disposition of him, the said A B, her intended husband, or be liable for his debts. And upon this further trust, that he, the said H K, his executors or administrators, shall and will pay, transfer, or deliver unto the said C D, or unto such person or persons, and at such time and times, and in such proportions, manner and form, as she, the said C D, may direct, by her request or order, made in writing, attested by three or more credible witnesses, all the rents, issues and profits of the said property, so conveyed as aforesaid. And that all the said separate and distinct estate, and the produce and increase thereof, shall be had, taken, held and enjoyed by such person and persons, and for such use and uses, as the said C D shall at any time or times hereafter, during her life, limit, devise, order or dispose of the same, or any part thereof, either by her last will and testament in writing, or by any other writing whatsoever, signed with her hand, in the presence of two or more credible witnesses. And the said A B, for himself, his heirs, executors and administrators, covenants, agrees and promises, to and with the said H K, his executors, administrators and assigns, by these presents, in manner following (that is to say,) that if the said intended marriage shall take effect, he, the said A B, shall and will permit and suffer the said C D to give, grant and dispose of her said separate estate, as she shall think fit, in her lifetime, and to make such will or other writings as aforesaid, and thereby to give, order, devise, limit and appoint her said separate estate, to any person or persons, for any use, intent or purpose whatsoever; and that he the said A B, shall and will permit and suffer such will, hereafter to be made by the said C D, to be duly proven by the executors in such will named or to be named, and probate of such will to be had and taken as usual; and that the person or persons to whom the said C D shall give or dispose any part of her said separate estate, by her will, or any other writing that shall be signed, sealed and executed by her in the presence of two or more credible witnesses as aforesaid, shall and lawfully may, peaceably and quietly have, hold, use, occupy, possess and enjoy the same, according to the true meaning of such gift, devise or appointment, without any hindrance or interruption of or by the said A B, his executors, administrators or assigns, or any of them; and that he, the said A B, shall and will, from time to time, and at all times from and after the said intended marriage shall take effect, upon every reasonable request, and at the proper cost and charges of the said H K, or his executors and administrators, make, do and execute all and every such further act and acts, thing and things, for the better settling, recovering and receiving the moneys, goods and estate of the said C D, allotted and declared for her separate use, benefit and disposal as aforesaid, as by the said H K, or his executors and administrators, or their, or any of their counsel learned in the law, shall be reasonably devised, advised or or required.[1]

In witness, &c. (as before on page 16.)

——— ——— [Seal.]

[1] See pp. 84–86 ante. The provisions in the deed there found may be inserted in a marriage settlement.

XXVII.

SURRENDERS.

Surrender of Dower.

This indenture, made and entered into this day of , in the year , between A B, of , widow and relict of C B, late of , deceased, of the one part, and E B, of (son and heir of the said C B), of the other part.—Whereas, the said C B died seized of the freehold and immediate inheritance of and in certain tenements and premises in the , of which tenements and premises the messuage and tenement hereinafter described were part, upon whose decease the said A B became entitled to her dower of and in the same. And whereas, the said E B, as heir of the said C B, (to whom the premises before mentioned descended), did, after the decease of the said C B, assign all that messuage and tenement situate, lying and being in , unto the said A B, as for and in lieu and satisfaction of her dower, and all right and claim to dower of and in the several hereditaments, &c., of which the said C B hath been seized of the freehold and inheritance from the solemnization of his marriage with the said A B, to the time of his death, which the said A B accepted in full satisfaction of her dower, right and claim to dower, as aforesaid. And whereas, it hath been agreed by and between the said A B and E B, that the said A B should, for the considerations and purposes hereinafter mentioned, surrender and yield up, all and singular the said messuage, &c., and all her estate, interest and claim of and to the same, unto him, the said E B. Now, this indenture witnesseth, that for and in consideration of the yearly sum of dollars, good and lawful money of the United States, to be paid out of and chargeable upon certain other premises of the said E B, by virtue of a certain deed, &c., she, the said A B, hath surrendered and yielded up, and by these presents doth surrender and yield up unto the said E B, all that messuage and tenement lying and being in , of which the said A B was entitled to as her dower as aforesaid; and all the estate, right, title and interest, as well of and in the said messuage and tenement, as also of and in all and singular other the hereditaments of which the said C B, her late husband, was at any time seized during the coverture between them. To have and to hold the said messuage and tenement to him, the said E B, and his heirs, to the intent that he may become actually possessed of the same, and that the estate and interest of. the said A B therein, may become merged and extinguished to all intents and purposes whatsoever. And also, all and all manner of actions, suits, &c., which, against the said E B, his heirs, &c., she, the said A B, her executors, &c., hath or have, or should or might have had or claimed, either at law or in equity, on account thereof.

In witness, &c. (as before on page 24).

―――― ―――― [Seal.]

Surrender of part of term of leased property—tenement having been destroyed by fire—by indorsement on the lease.

Whereas, the within mentioned messuage or tenement hath been lately burnt down and destroyed by fire, and the within named A A hath requested the within named W E to surrender to him, the said A A, the site, or piece or parcel of ground whereon the said messuage and tenement lately stood, for all the residue and remainder of the said unexpired term of years, by the within written indenture granted therein, to the intent that the same residue may merge and be extinguished, in the estate and interest of him, the said A A, in the same premises respectively, which he, the said W E, hath consented and agreed to do. Now, these presents witness, that in compliance with the said request of the said A A, and also for and in consideration of the sum of dollars, good and lawful money of the United States, to the said W E in hand paid by the said A A, at or before the sealing and delivery of these presents, the receipt whereof he doth hereby acknowledge, he, the said W E hath surrendered and yielded up, and by these presents doth surrender and yield up unto the said A A, his executors, administrators and assigns, all the said site, &c., and all the estate, &c. To have and to hold the said site, &c., and all and singular the other premises hereby surrendered and yielded up, or intended so to be, with their and every of their appurtenances, unto the said A A, his executors, administrators and assigns, from henceforth, for and during the rest, residue and remainder of the said term of years, by the within written indenture granted therein, now to come, and unexpired, to the intent and purpose that the same rest and residue may merge and be extinguished in the estate and interest of him, the said A A, in the same premises respectively.

In witness, &c. (as before on page 24).

——— ——— [Seal.]

XXVIII.

WILLS.

Will bequeathing portions to several children, and appointing guardian.

In the name of God, amen. I, T L, of do make this, my last will and testament, as follows (that is to say): My desire is, to be buried with as little expense as decency will permit, and that all my debts and funeral expenses be paid as soon after my decease as conveniently may be. And I give all my messuages, lands, tenements and hereditaments whatsoever, situate, lying and being in , with their appurtenances, unto my dear wife J L, for and during her life. And from and after her decease, I give and devise the same to my eldest son W L, and his heirs forever, and I give all the rents which shall be due and owing to me at my death, for the aforesaid messuages, lands, tenements and hereditaments herein before given to my said wife for life, and after her death, to my said son W, and his heirs, unto my said wife J L, for her own use. And I give and devise all that tract, piece or parcel of land lying in the county of , which I purchased from S B, unto my son H L, and his heirs forever. And I also give to him, my said son H, all the rents which may be due and owing me at my decease, for, from and out of the same. And I give unto my daughter C L, and my son R L, both minors, the sum of dollars each, to be paid them respectively, upon their attaining the age of twenty-one years. And I give all my household goods and furniture, plate, china-ware, household linen, books and prints, and all the household utensils in my house in where I now reside, and my house situate in , unto my said wife for her own use. And as to all the rest and residue of my personal and real estate and effects not hereinbefore mentioned, and which shall remain after payment of my debts, funeral expenses, and the aforesaid specific and pecuniary legacies, I give and bequeath the same to my said son W L, and his heirs forever. And I give the custody, tuition and guardianship of the persons of such of my children as shall be under the age of twenty-one years at the time of my death, to my said wife J L, during their respective minorities. And I nominate and appoint my said wife executrix of this, my last will and testament; and my will is, and I do hereby direct, that all the rent of the tract, piece or parcel of land hereinbefore given to my son H L, shall be paid to his guardian, during his minority, and applied for his maintenance, education and support, and that the said sum of dollars, bequeathed to my said daughter C L, and the said sum of dollars, bequeathed to my said son R L, shall be invested in stock, and the interests and dividends arising therefrom, shall be paid to their guardian during their minority, and applied for their maintenance, education and support.

On the qualification of my wife as executrix of this my will, I request and direct that no security be required of her.

In witness whereof, I, the said testator, T L, have hereto set my hand and seal on this day of 18 .

T L, [Seal.]

Signed, sealed, published and declared by the testator T L, as and for his last will and testament, in presence of us, who in his presence, at his request, and in the presence of each other, have hereunto subscribed our names as witnesses.

J M,
S S.

A general form of a codicil to a will.

Whereas, I, A B, of , have made and duly executed my last will and testament in writing, bearing date day of , in the year . Now I do hereby declare this present writing to be a codicil to my said will, and direct the same to be annexed thereto, and taken as a part thereof, and I do hereby give and bequeath, &c. And I do hereby revoke all former and other codicils by me made at any time heretofore.

In witness whereof, to this present writing, which I hereby declare to be a codicil to my last will and testament, bearing date the day of , in the year , and which I direct to be added thereto, and to be taken as part thereof, I have set my hand and seal, this day of , in the year .

——— [Seal.]

Signed, sealed, published and declared by the said A B, as and for a codicil to his last will and testament, in the presence of .

——— ———

——— ———

Commencement and conclusion of a nuncupative will.

This, the last will and testament of C D, of , written by H B, at the request of the said C D, who, by reason of sickness, was unable to write, and declared by him, on the day of , in the year , in the presence of us, who have hereunto subscribed our names as witnesses thereto. "My will is," (recite the *very* words.)

These words, or the like effect, the said C D declared in the presence of the witnesses whose names are hereunto subscribed, with an intention that the same should stand for and be his last will and testament, and he the said C D, bid the witnesses bear witness thereunto.

Provisions of Code of Virginia on the subject of Wills.

(Chapter 122.)

1. Nuncupative wills are of force only in the cases of a soldier in actual military service, or of a mariner or seaman being at sea. In other cases, the provisions of the fourth section of the chapter (hereafter cited) must be strictly complied with.

2. In all cases, whether of a devise of *real* or personal estate, the will shall be construed to speak and take effect as if it had been executed immediately before the death of the testator, unless a contrary intention shall appear on its face.

3. An executor is not an incompetent witness. A party attesting a will in which there is a devise to himself, will, in case the will cannot be otherwise proved, be a competent witness, and the devise will be void; but if such witness would be entitled to any share of the estate of the testator, in case the will were not established, so much of his share shall be saved to him as shall not exceed the value of what is so devised or bequeathed.

4. The power of disposal by will extends to any estate, right, or interest to which the testator may be entitled at his death, notwithstanding he may become so entitled subsequently to the execution of the will.

5. No person of unsound mind, or under the age of twenty-one years, is capable of making a will in Virginia, except that minors eighteen years of age or upwards may by will dispose of personal estate. Nor is a married woman capable of making a will except for the disposition of her separate estate, or in the exercise of a power of appointment.

6. The will of a person domiciled out of Virginia at the time of his death is valid as to personal property in Virginia, if it be executed according to the law of the state or country, in which he was so domiciled.

How Wills are executed in Virginia.

Sections 4th and 5th of chapter 122, Code of Virginia, enact—

§ 4. No will shall be valid unless it be in writing and signed by the testator, or by some other person in his presence and by his direction, in such manner as to make it manifest that the name is intended as a signature; and moreover, unless it be wholly written by the testator, the signature shall be made or the will acknowledged by him in the presence of at least two competent witnesses, present at the same time; and such witnesses shall subscribe the will in the presence of the testator, but no form of attestation shall be necessary.

§ 5. No appointment made by will in exercise of any power, shall be valid, unless the same be so executed that it would be valid for the disposition of the property to which the power applies, if it belonged to the testator; and every will so executed, except the will of a married woman, shall be a valid execution of a power of appointment by will, notwithstanding the instrument creating the power expressly require that a will made in execution of such power shall be executed with some additional or other form of execution or solemnity.

INDEX.

www.ingramcontent.com/pod-product-compliance
Lightning Source LLC
Chambersburg PA
CBHW030341270326
41926CB00009B/916

* 9 7 8 3 3 3 7 2 2 4 2 3 3 *